PR
HerVenture.com

"*HerVenture.com* belies the idea that it's mostly young male entrepreneurs who are starting and growing Internet businesses. This book provides a unique blend of practical advice, useful tips, and wonderful role models who will inspire any woman who wants to succeed. A must-have for women starting any type of business!"
> —JANET ATTARD, founder and CEO,
> BusinessKnowHow.com

"Wow! This book has it all. For anyone who dreams of profiting from the Internet. I wish I had read this years ago."
> —PAULA FUOCO DAVIS, founder and
> editor of Commitment.com

"*HerVenture.com* is *the* guide to transforming your small business into an online success."
> —LIZ FOLGER, author of *The Stay-at-Home Mom's Guide to Making Money from Home*, author and owner of bizymoms.com

"If you are looking to expand your business to the Internet market (and you should be), you will find just about everything you need to get started in *HerVenture.com*."
> —DR. ROBERT SULLIVAN, author of *The Small Business Start-Up Guide* and founder of The Small Business Advisor <www.isquare.com>

"Any woman looking for a great partner will find it in *HerVenture.com*. I believe that Priscilla's latest book offers women who are thinking about starting Web businesses (or who already have them) solid information and expert guidance."
> —DIANE G. SILVER, senior producer,
> Career/Business Channel, womensforum.com

PRISCILLA Y. HUFF

HerVenture.com

Your Guide to Expanding Your Small or Home Business to the Internet—Easily and Profitably

PRIMA SOHO
An Imprint of Prima Publishing

3000 LAVA RIDGE COURT • ROSEVILLE, CALIFORNIA 95661
(800) 632-8676 • www.primalifestyles.com

PRIMA SOHO and colophon are trademarks of Prima Communications, Inc. PRIMA PUBLISHING and colophon are trademarks of Prima Communications Inc., registered with the United States Patent and Trademark Office.

Disclaimer

This book contains information of a general nature regarding starting and operating a business. It is not intended as a substitute for professional, legal, or financial advice. As laws may vary from state to state, readers should consult a competent legal or financial professional regarding their own particular business. In addition, readers should understand that the business world is highly dynamic and contains certain risks. Therefore, the author and publisher cannot warrant or guarantee that the use of any information contained in this book will work in any given situation.

Library of Congress Cataloging-in-Publication Data

Huff, Priscilla Y.
HerVenture.com : your guide to expanding your small or home business to the Internet—easily and profitably / Priscilla Y. Huff
p.   cm.
Includes bibliographical references and index.
ISBN 0-7615-2528-9
1. Electronic commerce.   2. Women-owned business enterprises—Computer networks.   3. Business enterprises—Computer networks.   I. Title.
HF5415.126.K555   2000
658.8'4—dc21   00-062381

00 01 02 03 HH 10 9 8 7 6 5 4 3 2 1
Printed in the United States of America

HOW TO ORDER

Single copies may be ordered from Prima Publishing, 3000 Lava Ridge Court, Roseville, CA 95661; telephone (800) 632-8676 ext. 4444. Quantity discounts are also available. On your letterhead, include information concerning the intended use of the books and the number of books you wish to purchase.

Visit us online at www.primalifestyles.com

*To my family for their patience
and support and to Pam, my
best friend and favorite minister!*

CONTENTS

Preface

Becoming "Virtual"

It was bound to happen—as computers became essential tools for business and education, they opened up a "virtual world," in which the Internet enables us to have worldwide communication and now "virtual" businesses. Just when we thought we had it made, starting and running our small ventures, along came this new business frontier to challenge us in ways we never expected to be challenged, even five years ago!

Business owners everywhere are asking themselves such questions as: "Should I have a Web site for my business or not? If so, how will it benefit me and/or my business? Where do I start? How much is this whole Internet process going to cost? Help!" Fortunately, as you read about the women profiled in this book who have made the virtual "jump," you will see by their examples that:

1. You *do not* have to know everything about the Internet to get started. There are plenty of books, magazines, Web sites, Web-savvy experts, and other women "netpreneurs" who can provide you with the information you need.
2. You can start simply and build your Web business or presence as your own Internet knowledge grows.
3. Basic business principles of producing a good product or service and providing good customer service still apply, and maybe even more so with the Internet, if you wish to gain your customers' respect and trust.

This book is *not* a technical book. It is a book that introduces you to the concept of using the Internet to start or expand a business, or to use for promotional purposes for yourself or for an existing business. There are many excellent publications and Web sites that can help you go as far as you want with a Web business.

In my opinion, the strength of this book is in the women profiled. Their advice and tips are from women who are learning netpreneurship as they go and doing very well, thank you, in using the Internet in ways that best suit them. Not all of them have businesses listed on the stock market, but then many are happy just where they are in terms of their business's operations. It is my wish that you will be inspired by their stories, and by the entire women's entrepreneurial movement as it continues to pick up speed and as more and more women become business owners in this new century. May you, too, find the ideal venture for you—in both the real world and the virtual world of the Internet!

—Priscilla Y. Huff

ACKNOWLEDGMENTS

I wish to thank each and every one of the entrepreneurial women who are quoted and profiled in this book for taking the time to share their expertise and experiences with you, my readers. Their advice and tips are the result of the ingenuity and creative problem-solving tactics these women "netpreneurs" have used, and are still using, to overcome the many obstacles they face daily in their efforts to achieve business success.

Special thanks goes to Diane Silver of the Women's Forum <www.womensforum.com> for her referrals to a number of the WF's partner members whose profiles are included in this book. I also want to express my appreciation to those men who contributed their comments, and also to all those men—including those in my life—who support and encourage the entrepreneurial women in their lives.

Thanks, too, to the staff of Prima Publishing for all their efforts on behalf of this book!

INTRODUCTION

Why Your Business Needs the Internet

✦

Only a few years ago, the Internet was not taken very seriously by many business experts, but with the onset of online ventures, and the millions of dollars being bandied about in connection with them, the Internet is now in the forefront of the news every day. To help you decide if you want to invest in a "virtual venture," here are some facts and figures to consider.

Statistics: Past, Present, Future

Statistics and records help to reveal business patterns and trends.

STATS FOR WOMEN ENTREPRENEURS

The following information was compiled from the National Foundation of Women Business Owners (NFWBO)* and the U.S. Department of Labor.

- As of March 26, 1997, the substantial growth of women-owned businesses was showing significant impact on the economic health of their local communities.
- As of March 2, 1998, the primary reasons that women were launching new businesses were that they were inspired by an entrepreneurial idea and came to realize they

---

*You can visit the NFWBO Web site at <www.nfwbo.org> for more information about women-owned businesses, but *not* for information about starting a business.

BUSINESS PROFILE: Georganne Fiumara, Adviser to
                        Mothers Working at Home

What is your Internet venture?

Mothers' Home Business Network (MHBN) <www.homeworking mom.com>.

Is it solely an Internet business?

MHBN was an offline business for 16 sixteen years. Now 100 percent online.

When was the business started?

May 1984.

How did you originate the idea for your site?

I was a mother working at home as a means of combining mothering and work. At that time, flexible work options were not well-known or used. I decided to make the work-at-home option more available. MHBN was the first organization formed to help mothers choose home as a workplace.

Do you have a "vision statement" for your Web site?

Any mother who would like to work at home should be able to make that happen, whether it is by owning a business or by finding a work-at-home job. It is our mission to provide the information and resources to help make working at home an achievable goal.

---

could do for themselves what they were doing for an employer. However, more recently, women entrepreneurs give the reasons of "being downsized," "lack of challenge," or "hitting the glass ceiling" as their primary motivation for starting a business.

- From 1987 to 1999 the number of women-owned firms in the United States more than doubled.
- The number of women-owned businesses is increasing in every state, and over the past decade women-

How did you finance your start-up?

A little at a time, through personal income and savings and reinvesting in the business.

What resource helped you the most?

Books have always been the most valuable resource. Meeting a woman named Angela Smith in an online mailing list discussion group in 1996 was the first step to creating HomeWorkingMom .com. She was willing to share the vision of helping moms work at home, at first for very little pay. Today, she is HomeWorkingMom .com's Web master and special project manager.

Can you offer any tips for creating a successful Web site?

Believe in your topic and have a passion for learning online marketing. Spend at least one hour each day doing online marketing. The Internet is still so new that there is room for personal creativity. Focus on a specific subject, keep your Web design functional without too many "bells and whistles," and provide valuable information along with any product or service that you are selling.

Georganne Fiumara is the author of
How to Start a Home-Based Mail Order Business

owned businesses have experienced the most dramatic growth in cities such as Portland, Oregon; Seattle; and Vancouver.

- As of 1999, there were 9.1 million women-owned businesses in the United States (40 percent of all American businesses), employing over 27.5 million people and generating over $3.6 trillion in sales.
- The largest share of U.S. women-owned businesses continues to be in the service sector.

- More than 60 percent of U.S. women-owned small-business start-ups are based at home.
- Women-owned businesses are as financially sound and creditworthy as the typical firm in the U.S. economy, and are likely to remain in business longer than the average U.S. firm.

Women still face obstacles such as securing sufficient financing to take a business to the "next step," which remains one of the largest inhibitors to growth. Women's access to capital—both debt and equity financing—has been limited because many of their businesses are simply too small to meet the criteria of most venture capital funds. However, it is hoped that the recent establishment of women-owned capital funds over the past few years will help reduce such financial impediments. (See Financing Your Online Venture in chapter 3.)

Women of all ages continue to start businesses because they are still facing lower median wages in many jobs, dealing with child-care dilemmas, and—although this is improving—are still experiencing career advancement frustrations.

INTERNET STATISTICS

- By June of 2000, 106 million people were online—54 percent of the U.S. adult population. (The Strategis Group, Washington, D.C., <www.strategis group.com>)
- Consumers spent twice as much time online as they did during the previous year—spending about $3.6 billion for products and services over the Internet, compared to $1.6 billion at the end of 1998. (The Strategis Group's "Internet User Trend Report," March, 2000)
- The Internet is the fastest-growing source of mail-order sales. Consumers spent an estimated $14 to $15 billion on Internet-based goods and services in 1998—$5 billion dur-

ing the 1998 holiday shopping season alone. (Federal Trade Commission <www.ftc.gov>)

- There were 108 million Internet users in the United States and 300 million worldwide, according to a study released in March, 2000, by the Vancouver-based Angus-Reid Group, Inc. <www.angusreid.com>.
- A June, 2000, study by the U.S. Commerce Department found that information technology–related ventures have stimulated U.S. productivity, doubling from a 1.4 percent annual increase between 1973 and 1995 to 2.8 percent growth between the years 1995 and 1999.
- According to data from International Data Corporation <www.idc.com>, "the number of small businesses with sites on the Web will be 4.3 million by the year 2001; with the average overall revenues of small businesses using the Internet being $3.79 million."
- ActivMedia Research LLC's <www.activmedia.com> annual electronic commerce study, "Real Numbers Behind 'Net Profits 1999," and in their report, "Top 100 Retail E-Commerce Web Sites" (January 1999), show that many profits have already been realized:

Nearly half of all Web sites are already profitable.

Another one in four expect profitability within the next 12 months.

One in three are profitable in their first year of operation.

Most companies enter online in a limited fashion initially, experimenting and seeking to maximize profits and benefits as they go.

Typical B2C (business-to-consumer) Web sites focus on niche specialty products where product design and personal taste combine to create effective barriers that protect their businesses from predation by larger competitors.

- ActivMedia Research said in their June, 2000, report, "Real Numbers Behind 'Net Profits 2000" that $132 billion in revenues are generated worldwide by e-commerce.
- Women are increasingly going online and made 37 percent of all online purchases in 1999, according to eMarketer <www.emarketer.com>, a market research firm which studies the Internet economy.

Researchers agree that, at present, most Internet revenues are being made with online business-to-business sales as opposed to business-to-consumer sales.

RELATED RESOURCES

Internet Sites

<www.estats.com> eStats; Information on Internet facts and figures

<www.researchbuzz.com> Research Buzz; Internet research news

Books

Advanced Internet Research One-Day Course by DDC Publishing Staff and Curt Robbins (New York: DDC Publishing, Inc., 1999)

Web Site Myths

With all the hype and publicity surrounding the Internet, it is difficult to differentiate between truth and myth associated with Internet business ventures. Here are some common myths and the truths behind them:

Myth: Fast money can be made on the Internet.

Truth: It may seem that new "netpreneurs" start up today and make millions tomorrow, but starting a Web venture is more likely to follow an offline start-up business venture: It starts small and over a period of time builds a client base and following through focused marketing efforts and excellent follow-up customer service.

Myth: There are investors out there just waiting to lavish millions on my new business.

Truth: Even though there are a growing number of women-owned venture capital firms being formed to assist women's businesses:

1. A very small percentage of all "dot-com" start-ups receive venture capital.
2. Any funding is more likely to be invested in your business after it has a good sales record and you wish to expand it.

Myth: Once my business is online, I will have lots of new customers, resulting in a flood of online orders.

Truth: Just like an offline business, you will need to exercise daily marketing efforts to:

1. Make potential customers aware of your site.
2. Gain their trust that you will provide quality products and/or services.

Myth: The Internet is a totally free business experience and I can operate my business as I wish.

Truth: Wrong!! There are legalities, rules, and business procedures governing copyrights, children's privacy, obscenity, advertising guidelines, and other laws you must adhere to when you operate a business online. It is

your responsibility to educate yourself about them or you
can be taken to court and suffer the legal consequences.

Myth: It is impossible to compete with the big companies
that have all the money and resources already available
to them to serve their customers online.

Truth: It is *almost* impossible for you to compete with the
"big guys" using their marketing methods. However, you
will be more likely to succeed if you:

1. Search, instead, for a "niche"—a product or service
   that a group of customers needs.
2. Provide customers with excellent quality and service.

These are just a few of the many common Web myths being
bandied about every day. You have to create a plan and follow through on it to give something of value to your customers
if you want to achieve your own Web "Rags to Riches" business success story.

Related Resources

Books

*The E-Myth Revisited: Why Most Small Businesses Don't
Work and What to Do About It* by Michael Gerber (New
York: Harper Business, 1995)

*Net Success: 24 Leaders in Web Commerce Show How to
Put the Web to Work for Your Business* by Christina
Ford Haylock, Len Muscarella, and Steve Case
(Holbrook, MA: Adams Media Corp., 1999)

Internet Sites

<www.jaderiver.com/webmyth.htm> Jade River Designs' arti-
cle, "The 6 Myths of Web Marketing;" and other Web

marketing-related information, including a page, "The Marketing Manager's Plain English Internet Glossary."

Why Should a Self-Employed Businesswoman Use the Internet?

When Aliza Pilar Sherman,* the original Cybergrrl, founder of Webgrrls International, and copresident of EVIVA.NET, was asked, "Why do you think so many women are either starting to use the Internet or planning to use it to promote their ventures and/or themselves?" she said, "The Internet is a powerful communications tool, and women are discovering that power and are looking to make connections, get the word out, gain support, and communicate on many levels for the success of their businesses."

Georganne Fiumara, founder of Mothers' Home Business Network and creator of HomeWorkingMom.com, adds, "The Internet has opened up a vast array of opportunities for business ownership and finding employment that did not exist before. The best part is that individuals can create Web sites that are equal to or better than those being put up by corporations. The costs are affordable and the possibilities are endless. All of the information you need for start up is available to anyone willing to do the necessary research."

Internet Business Terms

Every industry and profession has it own vernacular. The Internet is no exception with its new "lingo." You'll find common

---

*Aliza Pilar Sherman is also the author of *Cybergrrl: A Woman's Guide to the World Wide Web* (New York: Ballantine, 1999) and *Cybergrrl at Work: Tips and Inspiration for the Professional You* (New York: Berkley Publishing Group, 2000).) See Sherman's profile in chapter 3.

More Good Reasons for Using the Internet for Your Business

- You can reach customers from all over the world.
- It can offer you new marketing opportunities.
- More and more people are going to expect a business to have a Web presence.
- It helps to establish your credibility as a business entity and gives you the opportunity to "introduce yourself and your business to potential customers."
- It can save you time and money; as your site can answer customer questions, help track their orders, permit you to market with free options such as newsletters, eliminate store rental, and automate some of your business's operations.
- It can give you creative opportunities for promoting your business.
- The Internet can provide you with opportunities for exchanging information and solving problems with networking input of other online entrepreneurs.
- You can do instant research to enhance your education in your industry.
- You can track customer responses.
- It provides you with many tools to help communicate better with your customers—which is vital to your online survival.
- It gives you a chance to grow from a tiny, one-page store to one that can develop into a portal or community site of many people with common interests and bonds.

terms to help you speak "Web-ese" in the "Glossary of Internet Terms."

RELATED RESOURCES

Internet Sites:

<http://cnnfn.cnn.com/resources/glossary> Glossary of business terms offered by Dearborn Financial Publishing and CNN

<www.rahul.net/lai/glossaries.html> Online dictionaries and glossaries; Contains 62 online language dictionaries

<www.smartcomputing.com> *Smart Computing* magazine's *Smart Computing Dictionary of Computer Terms*; Searchable dictionary of more than 4,500 plain-English definitions

<www.webopedia.com> Sponsored by www.internet.com; Contains an extensive listing of computer and Internet words and terms

Women's Business and Self-Employment Challenges

On March 4, 2000, more than 400 women M.B.A. students from across the nation came to Los Angeles to attend the Graduate Women in Business conference held at the Anderson School at UCLA. During the two-day conference, Anderson School staff conducted an informal survey of the conference attendees to ask them about their career plans, their views on work/life balance issues, and also to discover which individuals these women admire most.

Asked what they thought was the largest issue facing women today, 48 percent of all respondents wrote that balancing work and a personal life was the number 1 issue. Among the other key findings were that 58 percent plan on starting their own businesses; almost 90 percent plan on starting families, and of those, 78 percent plan to continue to work.

BUSINESS PROFILE: Azriela Jaffe, Author, Public Speaker, Business Coach

What is your Internet venture?

Anchored Dreams <www.isquare.com/crlink.htm>; information on books, free newsletters for entrepreneurial couples and business owners, and nationally syndicated column, *Advice from A–Z*.

Is it solely an Internet business?

No, I'm an author and columnist and professional speaker and business coach.

When was the business started?

1997.

How did you originate the idea for your site?

Every author needs one these days!

How did you finance your start-up?

Savings.

Azriela Jaffe, mother of three, columnist, and author of such books as *Honey, I Want to Start My Own Business; Let's Go Into Business Together;* and *Starting from "No"—10 Strategies to Overcome Your Fear of Rejection and Succeed in Business,* gives this tip to women who are trying to balance an Internet venture and their family's concerns: "Learn to type with a child on your lap!"

The Balancing Act: Family Concerns

When so many women have to work—it often takes two incomes to support a family, even in the present "good" economy—women wonder how they are going to achieve both work satisfaction and a harmonious home life. Younger

What resource helped you the most?
Other entrepreneurs, books, online lists.

Can you offer any tips for creating a successful Web site?
It must be continually updated, at least every quarter.

Do you have any additional comments?
Owning and managing a Web site is a much more expensive process than you realize. It will be [costly] if you don't learn how to do it yourself, since you must keep your Web site current. Either way, it's a wise investment.

Azriela Jaffe; Visit Fortune Small Business *magazine online <www.fsb.com> for Jaffe's syndicated column,* Balancing Act.

women are not the only ones of their sex facing balancing issues. Many of their mothers, aunts, and even grandmothers today are sandwiched between generations, caring for elderly relatives and their children or raising grandchildren for one reason or another.

Since the 1980s, the answer for many women has been to start a business, as the statistics presented in the "Introduction" demonstrate. More than 60 percent of U.S. women-owned small business start-ups are based at home.

How does entrepreneurship—as compared to being employed in a "regular" job—help women balance their lives? Here are several comparisons:

- Entrepreneurship gives a woman more flexibility. She can often arrange her hours around the needs of her family.

Even though entrepreneurship may require double the amount of hours than being employed does, it still gives a self-employed woman more control and choices of the working hours she has available to her.

- Entrepreneurship gives a woman a sense of fulfillment and pride. She can see the direct results of her efforts in helping her venture to grow and thrive. If she is earning money at something she loves to do, she is less likely to be frustrated with her work. She gains a sense of accomplishment, too, when she learns to "move on" and learn from any mistakes she might make, or be a creative problem solver when faced with a business dilemma.

- Entrepreneurship offers the potential to earn more money. Building a business that's profitable enough to support a woman and her family may take five or even ten years, but it also has the potential for unlimited earnings. According to the U.S. Department of Labor, nearly seven out of ten women in 1995 earned less than $25,000. But the top-ranked woman-owned company in *Working Woman (WW)* magazine's <www.workingwomanmag.com> June, 2000, issue had revenues of $6.5 billion, and the 500th-ranked company had $18.5 million!

Here are three other tips to help you "balance your home-business and personal life" from Evelyn Salvador (see her profile in chapter 2), who has owned and operated her home based business, Desktop Publishing Plus—a graphic design and resume services business—in Coram, New York, since 1990.

Melding a home business and personal life can be far from the fantasy of a work-at-home business that one may originally think. At least it was for me. What I quickly learned is that one cannot do both optimally. Starting up and operating a home business requires dedicated, separate, and uninterrupted quiet time. Something not easily obtained with children at home. Raising children requires dedicated and separate quality time with each. Something difficult to do when you have a business to run. I found that instead of the children feeling great that you are home, the all-too-often knocks on your office door result in turning them away, which can leave them feeling rejected.

As a result, I would say that the three biggest tips I would offer someone starting up at home would be to:

1. Carefully select the setting for your home office so that it includes quiet work space with the ability to view or monitor the children's play area.
2. Schedule activities with the children during the day so that you can spend some quality time with them, and arrange activities to keep them busy.
3. Arrange part-time child care so that you are able to conduct important business and phone calls while the children are occupied and supervised.

Jennifer White, the founder and president of the JWC Group, a success-coaching firm, and the author of the best-selling book, *Work Less, Make More,* says "integration" is more important than balance.

What I see every day is women who define their lives by time. They're always comparing how everything balances out against work as if their lives only have two focuses: work versus everything else. Give me a break. Your life is much more than just juggling work with the other areas in your life. That's where integration comes in.

Integration means you're not defining your life by time. You're doing what is the right thing to do at that moment. Yes, it's about designing your life around priorities. It's about making choices on how you spend your time, energy, and passion. And it's about loving the choices you make. There are times when work becomes the priority, and there are times when family or fun or you become the priority. The

---

BUSINESS PROFILE: Jennifer White, Professional-Success Coach

What is your Internet venture?

The JWC Group <www.jwcgroup.com>, an international success-coaching firm.

Is it solely an Internet business?

No. We use the Internet to sell products that support our success-coaching services on jwcgroup.com, and our worklessmakemore .com site supports the national phenomena started by my best-selling book, *Work Less, Make More* <www.worklessmakemore .com>.

When was the business started?

1993.

How did you finance your start-up?

Personal resources.

What resource helped you the most?

Gosh, no idea. . . . I've used so many resources. . . .

Can you offer any tips for creating a successful Web site?

Never be cheap when doing your Web site. The best thing we did was hire the right designer, the right hosting company and the right technical programmer to make our sites well designed and well run. So many people on the Internet today are doing it themselves, and the sites look terrible. Be prepared to really invest in your site if you want to make it work.

*Jennifer White works with high
achievers to help them create successful
careers and richly satisfying lives.*

---

point is: At the end of the week, month, or year, did you invest your time in the areas you wanted to? Then you've been successful integrating what you want in your life. If you didn't, you have some work to do.

Best (or Worst) of Both Worlds?

Working for yourself can be the best or worst of both worlds. Liz Folger, author of the bestselling book, *The Stay-at-Home*

Mom's Guide to Making Money from Home, and owner of the Web site Bizy Moms <www.bizymoms.com>, says that for her the worst aspect of having a home-based Internet business is, "It's lonely! You're basically sitting in front of your computer screen all day. It's imperative that you get out at least once a week with friends. If you can manage it, maybe even once a day go out and have coffee and chat with people before you get to work."

Kristine Kirsch of PetVogue.com says that for her the best part of having an Internet business is that "it works for you 24 hours a day. Worst? Relative to a traditional business, there is little to complain about." (See her business profile in chapter 2.)

Deborah McNaughton of Financial Victory.com and publisher of *Financial Victory,* a monthly newsletter, says the worst is that "I believe you lose the personal touch of talking to a person either on the telephone or in person. If there is competition for your service or product the Internet information may not have the answers you need to make the customer feel secure." The best "is having Internet access can give a customer quick information and hopefully a sale." (See McNaughton's profile in chapter 3.)

Whether you work for yourself or as someone's employee, there will always be pluses and minuses to the situation. Here are just a few of the arguments for and against being self-employed:

Pro: As mentioned previously, the earning potential in working for yourself is unlimited.

Con: There is no regular paycheck, and it can take years before your business makes the profits you need to support yourself or your family.

Pro: Working for yourself allows you the flexibility to arrange your hours around your family's needs. Plus,

BUSINESS PROFILE: Liz Folger, Author, Columnist, Public Speaker

What is your Internet venture?

Bizy Moms <www.bizymoms.com>, a Web site featuring entrepreneurial ideas and resources for stay-at-home moms.

Is it solely an Internet business?

It's an Internet Business/Online Site.

When was the business started?

March 1997.

How did you originate the idea for your site?

I first created the site to help promote my book; however, the site soon became a wonderful resource on it's own.

How did you finance your start-up?

It costs me about $15 a month to have my site up each month. I taught myself HTML so I didn't have to hire anyone. I used a free software program called HotDog to create my site. There wasn't a whole lot of cost involved at first. Three years later I have hired my own Web designer, and pay $60 a month to have my site up, along with other miscellaneous costs. However, I'm now making enough money off my site to pay for these expenses.

What resource helped you the most?

Since I really didn't have a clue how HTML worked, I would look at other sites' source code to see how and why the code worked the way it did. This was a wonderful way to learn, and cheap.

home business owners are resourceful in finding ways to "cover" family needs. For example, a group of entrepreneurial mothers in one neighborhood have a daily "revolving" play group, in which each woman watches the others' children for an hour or two. This frees up blocks of time for work, business calls, or running errands.

Can you offer any tips for creating a successful Web site?

Give your readers a good reason to come back to your site on a monthly, weekly, and even daily basis (this all depends on how often you can update new information). I could have created a one-page site that just talked about my book. Instead, my site became a wonderful resource on it's own. At first I used to get excited when I had 50 page impressions a day. Now I'm looking at over 250,000 page impressions a month.

One great and inexpensive way to get people back to your site is to send out a free e-newsletter. I send one out each week. This is a great way to remind people that your site still exists and that there's new information available to them on the site.

Do you have any additional comments?

At this time I do not sell anything on my site. It's a free resource. I make my money via advertising. So you don't necessarily have to have something to sell. If you know a lot about a certain topic, there's a good chance there are others out there who would love for you to share with them your wisdom. A Web site would be a wonderful way to share that wisdom and make money with it at the same time.

Liz Folger works as a full-time mom, wife, columnist and public speaker. She manages her Web site for stay-at-home moms, Bizymoms.com, from her home in Napa, California.

Con: It is difficult to work from home while trying simultaneously to balance the needs of small children, teenagers, elderly parents, and other loved ones.

Pro: You get a chance to earn money at something you love to do. You look forward to your work instead of dreading it.

Con: There is no guarantee that your business will be successful.

Pro: You can start your own local support network in your community, as well as network with millions of other entrepreneurs via the Internet's news groups, forums, Web rings, and online entrepreneurial "communities."

Con: You often feel isolated and overwhelmed working by yourself.

Pro: More entrepreneurs than ever before—especially women—are using their businesses to help support community activities and nonprofit organizations with sponsorships, internships, and donations of products and services.

Con: You do not have the time you once did to volunteer for school, religious, or community activities.

Pro: Along with the growth of home businesses has come the growth of business-support experts who support these home and online industries, a "network" of professionals to help you handle your business activities successfully. You make the creative decisions—you do not have to run it by a boss or a board of directors.

Con: You are responsible for overseeing all your business's operations—accounting, marketing, billing, advertising, production, and so on.

Pro: Women have always been creative with their business's financing, plus more and more options are opening up as we enter into the twenty-first century, as financial lenders and institutions recognize the value of investing in women's businesses.

Con: Financing can be one of the biggest obstacles to overcome.

Darcy Miller, owner of the online site, Little Did I Know .com, advises women who are contemplating an online business, "Find a business that you are so passionate about that you don't want to go to bed at night and you can't wait to get up in the morning. I say this because having a toddler child during the start-up of a business, you more than often have to work when they are sleeping. I do most of my work late at night and during nap time because that is uninterrupted time. I go to bed at 2 A.M. and get up at 7 A.M. It's truly passion and adrenaline that keep me going!"

Working for oneself is not perfect, but as you read the profiles of the women in this book, you will begin to pick up the enthusiasm, the enjoyment, and the pride they have in their ventures. Work defines us and who we are, so why not do something that we truly love and are passionate about? The word failure is not in a true entrepreneur's dictionary—but persistence is, because statistics demonstrate that it takes an average of three business start-ups for one to succeed. And many entrepreneurs start more than one business, the result of "spin-off" business ideas and markets that open up as their first business grows.

According to the National Foundation for Women Business Owners (NFWBO), nearly half the women business owners surveyed (45 percent) talked about issues related to gaining control and independence as the greatest rewards of business ownership. Weigh the pros and cons, talk to other entrepreneurs, thoroughly research your business idea, and then "take the entrepreneurial plunge," to find your own best reasons for working for yourself.

Preparing Your Family

One of the drawbacks of starting a business is that a new venture will often take twice the number of hours committed to get it up and running. Preparing your family for this onslaught

---

BUSINESS PROFILE: Darcy Volden Miller, Mom on a Mission (M.O.M.)

What is your Internet venture?

Little Did I Know (LDIK) <www.littledidiknow.com>, an online gift shop and directory of unique gifts for baby, child, and mother. Everything that is for sale is either handmade or distributed by a stay-at-home mother.

Is it solely an Internet business?

Solely an Internet business.

When was the business started?

Concept, February 1999; open for business January 2000.

How did you originate the idea for your site?

I felt so fortunate to be able to stay at home with my new baby that I in turn wanted to help mothers everywhere to be able to work from home, so that they too could stay at home to raise and nurture their little ones.

How did you finance your start-up?

I did direct sales with several companies.

What resource helped you the most?

The best resource that helped me was a book called *How to Start a Business for $1,000 or Less* by Will Davis. Excellent. My other

---

of work hours will help prevent their resentment—though not eliminate it completely—and gain their support. Here are some other preparation tips:

- Stress the benefits of running your business from home— that you will be at home and available for them if needed; you will have a more flexible schedule so that you can attend some of their activities and special events. But do not make unrealistic promises like, "I'll be able to buy you anything with the profits I make." One woman who owns

favorite resource has been Home-Based Working Mothers
<www.hbwm.com>.

Can you offer any tips for creating a successful Web site?

Start talking and never stop! Tell absolutely everybody and any-
body about your site and ask them to tell other people. After all,
five or twenty mouths are louder than one. Somebody somewhere
knows somebody. Also, list your site absolutely everywhere. There
are hundreds if not thousands of places on the Internet to list your
site for free. A great place to find a list of tons of places to list your
site for free is <www.the1000.com>.

Do you have any additional comments?

My favorite personal quote that has helped me to keep my spirit
up is, "Keep your chin up. . . . You can see further down the road
that way." (author unknown)

> *Darcy Volden Miller, founder of Little Did I*
> *Know.com whose ultimate mission is to*
> *help mothers everywhere to be able to*
> *stay home through the support and*
> *encouragement of self-employment.*

a bookkeeping business "rewards" her family for their
patience after every tax season with a weeklong stay at a
nearby family resort.

- Ask them for their help—and then give them a list of
  household chores that you would be willing to delegate
  to them.
- Set the ground rules for being disturbed, even to the point
  of posting your working hours on your office door. This
  may sound harsh, but you will need to work in undisturbed
  blocks of time. This will depend on the age and condition

of those for whom you care in your home (many Baby Boomers also have their parents and/or in-laws living with them these days). One mother with a home business asks when her teenagers interrupt her during her (set) working hours, "Is the house on fire? Is anyone bleeding? Has anyone stopped breathing? No? Then it can wait until I am finished here!"

Pat Cobe and Ellen H. Parlapiano, work-at-home specialists for the women's site iVillage and authors of the book *Mompreneurs: A Mother's Practical Step-by-Step Guide to Work-at-Home Success,* share this tip:

Include your family in your business plans from the very beginning. Welcome their ideas, feedback, and concerns. For example, ask your husband and children for input when designing your marketing materials (even a two-year-old can vote on his favorite color or font style for a brochure). Give the kids office jobs (like stamping and stuffing envelopes or delivering the mail to your desk) so that they feel like they're contributing to your work. Most important, make a covenant with your family about your work schedule. (Promise that you won't answer the business phone during dinner or bring your laptop to bed every night!) If you write down on paper the hours you plan to work (and those you plan to spend with your family) and then post the schedule in a prominent place, it will be easier to keep work and family in balance. And your family will be more respectful of your work time, too.

Eunice Lawson, inventor of Seat Belt Buddy <www.umed.net>, was asked how she convinced her family of her decision to go forward in developing her unique idea. She says:

I had talked about my idea for many years but did not actively pursue it nor put my personal lifesavings into it until

I had completed a public opinion survey and felt fairly sure it would be successful. My family thought I had lost all sense of reality when I quit the most satisfying job I ever had to start my own business. For two years it was a constant battle to prove the validity of my invention. It was not until medical, fire, rescue, legal, and educational professionals validated my prototypes that my family finally believed in my idea and my ability to bring it to market. Now they support me 110 percent and work alongside me every day.

INVOLVING YOUR FAMILY IN YOUR ONLINE BUSINESS

- Give your children tasks appropriate to their ages and reward them with payment and/or special times together. Check with your accountant for the current guidelines about taxes regarding the hiring of your children.
- Hold periodic discussions with family members to hear concerns they might have about your entrepreneurial tasks. Some family members may not readily accept your decision to start a business and may not want to be involved at all. Respect their decisions, but let them know you are determined to go ahead.
- Do not be afraid to ask family members for feedback at times when you have a business dilemma. They may offer some unexpected insight in helping to solve your problems.

Stacy and Richard Henderson's publishing and editing business, *Home Business* magazine <www.homebusinessmag .com>, involves their entire family. Stacy Henderson says, "My husband Richard and I both work together on our business from home. One of my daughters plays in her playpen right next to the kitchen table where I work. My other four daughters do their homework at the kitchen table right next to me while I work, and I am there to help them whenever they need me. The experiences I've had with my children and spouse have

---

BUSINESS PROFILE: Stacy Henderson, Magazine Publisher

What is your Internet venture?

Home Business magazine <www.homebusinessmag.com>, *Home Business Magazine Live* <www.homebusinessmagazine.com>.

Is it solely an Internet business?

50/50. We publish *Home Business* magazine, a printed bimonthly, international newsstand/bookstore/subscription magazine, $7\frac{1}{2}$ years in circulation. We also publish *Home Business Magazine Live,* the online version of our magazine, which is continuously updated with information on home business–related topics, and home-office products and services.

When was the business started?

1996.

How did you originate the idea for your site?

We wanted to reach and provide helpful information to new and experienced home-business owners online as well as on the newsstands and in the bookstores.

---

also influenced the creation and selection of many articles that have appeared in the print and online versions of *Home Business* magazine."

Discussing beforehand with your life partner and family the impact a business start-up could have on their lives will help garner their support. Their backing will be important to your business's success.

RELATED RESOURCES

Books

Honey, I Want to Start My Own Business: A Planning Guide for Couples by Azriela Jaffe (New York: HarperBusiness, 1996)

How did you finance your start-up?
Personal savings.

What resource helped you the most?
Articles and books written by other home-based business owners, who practice what they publish.

Can you offer any tips for creating a successful Web site?
We continuously update our Web site with interesting and current information that keeps our visitors coming back over and over again.

Do you have any additional comments?
We've learned it's not the jazzy graphics, but rather the high-quality information on one's Web site that visitors will value most.

Stacy Ann Henderson, editor-in-chief
of Home Business *magazine.*

Let's Go Into Business Together: Eight Secrets to Successful Business Partnering by Azriela Jaffe (New York: Avon Books, 1998)

The Missing Middle: Working Families and the Future of American Social Policy by Theda Skocpol (New York: W. W. Norton, 2000)

Mompreneurs: A Mother's Practical Step-By-Step Guide to Work-At-Home Success by Ellen H. Parlapiano and Patricia Cobe (New York: Perigree, 1996)

The Stay-at-Home Mom's Guide to Making Money from Home, 2nd ed., by Liz Folger (Roseville, CA: Prima Publishing, 2000)

Work Less, Make More: Stop Working So Hard and Create the Life You Really Want! by Jennifer White (New York: Wiley & Sons, 1999)

Internet Sites

<www.athomemothers.com> At-home mothers resource center; Association, magazine, and resources to support mothers working at home

<www.hbwm.com> Home-Based Working Moms; "A professional association and an online community of parents who work at home and those who would like to"

<www.homeworkingmom.com> Mothers' Home Business Network; "The best resource for mothers who choose to work at home"

<www.momsnetwork.com> Moms Network; "Celebrating Moms at Home in Business"

<www.wahm.com> Work-at-Home Moms; Online magazine for work-at-home moms

Time Management

How to Say "No!"

Let's face it: Some women are better at saying "No" than others. Starting a business on- or offline is going to take a major commitment of time—something that many of us do not have enough of these days—so you will have to free up time to dedicate to your business. One woman home-based business owner has the word "NO!" on a 3 × 5 card taped next to every phone in her house and even typed into the message of her cellular phone. Some other tips:

- Instead of making a weekly volunteer commitment, try volunteering for projects instead—like a hoagie sale or a one-day workshop.
- Pick one (or maybe two) nonprofit organizations whose principles you feel strongly about, and support them; tell others who ask for your support that you are already involved.
- Write down what you need to say before someone calls you with a request. A "script" of sorts that reads, "Gee, I wish I could help, but presently I am already helping . . . "
- Foster independence among your family. Encourage children to clean their own rooms (just close the door and do not peek!) and older ones to do the research for their own homework.

LaDonna Vick, owner of the online site, Mommy's@Work <www.mommysatwork.com>, gives a tip for a woman and mother running a business from home on how to say "No!" (without feeling guilty!) so she can focus on her family and then her Internet business.

Vick says, "Hmmm, saying 'No' without feeling guilty—that's a tough one. I believe women and mothers in general tend to feel guilty when they have to say 'No' to a project or to helping someone, but when you consider the cost of saying 'Yes' and how that decision can affect your family, it would be a smart thing to say 'No.' Know your limits and what tasks you can take on without sacrificing time with your family and/or Internet business. Saying 'No' is just another part of making smart business decisions. Those guilty feelings will eventually go away, but your family will be there forever."

Recording Time

We all have the same 24 hours in a day—but some of us maximize those hours better than others, especially when we are

---

BUSINESS PROFILE: LaDonna Vick, Author, Publisher,
Home Business Resource Specialist

What is your Internet venture?

Mommy's@Work <www.mommysatwork.com>; Your Online Home Business Resource Place.

Is it solely an Internet business?

Solely an Internet business.

When was the business started?

January 1999.

How did you originate the idea for your site?

I often found myself on the other end of the phone line talking to my daughters, and they would ask, "Where are you Mommy?" and I would say, "Mommy's at work; I'll be home soon." It always broke my heart and I knew that I somehow needed to get back home. Working outside the home no longer appealed to me and I wanted to be a part of my daughters' lives, not just for an hour in the morning getting ready for work and then maybe a couple of hours at night before they went to bed. So came the name for my new business, Mommy's@Work, Your Online Home Business Resource Place.

How did you finance your start-up?

Initially I worked full-time and worked my home business part-time. I was able to use the income from that job for my business start-up costs. Now that I run my business full-time and use the many free and low-cost ways to operate my business on the Internet, I am able to manage without obtaining a loan from a bank and minimal use of my savings.

---

managing a home business operation amidst all the other demands on our lives. Time management experts recommend that you take an assessment of the hours you spend each day, for a week. Here are some suggestions:

- Do a Time Journal. For seven days, keep a log of what you did every half-hour, on the hour. Do not cheat just to make

What resource helped you the most?

I would have to say the Internet has been my greatest resource. It is so vast when it comes to finding out just about anything you need to know on any subject.

Can you offer any tips for creating a successful Web site?

A well-planned-out promotion strategy has to be the one most important reason for a successful Web site. If people don't know you are there, they won't come. It is important to take steps toward finding out who your target market is, and take every measure to market to them, using methods like exchanging links with other Web sites, swapping ads in newsletters, posting your Web site URL to search engines, participating in discussion groups, and becoming an expert in your field.

Do you have any additional comments?

Most new business ventures fail mainly because of lack of sufficient capital and inadequate funds devoted to marketing. But the Internet is changing things for those with dreams of owning their own business, giving them a better chance to become entrepreneurs. With small amounts of capital and low overhead costs, you can open your computer-based business today. Businesses on the Internet continue to break records in sales and volume.

> *LaDonna Vick is the author and publisher of* Your Guide to Operating a Computer-Based Business at Little or No Cost! *You can subscribe to her free "Mommy's@Work Newsletter" by e-mail: mommysatworknews@smartbotpro.net.*

yourself look good, because you want to get an honest and clear picture of how you use your time in a typical week in your life.

- Evaluate that week's activities. Break your activities into various categories like eating, sleeping, meal preparation, errands, family concerns, work and/or business hours. Total each of the hours spent doing those activities.

- Group those activities into broader, important categories such as family, religious, business, community, and personal, and any other major time commitments in your life. You can write these down and place into a file or computer folder for each.
- Now, take some time to mull over your goals and your loved ones' goals. List them under each of those priority categories.
- Based on these categories and goals, at the beginning of each week make a weekly To Do list.
- Each day, use this weekly list from which to plan your daily To Do list.
- Keep a Work Diary to record what transpired during your day.
- Analyze each week. Look over your week's activities, Work Diary, and To Do lists and see what you were and were not able to accomplish. This analysis will aid you in revising and planning for the upcoming week.
- Analyze your goals periodically—monthly, semi-annually, or as needed. Make sure you are focusing on the activities that will lead you to achieve your set goals.

Other home business experts recommend that you set apart blocks of time to carry out specific tasks. For example, block out a specific day and hour(s) to run business errands, and assign yourself as many as you can do into your designated time period in order to save time and gas money. Using your time wisely and productively, especially if you decide to start that new online business venture, will greatly increase your chances for business success.

Nita Jackson (see her profile in chapter 3), owner of Organize Tips <www.organizetips.com>, a site offering free planners, organizers, and software, says, "You must make time to be organized—it will save you so much time in the long run as well as give you a sense of well-being that will benefit your business. The benefits of being organized are endless!"

COMMON TIME WASTERS (AND HOW TO ELIMINATE THEM)

Here are several tips from other home-business owners and experts on how to avoid wasting your precious time.

Juli Shulem, author of *Home Based Business Mom,* as well as a professional organizer, time management consultant, and speaker says:

> In my experience it [the problem] seems to be keeping work-related items in the office area and keeping them from being scattered about the house. This leads to wasting time running around from room to room looking for items rather than actually doing the work that needs to be done on them. An obvious way to prevent this problem is to keep all work in the designated office area at all times—no exceptions. It takes self-discipline in order to keep work from getting past the threshold of the office door.
>
> Another situation that often accompanies this problem is not setting specific work hours. This leads to work being "carried about" the house while tending to other matters because the work isn't getting done in the office. By setting specific hours in which to work and doing the highest priority tasks while in the office with good focus, the desire to carry work items around will often cease. It is important to set aside time to do the important tasks, and with children around, it is especially crucial to do work at times when distractions will be at a minimum. This is often very early in the morning or late at night.

Packy Boukis, owner of Only You Wedding and Event Consulting says:

Not having a "plan of action" is a great time waster. How can I be more productive? If you were suddenly given two tickets for a "free" destination of your choice, most of us would start with a "plan of action," making lists, checking off tasks, and so on. We would list the most important and non-negotiable tasks first, and then list things we would like to get done, but the world won't end if we don't get them done. Our first task of the day would be the first priority on the list, and continue through to completion. We would proceed through the list with great excitement and anticipation. Even though we are not going on a free trip to a destination of our choice, we still need to incorporate this same organized, and well-thought-out plan and enthusiasm for our business.

Do you have a time waster, of which you are guilty? Mine is being on the Internet too long (even though I write for a number of Internet sites!). I find that if I go online at the end of my work day, or at least after I finish the most important tasks of the day, I am more productive and less likely to "wander" in cyberspace. Another tip is to place next to your computer a sign saying, "Is what I am presently doing one of my day's prioritized tasks? If not, stop procrastinating and get back 'on task'!"

Debbie Williams, founder of Let's Get It Together <www .organizedtimes.com>, an online organizing forum, says, "The best advice I can give a woman running a business from home is to limit interruptions as much as possible—screen phone calls with voice mail during busy or noisy times, consolidate tasks, don't have an open door policy, and turn off your cell phone. Remember that you are in charge of your time, not someone else, and take a proactive stand against time wasters."

Being aware of how you use your time can help you be more productive and organized, thus increasing your business's profits, while possibly even finding more time to spend with those people who are most important to you.

RELATED RESOURCES

Books

Creative Time Management for the New Millennium by Jan Yager (Stamford, CT: Hannacroix Creek Books, 1999)

Home Based Business Mom: A Practical Guide to Time Management and Organization for the Working Woman by Juli Shulem (Santa Barbara: Newhoff Publishing, 1996)

Time Tactics Survival Guide by Arthur A. Hawkins II (Evergreen Park, IL: Information Research Lab, 2000)

Internet Sites

< www.thebusywoman.com/index.html>; Susie Glennan's The Busy Woman's Daily Planner (time-saving tips and products); Or write The Busy Woman's Daily Planner, P.O. Box 3424, Ventura, CA 93006

<www.organizetips.com> Free planners, organizers; Free software for home, office, wedding, pregnancy, holiday, and budget

Software

ACT! 4.0 (PC and Mac), Symantec Corporation <www.symantec.com>

Lotus Organizer 6.0, Lotus Development <www.lotus.com>; Also has a Web interface that enables you to save Web

---

BUSINESS PROFILE: Debbie Williams, Professional
Organizing Consultant

What is your Internet venture?

Let's Get It Together <www.organizedtimes.com>, an online organizing forum.

Is it solely an Internet business?

Solely an Internet business but I also provide local consulting and off-site training.

When was the business started?

March 1998.

How did you originate the idea for your site?

My husband suggested it, actually, after I successfully helped a family member create a filing system. In the past, I have organized files, created procedure manuals, and helped women organize their homes, and he thought this was a perfect home business for me.

How did you finance your start-up?

I'm happy to say that my start-up was nominal. I launched this business with an Internet home page and $320 from our personal bank account.

---

addresses, post daily calendar and client contact information on the Web, and other helpful features

Outlook 98 (PC only) Microsoft Corporation
<www.microsoft.com/outlook>

From Dream to Goals

A dream is like that pot of gold at the end of the rainbow: You know what you would like—riches, fame, independence—but a dream does not provide you with the path you need to find it. You should realize, too, that though nothing happens

What resource helped you the most?

Without a doubt, the best resource that has helped me is online women's communities. I built an entire network of friends, colleagues, and clients from participating in forums and chats. It's a great way to test a product or service idea, conduct marketing research, and build a strong Internet network for marketing and publicity.

Can you offer any tips for creating a successful Web site?

Keep it simple, easy to navigate, and well organized. It's a living breathing entity, so make it as dynamic and interactive as possible.

Do you have any additional comments?

Treat virtual customers as you would those you meet in person—try to respond within a 24-hour period. Customer service is key in a virtual environment; you don't get a chance to make another first impression, so make yours a good one.

Debbie Williams, syndicated columnist of Organized Times *and founder of OrganizedU* <www.organizedu.com>.

overnight, each day can be a step closer to realizing your dream. That is where goals come in. Goals define the steps you will need to take to reach your dream—or something more than just a fantasy—a life and business you love. Here are some general goal-setting tips:

1. Write down your dream or end objective first, that is, having a thriving business or Web site, or being head of a major corporation.
2. Also decide your personal and financial goals. Do they "mesh" with your main business objective or goal?
3. Now, write down the steps you will need to reach the first of those goals. Whether it is to read a book about starting

---

BUSINESS PROFILE: Jenny Wanderscheid,
Fun Resources for Parents

What is your Internet venture?
ChildFun Family Website <www.childfun.com>.

Is it solely an Internet business?
Solely Internet.

When was the business started?
April 1997.

How did you originate the idea for your site?
It started with a "flame-free" discussion list and a personal home page full of links. Gradually, I added crafts, then e-cards, then recipes, and so on.

How did you finance your start-up?
I never really started up! It just grew over the last three years from a small page of links on a local ISP to the monster it is now.

---

an online business or to talk to another woman entrepreneur, make each step manageable so you feel you have begun taking the steps toward reaching your dream.

4. Keep your vision on your long-range goals, so you do not get sidetracked.

5. Review your goals regularly and evaluate your progress.

6. Be flexible, because sometimes your interests will change as you mature or experience life; do not be afraid to change and head for another "mountain."

7. Remember the adage, "Anything worth something is worth the effort." You may hear of overnight success with Internet companies, but in reality, a successful off- or online business takes long hours and hard work. For example, Jenny Wanderscheid, founder of ChildFun Family Website <www.childfun.com>, says, "A lot of people write to me

What resource helped you the most?

WomensForum.com has been an amazing help! The Web masters of the other sites there have been the best resource ever. We trade articles, links, and newsletter ads.

Can you offer any tips for creating a successful Web site?

Keep it fresh. New content, new graphics, new content, new writers, new content, newsletters, oh, and did I mention new content? Ha! People won't come back to read the same things over and over. Keep it fresh and give them a reason to come back every day.

Jenny Wanderscheid,
"Who says parenting can't be fun?"
<www.childfun.com>.

wanting to know how I did it. They are looking for a 'get rich quick' scheme. There isn't one. Four years of hard work, sleepless nights, and surviving on peanut butter and mac and cheese have paid off. I worked hard to get where I am."

8. Be realistic. You may dream of being the owner of a multi-million-dollar business, but first you have to achieve the goal of being profitable.

However you fare in achieving your goals, remember to enjoy the ride. Although money is important and will validate your business, the WWW—the "Wild, Wild Web"—will present you with challenging and exciting experiences, plus the chance to be involved in a new business frontier of unexplored entrepreneurial opportunities!

RELATED RESOURCES

Books

The Millionairess Across the Street by Bettina Flores and
   Jennifer Basye Sander <www.goalsandjewels.com>
   (Chicago, IL: Dearborn Financial Publishing, 1999)

Seven Secrets of Successful Women by Donna Brooks, Ph.D.,
   and Lynn Brooks (New York, NY: McGraw-Hill, 1999)

Women's Tips for Meeting the Challenges of "Netpreneurship"

The women "netpreneurs" profiled in this book all have important advice for anyone who wants to have a successful Web site. Here are several of their tips for meeting the challenges of "netpreneurship."

La Donna Vick of Mommy's@Work says:

> Now is the time to establish your business on the World Wide Web, while it is still considered new. Begin by finding something you enjoy doing. In other words, find your purpose or passion in life. Find out how you can turn your passion into a business and profit from what you love doing. It takes a lot of hard work and persistence to stay in the "game." Doing something you enjoy will help you stick with it when times are slow. It no longer takes substantial capital to start your own business, but it does take determination. With little or no cost, you can be in business on the Internet within hours, so it is important to be prepared so your venture will be successful.

Doree Romett, owner of Presentasia Gifts, Inc., says, "Investigate, investigate, investigate. So many people have jumped on the 'Web bandwagon.' So many people claim to be 'Web experts.' Keep an open mind and carefully choose the best Web designer, Web host, Web server for your particular business and personal needs. You tell them what you want. Don't let them talk you into what they want. You know your business better than anyone and only you can make your dreams come true."

Shannan Hearne of Success Promotions <www.success promotions.com> (see profile in chapter 4), an online marketing service specializing in helping people build their e-businesses, sees firsthand how women today are taking advantage of the Internet. Shannan says, "Some 85 percent of my clients are women doing business via the Internet from their homes."

RELATED RESOURCES

Books

The 21st Century Internet by Jennifer Stone Gonzalez (Upper Saddle River, NJ: Prentice Hall Computer Books, 1998)

Business Basics

Once you have told your loved ones that you will be living and working under one roof, you will have other business considerations to handle before you ever make one click on the Internet. Here are a few of the major ones.

CHOOSING YOUR BUSINESS

It can be home-based or located in a retail area's storefront; it does not really matter where your office is located for an online business site.

Here are some important considerations to help you choose the best business idea(s) for you:

BUSINESS PROFILE: Doree Romett, "Giftologist"

What is your Internet venture?

Presentasia Gifts, Inc. <www.presentasia.com>, a gift business with an online site used to complement it.

When was the business started?

1995.

How did you originate the idea for your site?

I wanted my site to be an extension of the already successful gift business I established. I worked along with a Web design company to bring my ideas to life.

How did you finance your start-up?

It was started with personal finances. This was too small of a project for a bank or financial institution to be interested.

What resource helped you the most?

The resources available in the gift industry itself and the local chamber of commerce. I greatly appreciate the experiences of other entrepreneurs and I am very involved in many professional networking organizations.

- Assess you—the background and experience you bring to this idea, and your likes and dislikes. You also need a passion for your work to sustain your enthusiasm and perseverance through the long hours a new business start-up will take.
- List the business ideas that interest you and decide if they fit you, your skills, and your preferences.
- Research the business outlook for growth industries and see if you can choose a business idea related to that industry, using your interests and skills.
- Look for a niche, an untapped market whose needs have not yet been supplied.

Can you offer any tips for creating a successful Web site?

Never stop learning about the World Wide Web and all that is involved regarding Web sites. The WWW's like learning a new language and lifestyle. Best advice for a site is to keep it simple, user-friendly, and give 'em reasons to keep coming back for more!

Do you have any additional comments?

My site is a continual work-in-progress and a labor of love. I am continually learning about the dos and don'ts. . . . It's very challenging, but at the same time rewarding; like when a new customer contacts you from Italy. How cool is that?!

Doree Romett,
Giftologist of Presentasia Gifts, Inc.,
<www.presentasia.com>.

RELATED RESOURCES

Books

The 101 Best Businesses for the 21st Century by Gregg Ramsay and Lisa Rogak (Grafton, NH: Williams Hill Publishing, 2000)

101 Best Home-Based Businesses for Women, 2nd ed., by Priscilla Y. Huff (Roseville, CA: Prima Publishing, 1998)

101 Businesses You Can Start on the Internet by Daniel S. Janal (New York, NY: Van Nostrand Reinhold, 1996)

121 Internet Businesses You Can Start from Home: Plus a Beginner's Guide to Starting a Business Online by Ron E. Gielgun (Santa Rosa, CA: Actium Publishing, 1997)

The Best Home Businesses to Start in the 21st Century: The Inside Information You Need to Know to Select a Home-Based Business That's Right for You by Paul and Sarah Edwards (Los Angeles: J. P. Tarcher, 1999)

Finding Your Perfect Work: The New Career Guide to Making a Living, Creating a Life by Paul and Sarah Edwards (Los Angeles: J. P. Tarcher, 1996)

Internet Sites

<www.onlinewbc.org> Online Women's Business Center; "Learning about Business"

<www.toolkit.cch.com> Business Owner's Toolkit's SOHO section, "Starting Your Business"

<www.score.org> Senior Core of Retired Executives (SCORE); Offers helpful business information and location of local offices where you can pick up a free copy of "How to Really Start Your Business"

MAKING A PLAN FOR YOUR BUSINESS

You need to create a business plan (more on this will be discussed in chapter 3), which is a "road map" or "blueprint" for you to follow in getting your business up and running. Here are some tips:

- Review samples of business plans in books, on the Internet, or from other online business owners if they will share theirs with you, to get an idea of a business plan's structure, language, and organization.

- Write a preliminary business plan to determine an estimate of your start-up expenses and to assist you in doing a search for the existence of potential customers.
- Evaluate the results of this introductory plan to your business idea because it can reveal if this venture shows a market potential, and if it is practical for you to start up at this time or if more research, money, and/or time is needed.

RELATED RESOURCES

Books

Anatomy of a Business Plan: A Step-by-Step Guide to Starting Smart, Building the Business and Securing Your Company's Future, 3rd ed., by Linda Pinson and Jerry Jinnet (Chicago, IL: Upstart Publishing Co./Dearborn Trade, 1996)

Online Business Planning: How to Create a Better Business Plan Using the Internet, Including a Complete, Up-to-Date Resource Guide by Robert T. Gorman (Franklin Lakes, NJ: Career Press, 2000)

Internet Sites

<www.business-plan.com> Out of Your Mind . . . and into the Marketplace; Business planning software and materials by Linda Pinson, business-plan expert

<www.onlinewbc.org> Online Women's Business Center; Has detailed information about business plans; Information on e-commerce in their "Technology Tower"

<www.sba.gov/shareware/starfile.html> The Small Business Administration; Offers several free business-plan shareware and public domain software programs you can download

Software

Following are just two of the many existing software programs designed to help you prepare business plans

BizPlanBuilder Interactive by Jian <www.jian.com>

Business PlanPro 3.0 by Palo Alto Software <www.pasware .com>; This site provides sample business plans

YOUR BUSINESS OR DOMAIN NAME

When Shane Brodock, a certified professional virtual assistant (V.A.), was asked how she chose her domain name, AskShane .com, she said, "I found the name by 'virtual brainstorming.' I tossed names around with several colleagues and mentors across the country using e-mail and instant messaging. We came up with some pretty interesting names and finally someone came up with AskShane. I have to admit I was a little hesitant at first, but everyone else loved it as soon as they heard it. Good thing I listened to my advisors."

Here are some other tips:

- Your name should designate what your business does, for example, Smith's Desktop Publishing and Design. It will be easier for potential customers to recognize what your company does than with a generic name like Smith's Enterprises, which could offer anything.
- If this is a new business start-up and you plan to have a Web site for it, take into consideration what you will use as a domain name and:
  1. Whether that domain name is still available.
  2. That your name is not similar to or the same as that of another business.
- Consider the image you would like your business's name to convey and incorporate the appropriate attributes, such as quality, low cost, service.

- When you decide on a name, and if you plan to do business under any name that is not your own, you are required to file a fictitious name statement, also known as DBA, "Doing Business As," with your county and state. Then it is to be published in the legal section of a local, general circulation newspaper. Generally, you can do this filing yourself or hire a lawyer to do it.

- If you will be selling items in a state that collects a sales tax, you will need to register the name of your business and get a sales tax number.

- Decide if your name and identity will lend itself to obtaining a trademark to protect it. You can trademark both text and graphics. Go to the U.S. Patent and Trademark Web site for more information <www.uspto.gov>.

- Do not include the terms "incorporation" and "corporation" unless your business actually is incorporated.

More on obtaining domain names is covered in chapter 2.

RELATED RESOURCES
Books

Names That Sell: How to Create Names for Your Company, Product, or Service by Fred Barrett (Portland, OR: Alder, 1995)

Trademark: Legal Care for Your Business and Product Names, 4th ed., by Kate McGrath and Stephen Elias (Berkeley, CA: Nolo Press, 1999)

YOUR BUSINESS'S FINANCIAL PROGRAM

An accountant should be one of the professionals included in your network of experts. A consultation with one is recommended before you start a business, to help guide you in setting up your   ; accounting, bookkeeping, record-keeping, and tax-keeping financial system.

Accounting and Bookkeeping

There are several accounting methods* that small- and home-business owners use, such as the following:

1. **Cash method:** This is the most commonly used method by small business owners; income is recorded as it is received and expenses are deducted when they are paid.
2. **Accrual method:** This method must be used by businesses that carry inventories. Expenses are reported when you have them, instead of when you pay them; your income is reported when you earn it, not when you receive it.

Record Keeping

It is imperative to have an efficient recording system for your business's income and expenditures. Here are some of the most important components in your record keeping:

- **Income:** You should keep a detailed account of all money that comes in, noting the amount, the source of that money, transaction date, form of payment (check, credit card, other), sales tax collected (if any), the products and/or services you rendered, and your customer's name.
- **Expenses:** List the date, description, and to whom you made business expenditures for tax deduction purposes, and keep all the receipts in one folder.
- **Business-owned resources (assets):** Keep records of each purchase, model and make, costs, use, and length of use for all business-related equipment. This will be used for determining the depreciation of that piece of equipment for the year.

---

*If you are unsure which accounting method is best for your business, consult with your accountant.

Recording Deposits

Jan Zobel, tax preparer and author of *Minding Her Own Business: The Self-Employed Woman's Guide to Taxes and Recordkeeping,* says:

> While most business owners realize they should keep track of the money going out (their business expenses), they're often unaware of the importance of recording the source of all money coming into their business. One crucial reason for keeping records of all deposits is that entrepreneurs have a greater-than-average chance of being subjected to an IRS audit.
>
> In the course of an audit, all deposits shown on the taxpayer's bank statements for that year are added together and compared to the income shown on the tax return. Unless you can explain where extra money came from, any discrepancy will be assumed to be unreported business income and will be assessed taxes and penalties. Not only do you want to avoid the possibility of criminal charges for underreporting income, but you also do not want to end up paying taxes on such nontaxable money as loans and gifts.

- **Employees and/or subcontractors:** Keep records of any payments to employees or independent contractors (ICs) with whom you may subcontract work. Make sure you have invoices from those ICs you may have hired.

Become familiar with the latest rules for business deductions—like the expenses of travel, promotions, education, and training, and other activities—that your business is permitted

Internet Taxes

In October 1998, Congress passed the Internet Tax Freedom Act, which includes a three-year freeze on new taxation of e-commerce. Also in 1998, the federal Advisory Commission on Electronic Commerce (ACEC) <www.ecommercecommission.org>, chaired by Virginia Governor James Gilmore, was set up to examine the issue of e-commerce taxation and to send to Congress its recommendations.

The publication *Inter@ctive Week* <www.inter active-week.com> reported in its March 27, 2000, issue that after the ACEC's final meeting was held the third week of March 2000, the board planned to send to Congress its findings that the majority of the eleven members supported a plan that would make it virtually impossible for online commerce to be taxed.

However, even the ACEC was divided about this decision because U.S. states will lose out on sales taxes, which the U.S. Department of Commerce (www .doc.gov) says makes up about one-half of their revenue. Experts fear that as more people do online shopping the states will lose income, despite the fact that, according to the law—called the "remote sales tax" or "use tax"—people should remit to their state governments taxes due from most out-of-state purchases. The fact is, though, that most people do not voluntarily pay this tax to their state, and states cannot force out-of-state businesses to collect it. As a result, experts predict the rise of other taxes, but for now e-commerce is tax-free.

to take. Keep the appropriate receipts and dc   tion and
supply them when it is time to file your tax   an take
photographs of the space you use in your home for your home
office to prove to the IRS that space is used for your business.
On the photos, circle business equipment, materials, and any
stored inventory.

Taxes

You will benefit (and help your accountant) if you educate
yourself in the basics of your business's taxes: how to report,
record, and know to whom you owe what tax.

Here are some programs and sources that can assist you
in obtaining the tax information you need.

FEDERAL TAXES: INTERNAL REVENUE SERVICE (IRS)

STEP Program

At certain times during the year, the IRS offers a Small Business
Tax Education Program (STEP), which is a partnership with
local organizations that provides (usually free) workshops or
in-depth tax courses covering starting a business, record keeping, preparing business tax returns, and other topics. An IRS
spokesperson says the program discusses tax obligations and
provides materials consisting of sample tax forms the business
owners will be using. For course information, call your local
IRS office and ask for the Taxpayer Education Coordinator,
or call 1-800-829-1040.

IRS Web Site

The IRS Web site <www.irs.ustreas.gov> offers the following
materials that you can order:

- Publications: "Tax Guide for Small Business," "Self-Employment Tax," "Starting a Business and Keeping Records," "Business Use of Your Home (Including Use by Day-Care Providers)," "Guide to Free Tax Services," and others pertaining to your particular business. The Business Tax Kit, Publication 454-A, contains various forms and publications for persons in business or for those starting a business.
- Small Business Resource Guide: CD 2000, a CD ROM that provides critical small-business tax information.
- Tax forms and publications can also be ordered directly from the IRS by dialing 1-800-829-FORM, or online at <www.irs.gov/prod/forms_pubs/index.html>.

State Taxes

- Contact your State Department of Revenue (which goes by different names in different states) to get information about available tax workshops. Jan Zobel says, "Some states have tax education programs, sometimes in conjunction with IRS workshops. I'd also recommend that people contact their local Small Business Development Centers (SBDC) for general information about taxes and record keeping."
- Online: This URL <www.irs.ustreas.gov/prod/forms_pubs/ftaframes.html> provides a link to state sites from the IRS's Web site.

Local Taxes

For information about local taxes, check with your city, borough, or township office; or at your county courthouse.

Judith E. Dacey, C.P.A., owner of Small Business Resources, Inc. <www.easyas123.com>, says, "Technically the only truly 'local' tax would be a city income tax if you are in the rare state where cities have them (like some cities in Ohio)

Small Business Development Centers

Small Business Development Centers (SBDCs) offer business counseling, classes, and other services, including tax information at all three government levels. They are located in most U.S. major cities on university campuses. The closest location to you can be found at <www.sba.gov/SBDC>.

or a tangible personal property tax like the counties in Florida have. In those cases the city or county taxing authority will provide information (usually in the form of pamphlets or one-page instructions)."

Do not let tax issues discourage you from starting or having a business. You'll find plenty of assistance to help you comprehend and meet your tax responsibilities.

RELATED RESOURCES

Books

422 Tax Deductions for Businesses and Self-Employed Individuals by Bernard B. Kamoroff, C.P.A. (Willits, CA: Bell Springs Publishing, 2000)

J. K. Lasser's Your Income Tax 2000 (consumer edition) by J. K. Lasser Institute (New York: Macmillan General Reference, 2000)

Minding Her Own Business: The Self-Employed Woman's Guide to Taxes and Recordkeeping, 3rd ed., by Jan Zobel (Oakland, CA: EastHill Press, January 2000); Order from EastHill Press, 6114 LaSalle Avenue, PMB 599, Oakland, CA 94611

BUSINESS PROFILE: Judith E. Dacey, C.P.A.,
                     Motivator and Adviser

What is your Internet venture?

Small Business Resources, Inc. <www.easyas123.com>.

Is it solely an Internet business?

No, a professional service business. The Net is used to attract new people to me and give me credibility with tech-savvy small businesses since they are a significant marketplace for me. I also use it to provide information for people who are considering using my services to set up their business or for clients who are considering me for a speaking engagement. My site has always been a marketing tool versus a selling or distribution system.

When was the business started?

My business started in June 1986, but I was the first C.P.A. on the Web in the southeast United States in 1992.

How did you originate the idea for your site?

In 1992, a tech client who had just established himself as an Internet Service Provider (ISP) convinced me I needed a site to be in the technological forefront.

How did you finance your site?

Personal savings and designing the business to generate money quickly so it could pay for itself.

What resource helped you the most?

With my Web presence, those who helped most were my tech client, my wonderful husband who is a contract programmer, and consumer tech magazines (books are just too out-of-date for current Net-tech issues), plus traveling the Web, learning how it works, experiencing it.

Streetwise Finance and Accounting: How to Keep Your Books and Manage Your Finances without an MBA, a CPA, or a Ph.D. by Suzanne Caplan (Holbrook, MA: Adams Media Corp., 2000)

Can you offer any tips for creating a successful Web site?
Number 1 key issue: Identify your marketplace. Who do you want to come to your site? What do you want them to do? Understanding this thoroughly will save you thousands of dollars by giving you exact decision criteria to use on everything—from the style of the Web site to the colors and logo to the type of marketing message and navigation mechanism.

What kind of bookkeeping system do you recommend for an Internet-related business?
First: Use an efficient manual checkbook/record-keeping system like the One Write System provided by Safeguard Business Systems (1-800-523-2422) or McBee Systems (1-800-526-1272)—for more information see the article on my Web site, <www.easyas123 .com/tensecond.htm>.

Second: Use a good computer accounting system. *QuickBooks* is very popular and costs about $60 when discounted. But the key here is you must use all its functions you need such as payroll and invoicing. Do not try to piecemeal it by using the software for accounting but doing the rest by hand. Also an accurate setup is vital to avoid problems that will plague you for years.

Third: You need to find a competitively priced credit card processor, because Web sales mean Web credit. (See chapter 5, "Processing Transactions," for Dacey's tips for finding a competitively priced credit card processor.)

Judith E. Dacey, C.P.A., motivator and adviser to small-business owners and the self-employed, a Mensan, and a professional speaker.

Internet Sites

<www.accounting.com> C.P.A. link; Information and directory of accountants and accounting firms in small business and specialized areas

<www.awscpa.org> American Woman's Society of Certified Public Accountants

<www.tax.org> Tax Analysts; A nonprofit organization providing the latest information on tax developments at the state, federal, and international level

<www.taxweb.com> TaxWeb; "The Internet's first consumer-oriented source for federal, state, and local tax-related developments"

Software

BusinessWorks for Windows 12.0 by Sage Software <www.us.sage.com>

QuickBooks Pro 6.0 by Intuit, <www.intuit.com>

Peachtree for Windows 6.0 by Sage Software, <www.peach tree.com>; Inventory and e-commerce features

TurboTax Home and Business 99 by Intuit, <www.turbotax.com>

Other

One Write System provided by Safeguard Business Systems 1-800-523-2422 or McBee Systems 1-800-526-1272; Manual checkbook and record-keeping system

The Legalities

Being a business owner involves many legal considerations. This section covers just a few of the major ones.

YOUR BUSINESS STRUCTURE

To determine which form is best for your business, you will need to decide under which auspices you will operate. There are a number of legal structures, each with its own guidelines.

Sole Proprietorship

This is the most common and simplest form of business structure. Your profits and losses are recorded on your tax return. A drawback, though, is if a customer sues, your personal assets can be at risk.

General Partnership

This is a business agreement between two or more persons for the purpose of making a profit. Unfortunately, a large percentage of partnerships disintegrate; it is important to have a signed, written agreement detailing each partner's contribution to the business and an "exit" plan if one partner should decide to leave the business. The advantages are that you can combine your strengths and skills to benefit your business; the disadvantages include differences of opinion on your business's direction and shared unlimited liability—each partner can be held responsible for the acts of the other. Many small-business owners use the alternative of joining with other business owners—partnering on projects but still remaining separate business entities.

Corporation

With this business structure, the corporation is an entity unto itself and is separate from your personal life. While it the most complicated form a business can take, it can offer protection for one's personal assets in the event of a lawsuit. It also involves more costs, paperwork, plus additional accounting and legal services. There are different corporate organizations, such as S Corporation and Limited Liability, and you are advised to consult with both an accountant and a lawyer as to which one will be the most beneficial to you. Judith Dacey (see profile) also has a helpful article on her site <www.easyas123 .com> about incorporating your business.

Permits, Licenses, and Zoning

According to the type of business you run—even one online—
you may have to have a business license or permit from your
local authorities, depending on your area's zoning regulations,
and also one from your state. Check with your local state representative or senator for a directory of agencies that handle
the licensing of your industry. Also, there are federal restric-
tions regarding some types of home work such as those involv-
ing certain types of sewing and jewelry production.

Zoning regulations for home businesses vary widely from
borough to township in one area, from restricting all home
businesses to permitting all home businesses. Though many
home businesses are "hidden," it is better to be upfront with
local authorities about your business, and for you and other
home business owners to work together to educate your local
officials about the benefits of having home ventures in their
jurisdiction. Contact your town clerk, building inspector, or
codes enforcement officer about a home-business permit.
Many objections to business use of your home or property
come from the amount of traffic and disturbance to your
neighbors, so you will need to explain exactly what your business's activities will and will not include.

Employees and Independent Contractors

If you are planning to hire employees or independent contractors, you need to know the difference between the two regarding benefits, withholding taxes, and other responsibilities you
are obligated by law to follow in each hiring situation. If you
have employees (or if your business name is different from
your own), you must get an Employee Identification Number
(EIN) from the IRS.

For more information, see Cyberlaw in chapter 2.

RELATED RESOURCES

Associations

National Independent Contractors Association (NICA)
<www.independent-contractor.com>; NICA is an alliance
made up of independent contractors

Books

Choosing a Legal Structure for Your Business by Stuart A.
Handmaker (Upper Saddle River, NJ: Prentice Hall
Trade, 1997)

The Legal Guide for Starting and Running a Small Business,
Vol. 1, by Fred S. Steingold, Mary Randolph, and Ralph
E. Warner (Berkeley, CA: Nolo Press, 1998)

*The Partnership Book: How to Write a Partnership
Agreement,* 5th ed., by Attorneys Denis Clifford and
Ralph Warner, (Berkeley, CA: Nolo Press, 1997)

*Teaming Up: The Small Business Guide to Collaborating
with Others to Boost Your Earnings and Expand Your
Horizons* by Paul and Sarah Edwards, Rick Benzel
(Los Angeles: J. P. Tarcher, 1997)

Wage Slave No More: Law and Taxes for the Self-Employed,
2nd ed., by Stephen Fishman (Berkeley, CA: Nolo Press,
1998)

Internet Sites

<www.nolo.com> Nolo Press; Publishes legal books and pro-
vides an online Legal Encyclopedia, including small business topics

< www.nolo.com> Nolo Press's site also has "FAQs for
People Working as Independent Contractors," articles,
books, and software helpful to the IC

<www.corporate.com> Corporate Agents, Inc.; Provides information on incorporating your business

Business Insurance

Whether you run a business out of your home, only online, or from a storefront, business insurance is a must. Do not assume your homeowners policy or even an endorsement added to it will adequately protect you from equipment loss or from liability lawsuits or some unexpected disaster. Talk to licensed insurance agents who are familiar with the type of business you own to find the best policy to cover both your personal needs as a business owner and your business itself.

INSURANCE AND THE INTERNET

As the Internet offers more opportunities for a business to increase its operations, it also may increase its susceptibility to certain losses. You should talk to an insurance agent familiar with Internet business terms to discuss if your business should have a policy with the following types of coverage:

- **Business interruption insurance:** in the event your business is affected by an ISP's interruption of service, power outages, flood, fire, or some other catastrophe.
- **Intellectual property coverage:** to protect against charges of copyright infringement about your Web site's content.
- **Electronic publishing liability:** you will want coverage should someone sue you for infringement of trademark, title, slogans, copyright, piracy, or the invasion of the right of privacy, or computer virus transmission and other items of this nature.
- **Loss of business income:** to help pay your expenses should a natural disaster or a personal illness or injury occur to cause your business' operations to stop.

- **Liability coverage against interruption of online service to clients:** you will need such coverage if your computer or server should be "down" due to a malfunction, storms, or some other occurrence.

The Insurance Information Institute (I.I.I.) "advises Internet service providers, Web site content developers and designers, and other Internet-related companies to evaluate risk exposures and insurance needs." Taking time to adequately insure your business as it goes online will help prevent expenses due to losses that could be the demise of your business.

RELATED RESOURCES

Internet Sites

<www.allmerica.com> Home-based business owners' insurance information by Hanover Insurance

ADDITIONAL BUSINESS INSURANCE CONCERNS

You should also consider the following types of coverage, but note that there may be other considerations that pertain only to your particular business.

Equipment

For coverage of computers and other office equipment vital to your online business, visit InsurePoint <www.insurepoint.com>, which offers a wide range of business insurance. Two other companies are Safeware <www.safeware.com> and South Coast Metro Insurance Brokers <www.coveragelink.com/PC_Ins/default.asp>.

Liability

Product   Against claims that your product caused injury or damage.

Professional   Also called malpractice or errors-and-omissions insurance, to protect you against claims that your advice or professional services were not performed as agreed upon. Note that you should consult with a business lawyer to help prevent any such suits by having a waiver or contract agreement for your clients to sign.

General Liability   To protect you in the event that someone, including a delivery person, is injured when they come to your home for business reasons.

Disaster   Against weather-related calamities, fire, earthquake, and others. Also it will help to have a disaster recovery if the unexpected should befall your business. The Federal Emergency Management Agency (FEMA) offers a free guide to help you reduce any business losses that may befall you. Visit <www.fema.gov/library/bizindex.htm>.

Personal Insurance

With all the start-up expenses involved with a new business, entrepreneurs often either neglect or avoid the costs of health, life, and disability insurance. However, you must seriously consider being covered by these types of insurances in order to protect yourself, your loved ones, and the continuance of your business. Again, talking to licensed insurance agents will help you get the best policies to fit your needs and budget.

Health Insurance

One of the drawbacks of being self-employed is having to pay for your own health insurance. You can deduct a percentage of your payments from your taxes (check with your accountant for the specifics), but the premiums can also be a strain on your business's budget.

As an entrepreneur, the quest is to find affordable health insurance that will best serve your needs. Here are some options you can investigate:

- **COBRA (Consolidated Omnibus Budget Reconciliation Act):** If your previous job gave you health benefits, a 1985 federal rule says a former employer must offer the option of continuing your health coverage for 18 months. Of course, you pay the premiums. Also be aware that there are other criteria that both you and your employer may have to meet to be eligible for this program.
- **Associations and Organizations:** Business-owner groups like local chambers of commerce, your national trade or industry group, or organizations for professionals like bar associations for lawyers may offer group-rate insurance as part of their member benefits.
- **Health Alliances:** These are set up just to purchase health insurance and offer members a number of plans from which to choose.
- **Individual Plans:** Experts recommend that you talk directly with an independent insurance agent. She can answer your questions and may be able to offer you a variety of plans to best fit your individual situation. Make sure the agent is licensed in your state and is knowledgeable in the area of health plans for the self-employed.

A number of Internet sites (see Related Resources following) now provide health insurance information, rate comparisons, quotes, and even the opportunity to purchase plans online (subject to state regulations). Again, make sure you thoroughly check to see that an online insurance company is licensed in your state and is following state guidelines for selling via the Internet. Also take the time to make sure that it is a legitimate company and not a scam!

The Web site of The Agency of Healthcare Research and Quality <www.ahcpr.gov> provides health insurance information, including such articles as "Checkup on Health Insurance Choices" and "Choosing and Using a Health Plan."

There is no perfect health insurance coverage, but taking adequate time to explore the different plans available will guide you in finding the best coverage for the best price, and more likely, the best plan for your circumstances.

RELATED RESOURCES

Associations

Following are two organizations (of many) that offer group health plans to members.

Women, Incorporated <www.womeninc.com>; Offers members an insurance program with multiple insurers and plan options

Working Today <www.workingtoday.org>; Offers access to group-rate health insurance for independent workers and their families

Books

The Confused Consumer's Guide to Choosing a Health Care Plan by Martin Gottlieb (New York: Hyperion, 1998)

Internet Sites

<www.healthinsurance.org> Insurancevalues.com; An online resource for individuals, the self-employed, and small businesses

<www.healthplandirectory.com/HealthPlans/Directory> HealthPlanDirectory.com; Provides contact information for health insurance plans in your state

<www.hiaa.org/cons/cons.htm> Health Insurance Association of America; Insurance consumer guides

<www.insure.com/health> Insure.com; Health Insurance basics, news, and rate-finder

Disability Insurance

If you are self-employed, you generally will not have workers' compensation to fall back on if you should be injured on the job. If your income is needed for you and your family's survival, check with your insurance agents and your accountant as to which kind of disability insurance is best for you and whether a certain business structure (corporation) will provide you with worker's compensation or unemployment payments. For more of an explanation, read the article, "How Disability Insurance Works" at <www.insure.com/health/disability.html>.

Life Insurance

Maintaining a life insurance policy that pays death benefits if you should die can help your beneficiaries sustain living costs and possibly continue to run your business after your death, should they choose to do so. Some policies allow individuals to borrow against them for the purpose of business start-ups (this should only be done after consulting with your insurance agent and your family). At <www.underwriter.com/analysis.asp>, you can use the site's tools to estimate life insurance levels—"Analysis of Your Life Insurance Needs."

An insurance agent for your business and personal needs is an important person who should also be included in your network of experts, to help protect you, your loved ones, and your business.

RELATED RESOURCES
Books

The Buyer's Guide to Business Insurance by Don Bury (Grants Pass, OR: Psi Research-Oasis Press, 1994)

The Complete Idiot's Guide to Buying Insurance and Annuities by Brian H. Breuel (New York: Alpha Books, 1996)

How to Insure Your Income: A Step-by-Step Guide to Buying the Coverage You Need at Prices You Can Afford by the Silver Lake Editors (Los Angeles, CA: Silver Lake Publishing, 1997)

Insuring the Bottom Line: How to Protect Your Company from Liabilities, Catastrophes and Other Business Risks by David Russell (Los Angeles, CA: Silver Lake Publishing, 1996)

Internet Sites

<www.iiaa.org> Independent Insurance Agents of America; "Protecting Your In-Home Business"

<www.iii.org> The Insurance Information Institute; Provides facts and assistance free of charge to the media, individuals, and organizations; Search this site for information of home and small business insurance and other insurance topics

<www.insure.com> A comprehensive resource of online insurance information for consumers including small and home business insurance, health insurance, and other related topics

Your Office

If your home is your castle, then your home office should not be a dungeon. It does not have to be elaborate, but it should be bright, comfortable, and arranged for your maximum efficiency. Here are some considerations for a new office setup or to improve the one you have.

PLACEMENT AND SPACE

Home offices are everywhere an individual can put them—under stairs, a corner in a living room, in the basement, in the garage—or are built as home additions or separate buildings. It all depends on what space is available, your budget, your personal and family needs and schedule, and availability of access to electricity and phone lines. The good news is that space-saving desks and work stations are readily available, and you can often buy good used office furniture.

SAFETY

If you have small children and/or pets, put a door on your office to keep them out; keep scissors, staplers, cleaning fluids, and other potentially harmful items out of reach or locked up. Some mothers have "Dutch" office doors in which the bottom half can be locked and the upper half open to the other part of their home so they can watch their children, but not have them underfoot. Be careful of too many pieces of equipment hooked up to outlets, and keep wires out of the way of traffic patterns.

Have adequate lighting for your work, using as much natural lighting as is physically possible. Experts also recommend using sound-reduction tools such as carpeting, weather-stripping, sturdy doors, and insulated windows.

EQUIPMENT

Affordable home office equipment and technology is one of the reasons for the millions of home offices. Make sure each piece of equipment vital to your business's operations has the basic features you need, a guarantee (unless you are a tech expert

BUSINESS PROFILE: Eunice Lawson, Inventor
of the Seat Belt Buddy

What is your Internet venture?

Seat Belt Buddy, a Universal Medical Emergency Device (UMED)
<www.umed.net>.

Is it solely an Internet business?

UMED is a click and mortar business. We use the Internet to recruit
sales representatives and showcase our products to wholesale pur-
chasers. If visitors want to purchase single items we direct them to
our affiliate Web sites.

When was the business started?

The idea to begin an identification business was born in the late
1970s when our daughter was misidentified as a person killed in
an auto accident. Actual production and sales began in early 1999.

How did you originate the idea for your site?

Having been an Internet user for several years, it was a natural
assumption that UMED would eventually have its own Web site.

How did you finance your start-up?

The start-up for UMED was from personal savings, family loans,
salary from my "day job," barter, WINGS educational scholar-
ships, and calling in favors.

yourself or have one close at hand!), and a phone number for
technical support—preferably 24 hours a day.

Ergonomically designed equipment and furniture—key-
boards, mouse devices, office chairs, and even staplers—will
help prevent repetitive motion strains and injuries. Protect your
equipment with surge protectors and uninterruptible power
supply (UPS) devices. If the power goes off, or even if it just
momentarily flickers, a basic UPS unit like American Power
Conversion's Back-UPS Office <www.apcc.com> switches from
utility to battery power, providing you with enough power to
save your work and safely shut down the operating systems of
your computer and other electronic equipment. This will help

What resource helped you the most?

My earliest supporters were people I met on the Internet. The first major resource and one that I continue to utilize is my local Small Business Development Center (SBDC). Other ongoing resources are the wonderful women at iVillage, particularly the Work from Home Moms message board.

Can you offer any tips for creating a successful Web site?

I feel that your own dot-com (or dot-net in my case—I'm still working on the dot-com one) makes a company look more creditable. Also, putting your Web site address on every piece of paper that goes out of your office is important.

Do you have any additional comments?

I cannot stress how my company has benefited and grown from both online and offline networking.

Eunice Lawson, owner of
Universal Medical Emergency Devices

prevent the loss of vital computer files, financial records, and documents or irreparable damage to equipment.

Home networking technology is also a future trend where multiple computers and peripherals in the home are interconnected. This sharing of peripherals, phone lines, files, modems, and Internet accounts will help save on additional phone line costs and equipment, as it enables dual entrepreneurs and other family members to work simultaneously doing research or other projects. Intel Corporation's The Intel AnyPoint <www .intel.com/anypoint> connects PCs via home telephone jacks without interrupting the ability to make and receive phone calls while sending data across the network. It is simple to install and priced to fit the budget of most computer families. If you are building a new home, some local phone companies offer to do wiring for present and future technology.

COMMUNICATION

You should have at least two phone lines for fax sending and receiving, your modem, and calls. An increasing number of home business owners are using cellular phones as business numbers so they can keep in touch with their customers while they are away from the office. (Do not use the cellular phone while driving, or at least use the microphones or phone holders that permit you to place both hands on the wheel of your vehicle. Be courteous, too, where you allow your cellular phone to audibly ring.)

Many phone companies are offering low-cost digital subscriber lines (DSL) as alternatives to dial-up and cable modems. If you sell products online, offer a toll-free ordering and customer service number for those customers preferring to order over the telephone or who have questions.

OTHER OFFICE CONSIDERATIONS

If you find your office setup is not working for you, try changing the arrangement of your furniture and equipment or look for another space in your home (or attached buildings). You want your office to be inviting and a place in which you are looking forward to doing your work—not dreading it.

RELATED RESOURCES

Books

Home Office Design: Everything You Need to Know about Planning, Organizing, and Practical Home Office Solutions by Neal Zimmerman (New York, NY: McGraw-Hill, 1998)

Organizing Your Home Office for Success, 2nd ed., by Lisa
   Kanarek (Dallas, TX: Blakely Press, 1998)

Internet Sites

<www.homeofficelife.com> HomeOfficeLife; Site of leading
   home office expert, Lisa Kanarek

<www.ideasiteforbusiness.com/org.htm>; Tips on organizing
   your office

<www.quicken.com/small_business>; Equipping your office
   and other information

<www.tipworld.com>; Many ideas from their Small Office/
   Home Office tips

<www.workspaces.com> WorkSpaces; Information on ergo-
   nomic home-office equipment and other home-office tips

Other

Small business publications often feature tips and photos of
many unique home offices and reviews of the latest home-
office equipment and technology.

Entrepreneur's Business Start-Ups <www.bizstartups.com>

Home Office Computing <www.smalloffice.com>

HomeBusiness magazine <www.homebusinessmag.com>

Smart Computing <www.smartcomputing.com>

Avoiding Internet Business Scams

scam   A fraudulent business offering or scheme, especially
   for making a fast, illegal profit.

SPAM   Unsolicited e-mail, usually to try to sell a business
   opportunity, or market a service or product.

Subject: Re: YOUR REQUEST!

Get over 50,000 Hits FREE—GUARANTEED!
This WORKS! You should definitely try this!

Subject: YOU CAN MAKE OVER $100,000 PER YEAR!
To: EVERYONE WHO WANTS TO MAKE MONEY!
HERE IS THE INFO YOU REQUESTED, THIS IS
NOT SPAM. . . .
EARN $100,000 PER YEAR SENDING E-MAIL!!

Dear Friend,
You can earn $46,000 or more in the next 90 days sending e-mail, seem impossible? Read on for details (no, there is no 'catch'). . . .

Just as legitimate businesses are using the Internet to start, grow, and expand their businesses, so too are scam and con artists using the Internet to bilk both consumers and businesses out of money. These two e-mail SPAMS are actual examples of the type of suspicious solicitations I receive every day in my personal and business e-mail boxes.

The National Consumers League (NCL) Internet Fraud Watch said in a press release released February 16, 2000, that consumers lost over $3.2 million to Internet fraud in 1999, with a 38 percent increase in Internet fraud complaints coupled with an average consumer loss of as much as $580. The NLC said the number 1 Internet fraud was online auction sales, 87 percent, with other top frauds being non-auction sales of general merchandise, Internet access services, computer equipment/software, and work-at-home plans.

Businesses of all sizes are also bombarded by unscrupulous con artists with such common scams as bogus invoices, fax frauds, charitable solicitations, Internet services, Nigerian money offers (I received that one!), and any number of others that may sound good but are definitely not legitimate.

It could be a scam if it:

- Promises huge profits running this business in your spare time.
- Asks for your money, credit card number, or bank account information before any of their information will be supplied to you.
- Refuses to give names and contact information of others who have invested in this deal.
- Wants to sell you this business opportunity but not to instruct you how to run this business.
- Refuses to send you a demo disk if they are selling business software.
- Sends you an e-mail that says you requested this message.
- Sends you e-mail solicitations in CAPITAL LETTERS.

These are just a few of these scam artists' tactics. Here are some tips to avoid being a scam victim:

- Only do business with those people and companies with whom you are familiar.
- Ask for references and any certifications that their industry gives to legitimate companies.
- Do not sign any contract without reviewing it with your lawyer.
- Do not give out financial or personal information.
- Do not even respond to unsolicited e-mails because experts say it is often how these people determine if your address is "live," and they will keep sending them.

If you have been SPAMmed or scammed or know someone who has, contact one or more of the following:

- The Better Business Bureau in the state of the location of the company. Go to <www.bbb.org> to find the offices.

- The state attorney's office where the company is located.
- Your ISP or Web host.
- The National Fraud Information Center <www.fraud.org>, or call 1-800-876-7080.
- The Federal Trade Commission (FTC) <www.ftc.gov>. The FTC cannot resolve individual disputes, but it can take action if there is a pattern of deception being committed by a company.

You may be anxious—even desperate—to make money with your idea or business, but take the time to thoroughly research your business ideas and do not spend a single penny until you are satisfied with the credentials of the people with whom you are dealing. Trust your instincts, and if you do not feel right about a transaction, just forget it!

The rule to follow—you know the one . . . repeat after me: "If it sounds too good to be true . . . "

RELATED RESOURCES

Internet Sites

<www.bbbonline.org>; The Better Business Bureau drafted a "Code of Online Business Practices," that will be a "roadmap for businesses engaged in e-commerce," to give consumers confidence in doing business online

<www.fraud.org>; The National Consumers League runs the National Fraud Information Center (NFIC) and the Internet Fraud Watch, which provides tips, articles, and other information concerning Internet fraud

<www.ftc.gov>; The Federal Trade Commission has a selection of e-commerce and Internet-related information regarding Internet scams, compliance with advertising, privacy protection rules, and other regulations for businesses

Developing a Business Web Site

The Federal Trade Commission <www.ftc.gov> states, "The Internet is the fastest growing source of mail-order sales. It is estimated that consumers spent $14 to $15 billion on Internet-based goods and services in 1998—$5 billion during the 1998 holiday shopping season alone." And according to data from International Data Corporation <www.idc.com>, "The number of small businesses with sites on the Web will be 4.3 million by the year 2001, with the average overall revenues of small businesses using the Internet being $3.79 million." And one more statistic: ActivMedia Research says in their annual survey, "Real Numbers Behind 'Net Profits 2000" <www.activmediaresearch.com/real_numbers _2000.html>, that e-commerce today generates $132 billion in revenues worldwide.

These statistics are enough to motivate any entrepreneur to immediately post some type of Web site for their business or business idea. But, as with all businesses, the more planning and preliminary research you can put into your Web site or presence, the more chances you will have for success. Throwing money at Internet avenues without study and calculated steps can be a waste of money and time. This chapter presents information and steps to help you enter the entrepreneurial Web "portal."

Determining the Purpose of Your Site

Knowing why you need a Web site and what you want it to accomplish should set the "template" around which you pattern and maintain your site. If you want your site to be primarily informational, you will need to supply regular Web content. If you are selling products, you will need to provide potential customers with access to easy and secure transactions. If you want your site to be interactive with its visitors, you will need to provide it with chats, message boards, questions, and other offerings that will encourage visitors to return to it on a regular basis.

Following are some considerations that will help you determine your Web site's purpose.

Your Mission Statement

What is a mission statement? A mission statement gives the reasons for your business's existence and its customer benefits. In other words, a mission statement declares your business's purpose. It will help you to refine your business objectives.

Debra M. Cohen, President, Home Remedies of NY, Inc., whose business provides "dependable, skilled professionals for any household task," says her business's growth directed the purpose of her Web site. "As the demand for Homeowner Referral Network services grew," says Cohen, "so did my workload. I needed to get word out about my business to a much larger audience but didn't have the extra time or financial resources to do it. Launching a Web site was the ideal solution. It's like having a full-time sales and marketing force to promote your business globally."

Here are several other reasons you should write a mission statement for your online venture:

- It will help activate your marketing plan by setting goals and objectives for the future.
- A well-written statement can be an effective marketing tool and be used as an attractive introduction to prospective customers. You should be able to explain your business's fundamental nature, merit, and its undertaking in one or two well-articulated sentences—which you can readily state to anyone who asks, "What is your business?"
- It can help you define the type of customers your business will most likely be serving.
- It can help you focus on the benefits you promise your customers.
- It can help you better understand the purpose of your business and give you the inspiration and nerve to withstand the rigors that a business owner often experiences.

Writing a Mission Statement

When writing your business's mission statement, include some of the following elements:

- A description of your business as you envision it—how you wish your prospective customers to think of your business.
- Examples of how your business meets the needs of your customers.
- Information about how customers will benefit from using your products or services.
- Descriptive and "active" words, and terminology that's easy to understand.

BUSINESS PROFILE: Debra Cohen, Homeowner Referral
Specialist

What is your Internet venture?

Home Remedies of NY, Inc. <www.homeownersreferral.com>.

Is it solely an Internet business?

Home Remedies is a home-based business which has expanded
nationally. I've used my Internet site to promote and support my
business outside of the local area where I operate.

When was the business started?

February 1997.

How did you originate the idea for your site?

My business is a Homeowner Referral Network (HRN) and links
homeowners with reliable, prescreened home improvement contractors. I market my business on a global scale now and wanted a
site that would be user-friendly and functional while promoting our
services in a professional manner. The HRN Web site serves two
functions:

1. It promotes the launch of other HRNs nationally.
2. It allows anyone in the world to find an HRN (and thus, reliable
   home improvement contractors) in their area.

How did you finance your start-up?

We financed my business by taking a $5,000 loan against our retire-
ment savings.

What resource helped you the most?

My husband. As with all aspects of my business, first I seek advice
from professionals in the field (Web designers, SCORE advisors, my
attorney, etc.) and bring the information back to him for a final

---

You may find it helpful to write your mission statement
with a "picture" of your target customer in mind.

After you have written your statement, put it away for a
few hours or until the next day, so you will have a fresh outlook on it when you reread it. To include all this in a paragraph
or a single page is not easy! Write and rewrite your statement,

decision. He always brings a new perspective to my business. I remember when we first decided that I should have a Web site, we sat down and sketched the format on a small notepad at our kitchen table!

Can you offer any tips for creating a successful Web site?

Have a clear focus of what you need your site to do. Many people launch sites just because they think they should have a Web presence. In order for your site to be effective you must have a purpose in mind. This will help you market your site better as well.

Also, a Web site requires an ongoing marketing effort. If your area of expertise isn't in Web marketing (or you don't have the desire to handle that aspect of your business), outsource it to a reliable Web professional. Finally, take some time to seek out and develop strategic Web relationships with others who provide complimentary services or products to yours. Like in an office, networking with others is a great way to learn while spreading the word about your business.

Do you have any additional comments?

Just because you have a Web site, do not let your business lose its "personal touch." Whether it comes in the form of personalized e-mails to your visitors or follow-up phone calls, the Web can be an anonymous place, and making that extra effort goes a long way in developing consumer trust.

> *Debra M. Cohen, president, Home Remedies*
> *of NY, Inc. E-mail: HomRemdies@aol.com.*

or write several and get feedback from other business owners, business experts, or friends and family.

When you have decided on your mission statement, read it to yourself on a daily basis, because it should be a valuable guideline when making decisions about your business's operations. It will help you keep a clear vision of your business's purpose and keep you connected to the customers you most want to reach.

RELATED RESOURCES

Books

The Mission Statement Book: 301 Corporate Mission Statements from America's Top Companies by Jeffrey Abrahams (Berkeley, CA: Ten Speed Press, 1999)

Say It and Live It: 50 Corporate Mission Statements That Hit the Mark by Patricia Jones and Larry Kahaner (New York: Currency Doubleday, 1995)

Internet Sites

<http://edge.lowe.org>; The Edward Lowe foundation's "Entrepreneurial Edge"; Search in its documents for "Mission Statement"

GOALS AND OBJECTIVES

The goals and objectives of your site will be determined by your business's overall strategy.

Stacy Brice, president and virtual maven, Assist University (AssistU) <www.assistu.com>, says of her business strategy, "Relationships drive results. Always choose love over fear." (See her profile in chapter 3.)

Some other tips for setting goals and objectives for your site:

- Determine the opportunities the Web presents to you and/ or your business and work out your objectives accordingly.
- Determine who is the Web "community" that you will be targeting with your site.
- Determine how your Web site's goals will be integrated into your overall business goals. Will it be a major player—get-

ting most of your customers via the Internet? Or will it be a sideline player—reaching customers that otherwise your business would not likely reach?

When asked how she set her goals and objectives when she first started, Kristi Kirsch, owner of PetVogue.com, said, "Realistically. Let's have a good time doing something we enjoy (pets) and generate income to boot!"

DEFINING AND MEASURING SUCCESS

After you list your goals and objectives, consider what a successful Web site will constitute for you. What will be your criteria that says your site is a "cybersuccess"? Will you measure its success by:

- The amount of money your site makes to sustain itself or support you and your family?
- The number of hits or impressions it receives per month?
- An increased number of nationwide and global customers?
- The number of inquiries you receive for promotional purposes?
- If your business is an organization, an increase in members?
- Being able to take your Web site public?

Of course, your measure of success may change as your Web site evolves, especially with the uncertainty of the e-commerce economy in this new century. Once you enter the Internet business world, be ready to immerse yourself in its latest trends and technology to keep your site competitive and working the best it can! Susan Abrams, author of *The New Success Rules for Women* <www.newsuccessrules.com>, says, "My advice to women to achieve success in their own businesses is: Be focused, be tenacious, and self-promote liberally but gracefully."

BUSINESS PROFILE: Kristine Kirsch,
                    Unique Pet Products

What is your Internet venture?
CoolPetStuff.com <www.coolpetstuff.com> was our first site;
PetVogue.com <www.PetVogue.com> is the new site.

Is it solely an Internet business?
Strictly Internet businesses.

When was the business started?
CoolPetStuff.com, April 1998; PetVogue.com, March 2000.

How did you originate the idea for your site?
My husband Steven and I wanted to work together. We chose
e-commerce, then a sector in which our interests lay.

How did you finance your start-up?
Bootstraps and $20,000 in savings.

YOUR VISION

Your vision of your site will be a combination of your mission
statement, goals, and objectives. While your mission statement
is the reason for your business's existence, a vision statement
describes what you strive for your business to become. Some
common characteristics of vision statements:

- They can list what will be unique about your Web business and what will differentiate it from its competitors.
- They can be pledges of what a site's owner will (and will
  not) attempt to present to those who visit the site.
- They can include statements of the business owners' ethics
  to help earn the respect and confidence of their customers.

Some Web site owners will share their visions with their
site's visitors on the pages called "About Us" or on a separate
page, "Our Vision."

What resource helped you the most?

Definitely other entrepreneurs. There were no books at the time, and few people knew anything about e-commerce and specifically marketing on the Internet.

Can you offer any tips for creating a successful Web site?

Best tip: Think hard, identify a market need, fill that need, and never forget who your customers are.

Do you have any additional comments?

As with any undertaking in life, I would recommend . . . having a good time!

Mrs. Kristine Kirsch is the owner of PetVogue.com and ManuPets.com <www.manupets.com>.

Your vision for your Web site may or may not be written down, but it should be clear in your mind before you begin the planning stage of your Web site or your business use of the Internet. Paula Davis, a reporter with 10 years of journalism experience and the desire to own her own women's magazine, knew that women want to read about truly inspirational, down-to-earth women who have overcome problems similar to their own. In 1995 she used this vision to start her online publication, *Commitment,* which strives to do something positive to help women.

Davis says, "Our goal is to inspire women instead of preaching to them. We don't dwell on weight or celebrity issues because we always want to be doing something different, and a little out of the ordinary."

In essence, a vision comes from you and is translated by how and what you will present to the entire Internet community on your Web site. Use it to help form your goals and guide

---

BUSINESS PROFILE: Paula Davis, Online Magazine Editor

What is your Internet venture?

Commitment <www.committment.com>, an online magazine for women.

Is it solely an Internet business?

This is solely an Internet business.

When was the business started?

November 1995.

How did you originate the idea for your site?

I was looking for women's sites, and there were not many I was attracted to. Women have a lot more to worry about than diets, celebrities, and movie-of-the-month, and women's magazines didn't seem to recognize the real-life responsibilities most women face.

How did you finance your start-up?

Personal savings.

What resource helped you the most?

Trial and error were my best teachers.

Can you offer any tips for creating a successful Web site?

Work hard every day. Never rest on your laurels. Be ready to give up a part of your life.

Paula Davis, Editor of Commitment
*" . . . featuring true-to-life content developed
with the reader—the everyday woman—in mind."*

---

you in the planning and maintenance of your site and its Internet activities.

RELATED RESOURCES

Books

The New Success Rules for Women: 10 Surefire Strategies for Reaching Your Goals by Susan L. Abrams (Roseville, CA: Prima Publishing, 2000)

Outsmarting Goliath: How to Achieve Equal Footing with Companies That Are Bigger, Richer, Older and Better Known by Debra Traverso (Princeton, NJ: Bloomberg Press, 2000)

Planning Your Web Site

Choosing Your Site's Host

Essentially, a Web site is a place on the Internet where you store information about your business or yourself, and from which you may offer services and or products. Your Web site can be established on an existing Web server, or you can have your own server—which is usually beyond the budget or needs of small or medium-sized businesses. Many small businesses start with a local ISP or with a member site's free personal page to get a feel for designing a Web site. You may also go to a larger commercial ISP that will host your Web site for a monthly fee, or start with free publishing sites like BigStep or Yahoo! GeoCities.

However, be aware that not all hosting companies provide the same level of service. That is one of the reasons that the Web Host Guild* (WHG) <www.whg.org> was founded by Jonathan Caputo—to set a standard its members would follow to protect consumers and benefit quality hosting companies. If the host company you are considering has the Guild seal on its site, you can be assured of high quality services.

Debra Traverso (profile in chapter 7), copartner of the writers' instructional site, WriteDirections <www.writedirections.com>, and author of *Outsmarting Goliath,* says in answer to the question, "How did you decide which host to use for your site?" "Shopping around. We have a virtual assistant

---

*The WHG regularly features member profiles in the print and online publication, *Inter@ctive Week* <www.interactive-week.com>.

who is just dynamite and she does the research for us. I used to be involved in crisis management and communication, so I'm especially sensitive to the potential for hackers, crashes, and so on. Reliability was a big factor with me."

Here are some other factors you will want to consider in choosing your Web site's host (local ISP or otherwise):

- **Their connection capacity:** If your host's connection capacity is at 50 to 100 percent, movement around your site may become too slow or stop completely. You will want the host's bandwidth to be able to handle the amount of traffic to your Web site.

- **Domain parking:** A host should offer free domain "parking" (the registering of a domain name that will not immediately be used for a Web site setup) and should not entice you into signing a contract committing you for a period of time to host it—you may want to choose another hosting company. Many Internet service providers offer complimentary "parking" or "holding" services for their customers.

- **Storage space:** Compare the amount of storage space (measured in megabytes, or MB—10 to 20 MB is most often offered by ISPs, which is usually adequate for most Web sites) you get for your price, and get the most for your money. E-commerce "eats up" that space quickly, and you will want some room for business expansion.

- **Others sharing the server:** Too many other Web sites on your server can cause slow loading of your pages.

- **The host's technical support:** Preferably 24/7. You may also want your server to have available Web site–building services to help you expand your site's offerings as demanded by your customers or your business's growth.

- **The host's equipment:** Naturally, the most up-to-date will deliver your pages more speedily than dated equipment will.

- **Back-up storage systems:** If your server should crash, you will want your information to be stored on a backup server! Do not rely on the hosting company to maintain backups of your data. You should keep copies of all your Web site pages on your own computer by using FTP transfer to download the files. Your hosting company* can give you details on how to do this.
- **Rates:** Get a figure of the total fees charged for setup, monthly maintenance, and extra services.
- **Modem speed:** If you use a local ISP, you will want to know if it can support the fastest-speed modem you are using.
- **E-mail:** You will want to know how many e-mail boxes you receive for your fees.
- **Software compatibility:** You will want your Web site–creation software to be compatible with your host or ISP.
- **Monitoring:** You may need or want to be able to evaluate the number of your site's visitors and how they use your site's offerings.

Do not forget to ask your server for references from satisfied customers, as well as asking other women who have Web sites what they like (or do not like) about their current hosts to help you in this important decision.

Selecting a Domain Name

A domain name is the part of the word address of a Web server. It usually ends with a three-letter abbreviation such as .com (commercial ventures); .edu (educational institutions); .org (nonprofit groups); .gov (government agencies); .mil (military); .net (most often for Internet service providers); and others that

---

*BSCNet <www.bscnet.com>, for example, is a hosting company that is friendly to small businesses and can provide excellent support.

designate a country, like .ca (Canada) or .nz (New Zealand).
Other extensions may be added in the future (if they have not
already been adopted) such as .store (e-commerce Web sites);
.info (for information-based Web sites); .nom (individuals);
and others. These new extensions will pose other dilemmas
for businesses that are trying to protect their trademarks and
intellectual property and will complicate Web searching, but
you can be sure there will be technology and solutions to overcome these problems.

The entire URL (uniform resource locator) would look
like this:

<www.your_domain_name.com>

If you lease space from another Web site, it will look like
Patricia Gallagher's business Web address:

<www.geocities.com/teamofangelpins>

Your selection of your domain name is extremely important, as it relates to you and your business and helps establish
your business's name and recognition. If your URL uses
another site's principal domain name, <www.their_company/
215453your_business_name>, as in Patricia Gallagher's case,
it may be more difficult for both your present and potential
customers to locate your site. Domain names should be for the
convenience of consumers, to help people remember them.

In actuality, computers recognize not a registered domain
name, but the numeric address, called the Internet Protocol (IP)
address, consisting of four groups of numbers between 0 and
255 separated by a period (such as 123.45.678.90). When someone types your URL into her browser software, the Domain
Name System (DNS) translates your URL into an IP address of
numbers, enabling the Web browser to locate your site.

As you read the profiles and quotes of the women featured
in this book, take note of how their domain names are suited

to the purposes of either their businesses or themselves. Some good examples are La Donna Vick's Mommy's@Work <www.mommysatwork.com>, author Susan L. Abrams' <www.newsuccessrules.com> for her new book, *The New Success Rules for Women;* and Shane Brodock's <www.askshane.com> a virtual assistant for authors and speakers. Other well-chosen names are <www.ucanride.com>, The American Association of (horseback) Riding Schools, Colleen B. Pace's franchised riding school; and <www.clubko.com>, Kids Only Clothing Club, Inc., a party-plan sales company offering clothing designed by mothers and founded by Cindy Eeson. You can see by these examples, that in choosing a domain business name, you are only limited by your creativity and, of course, the availability of the domain name you choose.

Registering Your Domain Name

You can register your domain name yourself or pay to have a company, like Domain Direct <www.domaindirect.com>, do it for you. The process:

1. Choose one (or more) names for your domain.
2. Search databases of registered names, like Network Solutions <www.nsi.com>, Register.com <www.register.com>, or BetterWhoIs <www.betterwhois.com>, to see if that domain name is available.
3. Provide your information, the IP address, and your ISP's primary and secondary name servers.
4. Fill out the registration form.
5. Arrange payment and await registration confirmation.
6. Start! After your domain registration has been completed, you are ready to proceed with your online venture.

Here are some other factors to consider when choosing a domain name:

The Domain Registration Market

Until October 1, 1999, you had to use Network Solutions (InterNIC) <www.networksolutions.com> to register your domain name, paying upfront for two years' registration ($70), and then renewing annually ($35). However, the U.S. Commerce Department ended this monopoly (Network Solutions still maintains the database). You can now use one of a host of other new companies, like BuyDomains <www.buydomains .com>, that offer competitive prices and services, for your domain registration. These new domain registrars are accredited by the Internet Corporation for Assigned Names and Numbers (ICANN) <www.icann.org>, the agency now responsible for the global Domain Name System. Internet experts recommend that before you sign up with any of these new registration companies, check whether they are accredited by ICANN and that this can be verified.

- **Trademark considerations:** You may want to trademark your name. Trademarks are unique words, catch phrases, symbols, marks, or other things that identify a product or service. In essence, trademarks are brand names. You can register your trademark yourself by going to the site of the U.S. Patent and Trademark Office <www.uspto.gov> and clicking on "Trademark Electronic Business Center," to use their new Trademark Electronic Search System (TESS). You can then file an application at <www.uspto.gov/teas>. If you are unsure, the best overall step may be to first consult with a lawyer who specializes in trademark law. Note, too, that trademarks transcend countries' boundaries, so be sure you yourself do, or hire someone to do, a thorough search, not just within your own country, but internationally as well.

If someone has already registered the name you prefer, you can, of course, choose another one or contact that person to see if they would like to sell or lease it to you.

• **Copyright:** Copyright protects literary, dramatic, musical, or artistic works, motion pictures, software, and other intellectual property. Make sure your name does not

---

Cybersquatting

Effective November 29, 1999, Congress signed into law the Anti-Cybersquatting Consumer Protection Act, which permits trademark owners to sue someone who has registered a domain name that is similar to or the same as a trademark owned by that company. In one example of this, reported by the Associated Press in the *Philadelphia Inquirer,* the well-known convenience store operator Wawa, Inc., sued a California woman for registering a number of domain registrations using the "Wawa" name.

The purpose of this law is to prevent people from buying up domain names of well-known companies for the sole purpose of making a profit by selling them back to that company. That practice is known as "cybersquatting," and it can result in fines ranging from $1,000 to $100,000. Some disputes are referred to the World Intellectual Property Organization (WIPO) <www.wipo.org>, which charges reasonable rates to individuals and small businesses to help defend themselves in domain disputes with larger companies.

---

infringe on someone's copyrighted name. For more information about formally getting a copyright, go to the Copyright Office's home page <www.loc.gov/copyright>.

- **Recognition:** Choose a name based on your business's products and services so that potential customers can recognize what you offer at your site. If you choose a generic name, such as "your_name_enterprises," people will not know what your business is offering ("enterprises" is too general), and you will have to increase your marketing efforts to establish the name recognition that you need.

- **Length:** Be careful about the number of characters used in your name—previously you could only register a name that was 22 characters in length; now it is up to as many as 67! Deciding the use of long or short names should be based on how it will benefit your business or how you intend to use the Internet.

- **Global awareness:** Because the Internet is global, make sure your domain name is not an offensive word in another language.

- **Legal issues:** You may also want to consider registering all similar names and marks to your domain name to prevent future possible litigation. Though registering and paying the annual fees gives you the exclusive right to use that Internet name, you do not own it. If you stop paying the fees and/or decide to let it go, someone else may then register that domain name. If you have questions, you should always seek legal advice for your business matters.

Your business and domain name (if they are different) should help promote your business, and give it the prominence it deserves. When asked, "Do you have a tip for a woman considering an Internet business in choosing a name/domain name for her business or herself?" Tania von Allmen of LogoLab <www.logolab.com>, says, "Yes. The very second you come up with a name you remotely like, reserve it! I hear tales from our clients every day where one day a name was available and 24 hours later it's gone. It's like the great land rush all over again. Names are like gold, and the best ones are going fast. Sometimes, the difference between a successful Internet business and an also-ran is how memorable and 'spellable' a name is on the URL."

RELATED RESOURCES

Books

Domain Names: How to Choose and Protect a Great Name for Your Website (Quick and Legal) by attorneys Stephen Elias and Patricia Gima (Berkeley, CA: Nolo Press, 2000)

Trademark: Legal Care for Your Business and Product Name by Attorneys Stephen Elias and Kate McGrath (Berkeley, CA: Nolo Press, 1999)

The Trademark Registration Kit: Quick and Legal by Attorneys Patricia Gima and Stephen Elias (Berkeley, CA: Nolo Press, 1999)

Internet Sites

<www.networksolutions.com> Network Solutions; Features glossary of domain-related terms

<www.uspto.gov> U.S. Patent and Trademark Office

DETERMINING YOUR INTENDED AUDIENCE

With any new business venture, you should perform thorough market research to find out:

1. Whether potential customers exist for your business.
2. Whether they use the Internet to find people and/or businesses like yours.
3. The reasons they go online.

BUSINESS PROFILE: Tania von Allmen, Company Identity
Specialist

What is your Internet venture?

LogoLab, Inc. <www.logolab.com>.

Is it solely an Internet business?

Our business began as a business-to-business venture and still is
today. The main difference the Internet has made is in how we market our services and how we deliver our service. (Logo designs can
be sent by e-mail easily and efficiently.)

When was the business started?

LogoLab started in October 1993.

How did you originate the idea for your site?

We based our site on a "lab" theme that is consistent with our
name, logo, and marketing materials. We believe in big-picture
ideas and encourage our clients to do the same.

How did you finance your start-up?

VISA. It's every place you to want to be.

4. If your audience does not yet use the Internet, will they be
   increasing their use in the near future? You can determine
   this by:

   • Reading your industry's and related associations' pub-
     lications and online articles and information concern-
     ing the Internet.

   • Reading Internet business publications that regularly
     quote the latest e-commerce studies by research firms
     (see the Related Resources for some of these).

   • Visiting government sites, for example, the U.S. Small
     Business Administration <www.sba.gov>, your state's
     or province's sites, or women-related sites like the
     Women's Online Business Center <www.onlinewbc
     .org>.

What resource helped you the most?

My partner and I read a lot and also talked to lots of other business owners. In addition, we sought the services of a business coach, and that has also made a difference.

Can you offer any tips for creating a successful Web site?

Make the site part of your total marketing strategy. We put our Web address on our Yellow Pages ad and our direct marketing pieces, so all of our efforts complement each other. In addition, you've got to be savvy to metatags and keep up the maintenance effort there. Finally, the site itself must be visually appealing, easy to navigate, and have worthwhile content or people will move on quickly.

Tania von Allmen, principal of LogoLab, "specializing in helping small to medium businesses discover identities that make sense for them."

- Visiting statistical sites like Cyber Atlas <www.cyber atlas.com>, which offers statistical information about the Internet.
- Visiting research sites like those of the Trends Research Institute <www.trendsresearch.com> and the Net Future Institute <www.netfutureinstitute.com>.
- Hiring an information broker or a research firm to do the research for you.

Global Considerations

When you develop an Internet presence, consider that your business can draw from a worldwide market. One owner of a chocolate-making business has a faithful customer list from Japan, so who knows from where in the world your business

---

BUSINESS PROFILE: Kate Frykberg, Internet Consultant

What is your Internet venture?
The Web Limited <www.web.co.nz>.

Is it solely an Internet business?
Solely Internet.

When was the business started?
April 1995.

How did you originate the idea for your site?
My husband Dave and I thought that Internet technology would change the way the world worked, and we wanted to help people use it effectively. So we started our Internet consultancy.

---

could come? Kate Frykberg, of the New Zealand Web development business, The Web Limited <www.web.co.nz>, says, "We have concentrated on New Zealand rather than globally; however, global opportunities seem to be coming our way anyway."

In answer to the question, "In your opinion, why is it important that an online entrepreneur be aware of the global market potential of the Internet?" Angi Ma Wong, owner of Angi Ma Wong Intercultural Consulting and Corporate Training <www.wind-water.com>, says, "The Internet is the flying carpet that will transport your business to where you want it to go, and your business is as large or small a universe as you dream it to be."

Here are some tips for establishing your Web site as a global presence:

- Establish payment terms for foreign customers, such as asking to be paid in advance and in U.S. currency.
- Yes, translation software exists, but it is not perfect, so you

How did you finance your start-up? (A bank loan? Personal savings?)

A bit of both.

What resource helped you the most?

A great accountant who is also a business advisor was a big help. I also found *Built to Last* and *The E-myth Revisited* useful books.

Can you offer any tips for creating a successful Web site?

Know who you are targeting and what they need. Then make it really easy for them to take the action you want them to take.

> *Kate Frykberg, managing director, The Web Limited,*
> *"Providing Internet and intranet solutions."*

might want to hire a person fluent in the language of the country to whom you are marketing, or contact a translation service.

- Consider the benefits of partnering with companies in other countries to take advantage of better pricing, marketing, production, and other opportunities that working together can bring.

- Consider the potential market growth of such countries as China and those in Africa, including Egypt.

- Be aware of cultural differences in expressions, dialect and idioms (even in the same language), and Internet laws. If you are not thoroughly familiar with the customs of the country with whom you are doing business, it can save you embarrassment and worse by hiring consultants or localization services to assist you in your global commerce.

- Is your business "consumer-friendly" for international commerce? The United States and 28 other countries, working together as members of the Organization for Eco-

BUSINESS PROFILE: Angi Ma Wong, Intercultural Consultant and Corporate Trainer

What is your Internet venture?

Angi Ma Wong, Intercultural and Feng Shui Consulting and Corporate Training Web site <www.wind-water.com> and <www .fengshuilady.com> and other domain names.

When was the business started?

Consulting business was founded in 1989. Pacific Heritage Books, founded in 1993. My Web site was established in 1998.

Is it solely an Internet business?

No, it is not solely an Internet business. I am basically a business service with an online site. My business service facilitates profitability between Asian and nonAsians through seminars, sales and marketing support and training, speaking, publishing, and writing.

How did you originate the idea for your site?

Through the support of community Internet service.

How did you finance your start-up?

I began my business with $350 of my own money.

nomic Cooperation and Development, have decided on new guidelines for those who do business in the global electronic marketplace. You can read these guidelines on the Federal Trade Commission's (FTC) site <www.ftc.gov> in the Business Publications section. Click on "Electronic Commerce: Selling Internationally, A Guide for Business" to read the guide.

RELATED RESOURCES

Books

Teach Yourself Web Publishing with HTML in a Week by Laura Lemay (Indianapolis: SAMS Publishing, 1995)

What resource helped you the most? (Other entrepreneurs? Books, agencies/organizations?)

All of theses and mentor/friends.

Can you offer any tips for creating a successful Web site?

When designing it, it is imperative that you know who your audience is and that your site "speaks" to that market. Know what you are trying to achieve with your site: inform, attract new customers and clients, sell product/services, keep in touch or . . . ? The site should be interesting and visual, match the service or products, and explain what your business offers. For example, on my site, I endeavor to sell my publications, correspond with visitors, and attract new business, which I have been successful in doing, although it's a fairly passive site without a lot of bells and whistles.

Angi Ma Wong is the author of
Feng Shui Dos and Don'ts,
Feng Shui Desk for Success Tool Kit,
and Feng Shui Garden Design Kit.

XML: A Primer by Simon St. Laurent (Foster City, CA: IDG Books Worldwide, 1999)

Internet Sites

<www.adero.com> Adero; Assists companies in implementing global e-business strategies

<www.elingo.com> e-Lingo; Develops and hosts real-time translations solutions for portals, e-tailers, and others

<www.freetranslation.com> FreeTranslation.com; English to and from French, German, Italian, Norwegian, or Portuguese

<www.quickclue.com> QuickClue; Lists top sites in several categories including computers

<www.worldlanguage.com> World Language Resources; Translation products and services

<www.wtexec.com> WorldTrade Executive, Inc. (WTE); Provides business information services to the international trade community and focuses on the practical issues concerning the mechanics, barriers and opportunities for operating in international markets

PREPARING TO BUILD YOUR SITE

Once your domain name is protected, then comes the construction of your site. The kind of Web site you build will depend on your business goals and the type of business you have or the kind of self-promotion you desire—what your present needs are and what you are planning for future growth. Here are some of the most common types of commercial sites presently online:

- **Professional services:** Consultants and professionals such as physicians, attorneys, psychologists, educational consultants, and others who have specialized knowledge and credentials in their fields.
- **Business-to-business:** Companies and individuals seeking to subcontract their products and/or work for other businesses, such as manufacturers of equipment, virtual assistants, professional organizers, software developers, and others.
- **Consumer items:** Businesses selling just about anything to consumers, from pet products and clothing to household items and artwork. Business "niches" in this category would include sites for hobbyists—fly-fishing, sports, collecting, and a myriad of other activities.

- **Information-based:** Community sites like iVillage.com, Women.com, and BizyMoms.com as well as online or print publications like *Commitment* <www.commitment .com> and *Home Business Magazine* <www.homebusiness mag.com>; family or children's sites like Parenting Humor <www.parentinghumor.com> and ChildFun <www .child-fun.com>, or even radio stations that broadcast simultaneously online such as Working Assets <www.working assetsradio.com>.
- **Creative ventures:** Writers and authors (Stephen King <www.stephenking.com>, Dana Stabenow, mystery writer <www.stabenow.com>); comedians (Jimmy Carroll <www .members.tripod.com/jimmycarroll>); artists, musicians, and singers (Jewel <www.jewel.com>).
- **Technology and Internet-based:** Computer and home- or small-office supplies like <www.matchpatchink.com> and technology, and Web-based services—design, hosting, marketing, maintenance, and others—offered to those who need the Internet for personal and business reasons.
- **Small retailers:** Selling decorative items like Bucks Trading Post <www.buckstradingpost.com>, cards and gifts like those by Kathy Davis <www.kathydavis.com>, and chocolates <www.chocolatefactory.com>; others that have storefronts and sell their products online.
- **Various combinations:** Some or all of the above.

It is a given that each type of commercial site varies according to its business offerings.

Build and Maintain It Yourself

The construction of a successful Web site depends on your technical knowledge, your familiarity with HTML language (and/or XML, an HTML upgrade), and the tools (software) you use. Generally the best Web sites are built by those with a thorough comprehension of HTML specifications and limitations. You can enroll in Web-related classes at local colleges or adult evening schools, or online courses; read publications on Web publishing and building storefronts; or follow the templates in site-building software like Microsoft *FrontPage,* Macromedia *Dreamweaver,* Adobe *GoLive,* and others. (See Essential Equipment and Technology, in chapter 3, for additional options.)

Hire a Web Designer

Designing your own Web site has its advantages, but unless you are knowledgeable in the design process, you run the risk of having an amateur-looking Web site, which could detract from your business's professional image. Thus, you may want to spend the money to hire a professional. Costs can start at $2,000 and increase from there, depending on your site's complexity. One designer I know has designed sites for a major company for as much as $100,000!

Judith Dacey, C.P.A., <www.easyas123.com> (see her profile in chapter 1), says from her experiences of having a site to promote her services, "Web site development takes three different skills:

1. An experienced marketer who can develop the right message.
2. A good Web graphics designer who can set up effective visuals.
3. A techie who programs the info and develops the Web site for efficient downloading and navigation.

"Sometimes," continues Dacey, "you find one person with two of the needed skills. It's almost impossible to find one person with all three. So ask your designer: 'Who performs these three vital functions and what skills and experience does each person bring to the project?' Trying to cut corners by using a friend of a friend who is a combo designer/Web tech is spending money, not saving it."

When asked if she had a tip for women who are choosing a Web designer to design and maintain their businesses' sites, Jen Czawlytko, owner of webJENerations, says, "The most important aspect of choosing a Web designer for your business is . . . compatibility. Be sure you pick someone you can work with in a professional manner. Your designer should be someone who understands what you want, offers help and guidance to improve upon your ideas for the site, and can take you step-by-step through the start-up phase of creating your business image on the Web. Nine out of ten times when a client–Web designer relationship fails, the cause can be traced directly to personality conflicts or a lack of professionalism by one party or the other."

ELEMENTS TO INCLUDE ON YOUR SITE

When you begin to think about your Web site design, keep in mind the purpose of your site. Remember the primary goals of your site—to furnish more information about you and your services, so people or businesses can contact you or you can sell your products.

Design Basics

Web designers recommend that you draw a flowchart or storyboard to organize your pages more effectively. Arranging your Web site's pages in a diagram can help you to plan the best organization to present to your site's visitors (see figure 2.1).

Here are some basic Web site components to include:

• **The home page:** This is the first page that will be loaded onto your visitor's screen. It is their welcome and map to your site's offerings, so have it set up so your visitors can easily find the information and/or products for which they

BUSINESS PROFILE: Jen Czawlytko, Web Designer

What is your Internet venture?

webJENerations <www.webjenerations.com>, web design and related services.

Is it solely an Internet business?

75/25. I do market both online and offline but primarily online.

When was the business started?

I officially registered my business in June 1999, but freelanced as a Web designer for $1\frac{1}{2}$ years prior to the registration.

How did you originate the idea for your site?

My site was designed with business owners in mind. I wanted a very professional site that told potential clients a little about why their business should be on the Internet, described the services I offer, and showcased my previous and current work.

How did you finance your start-up?

Personal savings.

What resource helped you the most?

Meeting other women business owners online, at Bizymoms.com and through my former job in the iVillage Work-from-Home channel on AOL.

---

are seeking. It is an important first impression, and you will want it to project the best image of you and your company. List on this page any awards and certifications you and your business may have acquired. If your site is updated regularly, add the date when it was last amended. Most home pages also contain a copyright notice at the bottom of the home page to protect your work.

- **Your directory:** This should be located on your home page so that visitors can click on the hyperlink (underlined text or icon) that will lead them to each secondary page listed.

Can you offer any tips for creating a successful Web site?

For my type of business, keep the site professional, showcase your work on the site, be clear on the services you offer, give at least a general idea of the fees involved, put your Web site URL on all your marketing materials (I even have a decal on the rear window of my car), get linked in as many places on the Internet that you can, and make it easy for prospective clients to contact you through your Web site. In addition, all of my client contracts include a statement permitting my link to be on the client's site for as long as my site design is used, even if I do not continue to maintain the site.

Do you have any additional comments?

When deciding on an Internet business, be sure it is something you love. You will need that love to inspire you as you get started. Also remember to set reasonable goals/expectations for your business. It can be tempting to think you will get rich overnight with some of the stories in the press, but as with any business it takes planning and hard work to make your Internet business truly successful.

Jen Czawlytko, owner of webJENerations,
"Bringing Your Business into the Global Marketplace!"

- **"About Us":** This is a page of information listing your and/or your business's names, address, description, your biography, business philosophy, and—very important— your contact information.
- **Your business's services or products:** This is a description of your offerings, prices, testimonials, your experiences or awards. From this page, you can provide references, or the first links in the ordering process of the products you have.
- **FAQs:** Frequently asked questions are just that—questions that your customers ask often of you. A good set of FAQs

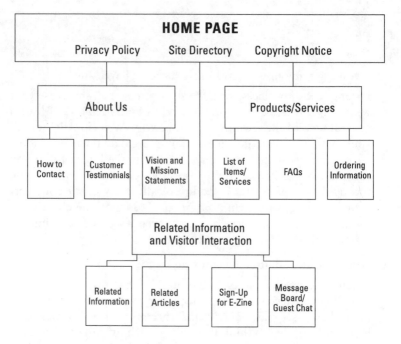

Figure 2.1   This is just a sample of how you can arrange your Web site's pages in a diagram to plan the best organization to present to your site's visitors.

will save both you and your customer time. Invite your site's visitors to add a FAQ of their own.

- **Privacy statements and policies:** List your policies about keeping any information you gather confidential and sharing or distributing it to other companies.

- **Terms of use:** If you offer a chat room or sponsor a forum, you should have what is and is not acceptable language, topics, and solicitations.

- **Guestbook and comments page:** Have a place for customers' feedback and their opinions to help you improve your site and your business's offerings.

- **Sign-up for more information:** If you offer an e-mail newsletter or send out periodic offers or sales, have a place where your site visitors can enroll to receive these.

- **Related information:** Providing helpful information and links related to your Web site will motivate visitors to return to your site often.

Your Web site may have some, all, or even more components than were mentioned here. Start with a basic, simple plan and expand it as your business grows and according to your customers' requests.

Judith Dacey, C.P.A. <www.easyas123.com>, adds to her previous comments about Web site development:

> It ain't TV. What you see is not often what another person gets. Browsers read data and generate the "picture." They do not reproduce it exactly as you see on your screen. Your Web designers will have the fastest system, an oversized monitor, and the highest evolution of the current Web browser. Do not be enthralled with what you see in their office. Be sure to look at your site on your neighbor's computer, your kid's, the one at the office, and have at least five good friends check it out and give you feedback.
>
> And the real kicker? It is estimated that almost 30 percent of the people run the Web with graphics turned off. So your beautiful pictures and logo are not even seen. Be sure that your Web site makes sense in a text-only format.

Here are some additional tips in designing your Web site:

- Design your site to have a logical progression for your visitors.
- Keep your pages short in length so that visitors do not have to constantly scroll down. Like a press release, have the most important information at the top of each page.
- Make your pages simple and fast to load by keeping your graphics and images simple, and not too many on any one page.

Frequently Asked Questions (FAQs)

Whether you sell products or provide information on your site, if your visitors repeatedly ask the same questions, or you want to help them navigate through your site's pages, you should include an FAQ section on your site. Having an FAQ section on your business site can better explain the purpose of your site and a synopsis of what you are offering. It will also save you time in answering oft-repeated e-mails. An FAQ section can also gain your customers' trust as you demonstrate to them that you understand their needs.

Here are some other FAQ tips:

- If your site is selling something, provide the following: descriptions of products or information, ordering steps, credit cards accepted and transaction security used, other ordering options, guarantees, exchange policies, and a site guide.
- Have a place where your customers can add their own FAQs.
- Place your most important questions at the beginning. Try to limit the number of FAQs. People do not want to scroll continuously.
- Update your FAQs as your information changes.
- Strive to keep your FAQ section organized and relevant, with the objective of helping your customers quickly find the answers they need.

Creative Considerations

Keeping your site interactive and innovative will be an ongoing challenge. More and more sites are offering interactivity for their visitors, such as hyperlinks to help them find answers to

their questions, surveys, contests, giveaways, regular announcements, chats, forums, virtual tours, and other features that
make sites interesting and give visitors reasons to return.

Be aware of your colors and backgrounds. Do not let them
contrast too harshly or overcome your content and text. Keep
your text in familiar fonts such as Courier, Times Roman, and
Arial, and do not "shout" at your visitors with too many
words in capital letters. Typeface should be 10 point or higher
for comfortable reading.

For pictures, you can have photos scanned and upload
them, or use Web graphics for free from ArtToday <www.art
today.com>. For more interactivity you can add these: If your
site has less than 500 pages but still provides a large amount
of content, an internal search engine can be added free
from Atomz.com <www.atomz.com>; and a chat, message
board, or other free tools for your site from Beseen <www
.beseen.com>.

Web designers caution that you do not get too caught up in
the design and forget the message you are trying to communicate to your target customers. Start with a simply designed and
streamlined site that is easy for visitors to use, and build on it
from there.

Evelyn Salvador of Desktop Publishing Plus says, "Just like
other advertising methods for print media, the content (copy)
as well as look (design) are important to attract your readers,
keep them interested, and keep them coming back."

Including a Catalog on Your Site

Not everyone can afford to start a mail-order business, but the
Internet is offering an affordable option for selling products
to both consumers and businesses. Despite the problems some
of the larger companies have had in fulfilling orders, many
people are successfully selling and delivering their products to
satisfied consumers. One example of this is Dianne Mayfield's

---

BUSINESS PROFILE: Evelyn Salvador, Resume and
Career Coach Specialist

What is your Internet venture?

Graphic Design and Resume Services <www.designerresumes
.com>, for resumes with guaranteed results; and <www.dtpplus
.com> for business-building advertising, design, and marketing
services (site currently under construction).

Is it solely an Internet business?

A retail business with an online site. I expect that the resume business will become more Internet than retail in the future.

When was the business started?

1990.

How did you originate the idea for your site?

Desktop Publishing Plus designed and wrote copy for the site and
Acorncreative.com developed it.

---

online gift boutique, Netique, Ltd. <www.netique.com>. Mayfield, a lawyer by trade, says she started Netique.com when
looking for an alternative to practicing law. Armed with the
desire to do something "positive," she came up with the idea
of a mail-order gift company.

Catering to people who enjoy unique gifts, but who lack
the time to leisurely browse looking for the perfect gift for a
family member, client, or employee, Mayfield's company now
offers more than 400 gift items as well as a customer collection
of products that can be special-ordered.

You may or may not have that many items in the online
catalog you want to include on your site, but starting with the
fundamentals and the right software, you can offer a basic catalog to get your products moving.

How did you finance your start-up?

Took out a loan for the computer setup ten years ago. Everything else we purchased from business proceeds as we grew.

What resource helped you the most?

My enthusiasm, expertise, creativity, and drive—at first. In 1997, I discovered the National Resume Writers Association (for the resume side of the business), and the Graphic Artists Guild (for the graphic design side of the business). I have found both organizations to be the best for advice, expertise, and member benefits.

Can you offer any tips for creating a successful Web site?

Use as many key words as possible so the search engines pick up your site through various search topics.

Evelyn Salvador, NCRW, JCTC, creative
director of Desktop Publishing Plus.

Related Resources

Books

Designing Web Usability: The Practice of Simplicity by Jacob Nielsen (Boston: New Riders Publishing, 1999)

Elements of Web Design: The Designer's Guide to a New Medium, 2nd ed., by Darcy Dinucci and contributors, Maria Giudice and Lynne Stiles (Berkeley, CA: Peachpit Press, 1998)

Learn HTML In a Weekend, Revised Ed. by Steve Callihan (Roseville, CA: Prima Publishing, 1998)

Web Navigation: Designing the User Experience by Jennifer Fleming, Richard Koman, Ed. (Sebastopol, CA: O'Reilly Associates, 1998)

Web Style Guide: Basic Design Principles for Creating Web Sites by Patrick J. Lynch and Sarah Horton (New Haven, CT: Yale University Press, 1999)

Internet Sites

<http://poorrichard.com> Poor Richard; Web site and creation help; Free information to help you set up your Web site; Newsletter; Order the book by Peter Kent, *Poor Richard's Web Site: Geek-Free, Commonsense Advice on Building a Low-Cost Web Site,* 2nd ed. (Lakewood, CO: Top Floor Publishing, 2000)

<http://webdb2.netobjects.com/netou/html/university.htm> NetObjects University; Provides Internet-related courses for both novices and professionals

<www.ehow.com> eHow; Search for "build a Web page"

<www.htmlgoodies.com> HTML Goodies; Primers, tutorials, and beyond HTML

<www.smartcomputing.com> *Smart Computing* magazine; Search for articles on "Web site construction"

<www.webdeveloper.com> Web Developer.com

<www.webmonkey.com>; Wired magazine's *Webmonkey*

<www.zdnet.com/zdhelp> ZDNet.com; Help and tutorials

Web Publishing Software

Adobe *Page Mill*

Claris *Home Page*

Cold Fusion

Microsoft *Front Page* (See also Microsoft's smallbiz Guide for Web site construction tips: <www.bcentral.com>)

There are other Internet-related software programs mentioned throughout this book. Of course, the latest Internet and Web design software programs are regularly reviewed by online business sites and print business publications.

Cyberlaw

There are a number of very important legal issues connected to doing business through or on the Internet. Some issues are common to all businesses, regardless of whether they are on- or offline, but some are applicable to the Internet only—primarily those dealing with intellectual property rights (trademarks, patents, copyrights). Consulting with a lawyer before you launch your Internet business may help you avoid possible litigation and legal disputes.

Stephen T. Maher, attorney <www.usual.com>,* says, "Consulting a lawyer familiar with the Internet is one way to assure that you are not missing important legal issues related to the Internet. But the reality today is that many lawyers do not yet know as much about the Internet as they should. I have been teaching courses for lawyers on Law and the Internet for five years now, and I anticipate that the need for such courses will continue to grow in the future. I think the profession has recognized the need to become more Internet-savvy, and is responding to that need."

Here are some of the Internet legal issues, presented for information purposes only. It is advised you seek legal counsel for precise advice on any legal matters concerning your business and promotional uses.

---

*Maher's Web site, "Law and Business As Usual on the World Wide Web," contains links to articles about Internet legal issues.

COPYRIGHT

The images, articles, and text that you originate for your Web site (including the site itself) all fall under the protection of copyright law. You should have a copyright notice on your Web site—most sites post it on or near the bottom of the home page and on every page thereafter. It should read © or the word "Copyright," the year of creation, and the word "by," followed by the name of the organization or person holding the copyright and the phrase "All rights reserved." An example: © 2000 by Priscilla Y. Huff. All rights reserved. If you are offering free use of your articles or materials or software trials to download, you should state that permission is given to use these materials, with the stipulation that your copyright notice should be used.

The same applies to your use of text, images, graphics, animation, or anything else that is the original work of another person. "Fair use" allows you to use small parts of a work for purposes of criticism or discussion without formally requesting permission (you should give proper credit), but if in doubt about whether your plans for the reused material constitutes fair use, contact the person or company holding the rights. Facts and ideas cannot be copyrighted.

TRADEMARK

Symbols, logos, images, or slogans that are the trademarks of other individuals or businesses should not be used or displayed without authorization, so that visitors do not think you are representing that company.

TERMS OF USE

You should have a Terms of Use section—especially if you have regular visitors or subscribers to your site—drawn up by your lawyer to protect yourself. A Terms of Use section will contain a set of legal statements and guidelines concerning how your site's subscribers or visitors can and cannot use your site. These can include a definition of your site's services, code of conduct, copyright claims to your site's materials and information, disclaimers, and other legal statements.

Your Opinions of Others

Just because on the Internet no one can "see" you or even know your name, you do not have the right to defame someone's reputation or use verbal abuse in online conversations—chats, forums, message boards. You could be sued for libel. You also cannot harass or "cyberstalk" another individual; this may constitute criminal behavior. If certain speech, written words, and actions are illegal in the offline world, they are illegal in the Internet world, too. At the least, you would be violating the terms of use agreements that most sites have that invite group participation, including those of your local ISP's service agreement.

Privacy Issues

Before visitors order anything or give you personal information about themselves, they will want to know how you will use this personal data, that you will keep it confidential and not distribute it to others. A statement of your privacy policy should be posted on your Web site (and once posted, make sure you adhere to it). Note, too, that some countries have laws regarding privacy issues and collecting information about their citizens.

If your site sells items for children, you must follow the regulations of the Children's Online Privacy Protection Act that became effective April 21, 2000, as it applies to the collection of personal information from children under age 13 and also to their participation in chats, e-mail, or instant messages in which they could give out personal information. For more information, go to the Federal Trade Commission's site to read their guide "How to Comply with the Children's Online Privacy Protection Rule" <www.ftc.gov/bcp/conline/pubs/buspubs/coppa.htm>. The FTC also has other information about consumer privacy in the online marketplace. You can also find more information at the Electronic Privacy Information Center <www.epic.org>.

DISCLAIMERS

If you give advice and tips on your site, you should have a disclaimer statement written by your lawyer and posted on your site, so that you will not be liable for some failure or misjudgment by an individual who has read your information.

CONTRACTS

You will need Internet-related contracts for subcontracting work, hiring Web experts, being an independent contractor, and other arrangements. Consult with your lawyer, and see Related Resources at the end of this section as well as The Legalities in chapter 1.

ADVERTISING

The Federal Trade Commission says if you're thinking about advertising on the Internet, remember that many of the same rules that apply to other forms of advertising also apply to electronic marketing. The FTC has a number of guides that you can access on their site, such as "Advertising and Marketing on the Internet," "Electronic Commerce: Selling Internationally. A Guide for Business Alert," "Selling on the Internet: Prompt Delivery Rules Alert," and others pertaining to privacy, Internet auctions, and the like.

Domains

Legal experts advise that when you hire a Web site designer to do your site you state in your contract that you are owner of your site's content, designs, logo, and other intellectual property.

International Law

Selling to foreign countries requires that you comply with all international export/import laws. Here are three Internet sites for related information:

<www.customs.ustreas .gov/imp-exp2/pubform/import/
index.htm>; The U.S. Customs Service has a book,
Importing into the U.S., that is published online

<www.sba.gov/oit> Site of the U.S. Small Business Administration's Office of International Trade; Links to offices, publications, trade events, and other resources for first-time exporters

<www.sba.gov/oit/info/guide-to-exporting>; Online publication of "Breaking into the Trade Game"; A free copy can be ordered from the SBA by calling 1-800-827-5722

Alana Webb of Love Stories.com says when she was planning her Web site, "My primary legal concerns were that we had a proper 'Terms of Service' notice since our audience is the general public. Also, we were concerned that our material wasn't copied by others."

Related Resources

Books

Cyberlaw: The Law of the Internet by Jonathan Rosenoer
(Sunnyvale, CA: Springer Verlag, 1997)

BUSINESS PROFILE: Alana Webb, Promoter of Love,
                        Romance, and Poetry

What is your Internet venture?

Love Stories.com <www.lovestories.com>.

Is it solely an Internet business?

Solely an Internet community.

When was the business started?

September 1997.

How did you originate the idea for your site?

After I had completed a large 18-month corporate project, working on contract, I decided to create a site of my very own, where I
could control everything. When I was brainstorming on domains,
I found that lovestories.com was available, and the ideas burst
forth.

How did you finance your start-up?

Personal savings, estimated at about $25,000, which financed it
for six to nine months. Plus, at times, credit cards.

What resource helped you the most?

My favorite HTML book is Laura LeMay's *Teach Yourself HTML
in 14 Days* (the original version). The best resource for me has

---

*Cyberlaw: What You Need to Know about Doing Business
   Online* by David Johnston, Sunny Handa, and Charles
   Morgan (North York, Ontario, Canada: Stoddart
   Publishing, 1997)

Internet Law and Business Handbook by J. Dianne Brinson
   and Mark F. Radcliffe (Menlo Park, CA: Ladera Press,
   2000) <www.laderapress.com>; Designed for the non-
   lawyer and lawyer, containing clear explanations of the
   laws applicable to the Internet; Includes a diskette containing 15 form contracts and resource appendixes

been people: from visitors who take the time to e-mail in feedback and suggestions, to a network of fellow Web masters whom I have met over the years—and now also Jodi Turek, founder of Women's Forum—to my channel producer, to other partner site owners.

Can you offer any tips for creating a successful Web site?

First, you have to have a passion for the topic. The passion of a site will shine through even with a poor design, although good Web design is essential. Plus, offer something that other sites do not.

Do you have any additional comments?

A lot of people think that you can make a quick buck on the Web, and maybe some do, but I've found that the Web is basically the same as other small businesses: The Web makes it easy to set up shop, but you have to put in a lot of work, be self-disciplined, and do things the "right" way in order to succeed long-term. You can't stay stagnant on the Web, or the site dies.

Alanna Webb of Lovestories.com, "a love, romance, and relationship community."

Internet Legal Forms for Business by J. Diane Brinson and Mark Radcliffe (Menlo Park, CA: Ladera Press, 1997) <www.laderapress.com>; Additional forms and contracts

Internet Sites

<http://law.about.com/medianews/currevents/law/mbody .htm> About.com's Law; Listing of various legal topics

<www.findlaw.com> FindLaw.com; A resource of Internet legal and e-business information and a listing of law

firms; Also has legal forms for e-business transactions <http://techdeals.findlaw.com>

<www.freeadvice.com> FreeAdvice.com; Explanations of various legal topics concerning business and other issues, plus a listing of lawyers

<www.ilpf.org> Internet Law & Policy Forum

<www.law.com> law.com; Updates of legal issues, including those affecting the Internet

<www.lawyers.com> Lawyers.com; Tips for hiring a lawyer and other related information

<www.nolo.com>; Nolo.com's Legal Encyclopedia; Find articles on legal topics A–Z

For samples of contracts and legal documents visit the following sites (some are free or charge low-cost fees):

<www.legaldocs.com> Legaldocs; Legal documents online

<www.quickforms.net>; QuickForm Contracts for the computer industry

Software

Small Business Legal Pro by Nolo Press <www.nolo.com>

Online Pricing

Pricing your products and/or services is a dilemma that all entrepreneurs—on- and offline—must handle. Their customers and clients want quality work and service, but at prices within their spending limits or budgets. Here are some considerations that can help you charge fair but profitable rates:

* Know your customers. Through your market research, you can discover not only potential customers, but what they are willing and able to pay. With the global Internet market, what some people pay for products and services in one country can differ greatly from that paid in another country.

- Scout your competition's offerings and rates to see if there are items and services they are not offering their customers that you could offer or specialize in. Check them out on a regular basis by monitoring their sites and getting some feedback from their customers.

- Know your business's industry pricing recommendations. You may be charging less than what is suggested. Keep abreast of their guidelines by accessing their online site's information and publications.

- Consult with a professional. If you need assistance, consult with business coaches, marketing specialists, or business experts at local offices of such federal government agencies as Small Business Development Centers, Women's Business Centers <www.onlinewbc.org>, and/or local chapters of SCORE (Senior Core of Retired Executives) <www.score.org>. For various Canadian small business links, visit <http://canadaonline.about.com>.

- Learn what value your products and services can bring to your customers. If your product or service helps them save time, provide helpful information, locate hard-to-find products, or assist them in improving their lives, emphasize these selling points in your online content copy, so they can decide if your prices are worth it to them.

- Consider all your operating and production (time) expenses, including shipping and handling, site maintenance fees, and other costs when determining your prices.

- Determine your break-even point. This is the dollar amount your business must make to break even; that is, sales income must equal costs. To stay in business, you must make a profit, so the price you charge, of course, must be higher than the cost of providing your services or producing your products. Your business plan, discussed in chapter 3, will help you determine this factor.

- Have a straightforward and easy-to-follow way for customers to find your pages that list your products and services and their corresponding prices.
- Understand your pricing strategies and how your rates will benefit your business. Your prices are a statement about your business, so take time in determining the best for you and your online business.

One business expert said, "It is impossible to offer low prices and high quality." Thus, pricing is an ongoing, variable process, and may take some time before you arrive at the rates that please your customers and satisfy your business's bottom line.

RELATED RESOURCES

Books

How Much Should I Charge? Pricing Basics for Making Money Doing What You Love by Ellen Rohr (Rogersville, MD: Max Rohr, Inc., 1999)

Money-Smart Secrets for the Self-Employed by Linda Stern (New York: Random House, 1997)

Pricing Strategy: An Interdisciplinary Approach by Morris Engelson (Portland, OR: Joint Management Strategy, 1995)

The Strategy and Tactics of Pricing: A Guide to Profitable Decision-Making by Thomas T. Nagle and Reed K. Holden (Paramus, NJ: Pearson, 1994)

Internet Sites

<www.onlinewbc.org> Women's Business Center Online; Under Marketing, "Pricing: How to Understand Costs and Prices for Profit"

<www.toolkit.cch.com> *The Business Owner's Toolkit; The SOHO Guidebook: Marketing Your Product/Services*

Internet
Start-Up Basics

The thought of starting an Internet business or of taking your present business online may (or may not) be daunting to you at first, but, as a rule, successful women entrepreneurs are not afraid to ask questions when it pertains to business. This was noted by Vanessa A. Freytag, director of Bank One's Woman Entrepreneur Initiative <www.bankone.com/women>, when she wrote *Wise Women: Success Strategies for Women Entrepreneurs*,* in 1999 for Bank One Corp. of Chicago.

Based on the interviews Freytag did for the 50-page booklet, she says, "When making business decisions, women seek more advice than other business owners."

Statistics also support the fact that the amount of time a person spends in researching and preparing for a business start-up has an impact on whether or not her

---

*The women featured in Freytag's booklet were among the national winners and nominees for the year 2000 Working Woman Entrepreneurial Excellence Awards that were sponsored by Bank One and *Working Woman* magazine <www.workingwoman.com>.

new venture will prosper. Thus, this chapter will present you with some fundamental questions and Internet basics you will want to consider *before* starting an Internet-related business, to enhance your chances of success.

Internet Business FAQs

Here are some frequently asked questions about using the Internet for business:

What is a business Web site?

A Web site is similar to an advertisement in the business advertising pages in your telephone directory. It is an interactive two-dimensional "store without walls," but because it is located on the Internet your goods and services are available 24/7/365 to potential customers and clients who have access to the Internet.

What is the difference between the Internet and the World Wide Web (WWW)?

The Internet and WWW are similar, but different. The Internet is a worldwide linkage of computers that was first used in the 1960s by the military and by universities for communication about research. It permits text-only information to be sent rapidly around the world. The WWW is what most people think of when the word "Internet" is mentioned. It enables graphics, photos, videos, and audio units to be transferred among different computers. The WWW project is an extensive multitude of worldwide, interconnected documents. It was started by Tim Berners-Lee while at CERN, the world's largest particle physics center, in Switzerland, and has evolved—and is still evolving—into the revolutionary medium it is today.

What are some of the programs available for accessing the WWW?

Here are some common ones: *Internet Explorer, NCSA Mosaic, Netscape Navigator.*

What are some good sources of the latest WWW news?

Most major newspapers such as the *New York Times* <www.nyt.com> and the *Wall Street Journal* cover daily Internet news highlights, in both their print and online publicatons, but here are just three sites (of many) that cover daily Internet news:

<www.zdnet.com/zdnn/internet> ZDNNEWS: Internet

<www.news.com > CNET: News

<www.wired.com/news> Wired News

As listed previously, *Inter@ctive Week* <www.interactive-week.com> is a good weekly print and online publication. For others see "Resources" and also visit your local newsstand for the latest in print publications covering the Net.

How do I create an online marketing survey for my proposed business idea?

First design your survey, and then send it to people who would not mind sharing their feedback on it. The site Zoomerang <www.zoomerang.com> offers this for free and also lists people willing to participate in various surveys.

Is there software out there that is easy to operate by a computer novice for a small retail operation that sells only 50 or 60 items?

There are many types of shopping-cart software available now. Many have "wizards" installed on them as well as templates from which to choose, enabling even a novice netpreneur to set up a Web shop. These include such features as adding and deleting items, viewing transactions, and other offerings to assist you in your online retail operations. Two recommended Web resource sites that offer free cart scripts (software) are the CGI Resource Index <www.cgi-resources.com> and Script Search <www.scriptsearch.com>. You can review them for properties that will best suit your purposes.

I have what I think is a great idea for a Web site, and have already obtained a domain name and some software programs to build my site as well as lining up several experts to help me. I would like this site to be the main source of my income; should I quit my full-time job so I can fully develop this site?

Starting an online business is the same as any business—do not go full-time until you have two or more years' savings to pay for your expenses (unless you have some other form of support, that is, a spouse or partner), and you have a solid customer base resulting in profits and demonstrating potential growth. In the meantime, do your research about what makes Web sites successful, through reading and talking with other online entrepreneurs, as well as gathering information to provide good content on your site. Then start your site on a part-time basis, while you are still working your full-time job or until your Web site is profitable enough to support you.

What are some ways to speed up my Internet connections?

Make sure you have an analog modem of at least 28.8 kilobits per second (kbps) or higher; or you can consider upgrading to a cable modem or to a Digital Subscriber Line (DSL).

What does it cost to get a Web site designed?

You can get software and do it yourself, or have a site designed for $2,500 and up. It depends on your finances and how detailed your site needs to be. Experts recommend you start small, keep it simple, and expand as you are able and according to the demand of your site's visitors.

Does every business or professional need a Web site?

No. It depends on what advantages a Web site will contribute to a business or a professional's practice. Just to have a Web site because every other business has one is not the right reason to go online. You need to know the purpose of your proposed site first. However, as more people are being connected to the Internet, the more they will expect a business or professional to have a site, so you may well need one in the future.

What is involved in getting a Web site up and running?

Whether you use an e-commerce software package to design and set up your site or a commerce hosting service, a business Web site selling products or services is comprised of four basic components: your Web site, building your store, taking customer orders, and processing your transactions. Costs for running your site's business operations will vary according to the memory your online venture requires and the number of products or services you are offering for sale. As discussed previously, to build a store you can hire a Web designer to create it; buy software and learn HTML and XML to build and maintain the site yourself, or register with a hosting service.

What is a good way to test-market a product online?

Many entrepreneurs start by selling items on a (legitimate) online auction to see the response to their products and the prices of those products.

These Internet business FAQs are just a sampling of the many you will ask in the process of learning to use the Internet to promote a business or yourself. The good news is that most all the answers to your questions exist on the Internet and from other online entrepreneurs. You just have to persist in finding the answers to the questions you and your customers have!

RELATED RESOURCES
Books

The E-Commerce Answer Book: A Survival Guide for Business Managers by Anita Rosen (New York: AMACOM Books, 1999)

Questions to Ask Yourself Before Going Online

Before you go online and invest in an online presence, you need to understand the capabilities of the Internet and what it can offer you and/or your business. Following are some questions you might want to ask yourself to determine exactly what you want.

FOR MARKETING

- Does your business belong on the Web? Is the Web the best place, the only place, to enhance you or your business? Or is it simply one marketing method?
- How do you plan to attract people to your site?
- How will you follow through with sales?
- Do you have a business plan (business plans are discussed later in this chapter)?
- Will your Web site drain other resources that are needed to promote yourself or your business?
- Can you use your site to do market research?
- What ways can you market your site to offset costs? Advertising? Associate programs?

FOR CUSTOMERS

- Are your products or services targeted to just your local area or can they be sold worldwide?

- Will your customers expect you to have a Web site business presence?
- Will you be able to fill a unique niche with your Web site or be the first with its idea?
- If you sell products, will you sell them directly to retailers or to consumers?
- Will you be able to use a Web site to present new sidelines or components or improve service to regular and/or potential customers?

FOR THE SITE MECHANICS AND PURPOSE

- What is your vision for your site?
- Do you plan to write and design your site or will you contract that out?
- Do you have the time and money to invest in getting a Web site up and running?
- If you presently have a full-time job and family commitments, will you have the time to devote to an online business?
- Do you project that your site will pay for itself?
- Will you be able to survive financially until your Web site becomes profitable?
- Do you have the equipment, technology, and know-how to access the Web and maintain your online presence?

These are only a few of the many, many questions you should ask yourself before you start a Web business. There is no right way that a person or business should approach using the Internet, but investigating the possibilities now rather than later will help you stay current and keep expenses down. A productive Web site should help you reduce costs, increase your sales, or both. It should also help improve communications and services and strengthen relationships with the most important persons related to your business—your customers.

Finding the Best
Online Niche for You

Forrester Research, Inc. <www.forrester.com> reported in 1999 that it expected online business-to-consumer (B2C) sales to reach $10 billion by 2003 and business-to-business (B2B) revenues to top $1.3 trillion. However, in this new business frontier of e-commerce, some of the most successful online entrepreneurs are those who have found a special niche on the Web—a market of untapped potential customers with well-defined interests or wants. How do you find the best online niche? When Terri Bose, founder of the site, Making Friends, was asked for a tip about how a woman can find the best business niche, on- or offline, she says, "Choose a product or service that you have not been able to find for yourself." Here are some questions to ask to help you choose an online niche:

- Are my products and/or services best suited to consumers or businesses or both?
- Are there people or smaller businesses that larger businesses or sites have overlooked?
- If so, who are these people whose needs are not being met?
- What are their interests, needs, or wants?
- Do I have a product or service that can fulfill their needs?
- Are these potential customers online?
- Can I create a brand or a recognizable association—symbol, slogan, phrase, or other notation—that will help new customers recognize my business or my expertise?
- If so, how can I use a Web site to attract them and convince them I can provide a solution to their problems or needs?

To answer these and other questions, your business plan formation and related market research will help you narrow your focus and find your best online niche. Take note, though, that the same applies to any business: Stay alert for a niche that

may open up as you go online—one that you may not even
have envisioned, and one that could possibly be more profitable than the niche market you originally started out with.

RELATED RESOURCES

Internet Sites

<www.wilsonweb.com>; Web marketing and e-commerce
information resource site where you can search for
articles on topics such as finding Web niches

<www.awssurf.com> A Woman's Shape Surf Company; An
example of a unique niche—an online wet suit/clothing/
surfboard venture founded by a woman surfer, Tracey
Hagemann

Internet Experts

When Stacy Brice, founder of a virtual assistant online training
and resource site, was asked for tips on choosing the right
experts for an online business she says, "It's hard to know
what you need, when you don't know what you don't know!
Working with an Internet-savvy business coach will give you
a guide to the road map leading to success. Once you start to
know more, you'll be able to guide yourself—knowing more of
what you need and want, and being able to choose the best
professionals to give it to you."

Brice continues:

I only work in collaborative partnerships with people—when
I choose a professional to work with me on any element of
my business, I want that person to be around long-term. It's
so much easier for me to invest time and energy on long-term
relationships, where the professionals get to know what I
need and want, almost before I need to tell them. So, I see my

BUSINESS PROFILE: Terri Bose, Creative Crafts and
Activities for Kids

What is your Internet venture?

Making Friends and Other Crafts for Kids <www.makingfriends
.com>.

Is it solely an Internet business?

Yes.

When was the business started?

February 1998.

How did you originate the idea for your site?

I looked for kid-friendly paper dolls online for my daughter but
didn't find anything. After designing my own, I posted them online
to share with others.

How did you finance your start-up?

There was very little set up cost. Just lots and lots of time.

What resource helped you the most?

The Women's Forum has been a great help. Before we hooked up,
I felt like I was flying alone.

Can you offer any tips for creating a successful Web site?

Find a niche that would interest others like you. Be prepared to
spend a lot of time providing good content to keep your visitors
coming back.

*Terri Bose is a mom, a stepmom, and the
author of three children's craft books.*

Web mistress as a partner, my coach, my attorney, my accountant, my printer—all partners for my success. That's one
reason why working with a virtual assistant is so fabulous.
I model what I talk about. I have two VAs who run my life
flawlessly. They handle everything I don't need to be doing
(e.g., e-mail, calls, scheduling, arranging travel, negotiating
with vendors, initial contact/screening of my customers, and
anything else that comes up) so that I can be free to focus

on the bigger picture, take advantage of opportunities, and move my business forward in ways I could never do if I had to handle *everything* myself.

Realize that you cannot handle all the aspects of business and also of going online. You will want to concentrate on the aspects of your business concerning the production of your goods and services—that is first and foremost, or you will not have any customers. Experts include a lawyer, accountant and bookkeeper, insurance agent, printer and/or desktop publisher, business coach, office support services (virtual and "real"); your Web experts—computer consultant, Web designer, Web master for maintenance, Internet marketing consultant, and anyone else who is essential to the operations of your business and online site.

Where can you find these experts? From referrals by other entrepreneurs, professional associations, business owners organizations, industry and entrepreneur conferences, and from the Internet itself. Some questions you should ask of any expert:

- What is your area of specialization?
- What are your rate terms? Do you offer a free consultation? Rates per hour or by the project? Ongoing or sliding scale? Extra charges for added services?
- Who are some of your clients?
- Are you a member of any trade associations or business organizations?
- What certifications and/or licenses do you have?
- If I do not feel we can work together, can I expect to have all or part of the fee refunded?

The best experts are the ones with whom you can work the best to accomplish your goals. Developing a good working relationship can give you peace of mind and let you concentrate on the work you do best.

BUSINESS PROFILE: Stacy Brice, Training and Support
for Virtual Assistants

What is your Internet venture?

Assist University (AssistU) <www.assistu.com> trains, coaches,
certifies, supports, and refers virtual assistants.

Is it solely an Internet business?

100 percent virtual.

When was the business started?

1997.

How did you originate the idea for your site?

I'd been working with virtual clients since 1988—before it was
easy or cool to do so. Nearly ten years later, in 1996, a journalist
did an article on my virtual work for a national magazine. When
that article was published, hundreds of women approached me,
very much wanting to learn how to work from home, doing virtual
assistance. It was then that I realized that there was a need for a
training program, and I decided to create it. Assist University
opened its doors in early 1997. Since then, we've doubled in size
each year, and quickly added additional services like professional
coaching for all VAs, a professional members association so that
each VA can have the ongoing support he/she needs, certification—
the highest in the industry, and free referrals to the public.

How did you finance your start-up?

Personal savings.

What resource helped you the most?

Fabulous professional coaches. I heartily suggest that all entrepreneurs work with amazing business coaches.

RELATED RESOURCES

Associations

Accountants: American Woman's Society of Certified Public
Accountants <www.awscpa.org>

Can you offer any tips for creating a successful Web site?

Build a community for your customers. Let them talk with you, and with each other. Find ways to give them what they want, as well as what they need—don't guess about it, you'll spin your wheels. Have terrific standards for your business, strong personal standards, and don't waver on them. Always put your own self-care first, or you'll burn out. Be willing to put a strong infrastructure in place to support your growth. Delegate everything you personally don't need to do. Listen to your heart over your head and you won't go wrong with any decision you make. Finally, focus on your own game rather than watching what others do. When you have one eye on other stuff, you can't be as successful with your own.

Do you have any additional comments?

So many people are looking for a quick buck. Find your passion, whatever that is, and do that. You'll be spending a lot of time with your business. If you are passionate about it, then every moment you work will seem like play. Without passion, you'll feel distanced from your dreams, quickly lose interest, money, and perhaps your self-respect. Working in a business you love is a key element in being truly successful.

Stacy Brice, president and virtual
maven of Assist University.

Coaches, personal and/or business: International Coach
   Federation <www.coachfederation.com>

Computer experts: Independent Computer Consultant's
   Association <www.icca.org>

Financial advisors: The National Association of Personal Financial Advisors (NAPFA) <www.napfa.org>

Insurance agents: Independent Insurance Agents of America <www.iiaa.org>

Lawyers: American Bar Association <www.abanet.org>

Virtual assistants: <www.staffcentrix.com> (see also Stacy Brice's Profile)

Internet Sites

<www.askme.com> AskMe.com; Expert advice (fees vary)

<www.demandline.com> Demandline.com; Lets small businesses name the price they would be willing to pay for products or services that are placed into a buying pool that is put up for auction for the best prices

<www.exp.com> EXP.com; Expert advice (fees vary)

E-Business Hatcheries

Business incubators are located around the United States and enable home and small businesses to expand and grow using the support of the incubators' business management and support services. With the recent growth of Internet-based businesses, special incubators—called e-business "hatcheries," such as the Annenberg Incubator Project at the University of Southern California (USC)—are being formed to support these new e-commerce ventures. Others examples include Idea Lab <www.idealab.com>, eHatchery <www.ehatchery.com>, and the Women's Technology Cluster (WTC) <www.womenstech cluster.org>, located in San Francisco and founded by Catherine Muther, a former marketing executive with Cisco Systems.

Besides providing a business incubators' typical services, e-hatcheries help draw the attention of seed capital from possible investors and venture capitalists who give their financial support in exchange for equity shares in the incubated start-up. Generally, for your business to qualify for inclusion in an incubator, you have to submit a business plan and fulfill other requirements as stipulated by each incubator. Before you enter an incubator, be sure to ask about the lease terms and length of stay, the available assistance services, who are the other tenants, and whether they allow for development.

RELATED RESOURCES

Associations

National Business Incubation Association <www.nbia.org>,
   20 E. Circle Drive, Suite 190, Athens, OH 45701

Essential Equipment and Technology

Technology has enabled small businesses to compete on a global level against much larger companies, but the small business owner still faces the many challenges of handling all aspects of an online business. According to the National Foundation of Women Business Owners <www.nfwbo.org>, home-based women business owners are just as technologically savvy as other business owners.

In a survey conducted in late 1999, Advantage Business Research Inc. <http://advantageresearch.com> says that the average amount of money spent by responding small businesses on Web computer products was $12,000, and during the coming year, these small businesses planned to increase their spending for Web products by 60 percent—to $19,000. Cahners In-Stat Group <www.instat.com>, in a report written by analyst Kneko Burney, predicts that by 2002, America's

8 million small offices and home offices (SOHOs) will spend $19 billion on computer hardware and software—up from $13 billion spent in 1998.

OFFICE FURNITURE

Keep costs down by using existing furniture or purchasing good used furniture; or use your woodworking skills (or a spouse's or friend's) to build your own. Buy your computer hardware first to make sure your furniture works with it.

Do not scrimp on a good office chair, which can run from $100 to more than $2,000. A good chair should have adjustable arms and seat, support your lower back, and have easily accessible controls. Its seat should be large enough to reach a few inches from behind your calves and have a good cushion that does not compact. If you work leaning toward your computer, you should buy a task chair, and if you typically work leaning back while on the phone, you should buy a management and executive chair with a higher seatback. Take some time to try out different chairs to find the best one for you. It will be worth the time and expense by helping you be more comfortable as you work and by helping to prevent back and neck strains.

In purchasing your equipment, visualize what operations you will be doing and your short-term and long-term needs. Shop wisely, and make your first purchases of good quality, with features that can accommodate future business growth.

COMPUTER SYSTEM

Buy the fastest, best-equipped, most upgradable computer you can afford. Your system should have between 32MB and 128MB of RAM, a fast processor—like a Pentium III or AMD chip, a CD-ROM drive (speed at least 16X), a 5GB or larger hard drive and at least one removable drive (such as a ZIP drive), to handle the operations and graphics you will need to conduct business. Most major computer manufacturers are online, and a number of them provide technological options for e-commerce: Compaq <www.compaq.com>; Dell <www .dell.com>; Gateway <www.gateway.com>; Hewlett-Packard <www.hp.com>; and IBM <www.ibm.com>.

Keyboard

Look for one that is ergonomically designed to help prevent repetitive injuries like carpal tunnel syndrome, and those that have added keys that direct your Web browser, e-mail, and your CD software.

Monitor

Purchase one that gives you high resolution (no less than 640 × 480), and is at least 15 inches to 17 inches diagonally.

Modem

Modems connect you to the Internet and have different speed capabilities. Your modem should be at least 36.6 kbps (kilobits per second). The type of Internet connection you choose (dial-up, cable, etc.) will determine what speeds you will have access to and what kind of modem you will need.* The following connection choices are available:

- **Dial-up connection:** You use an existing phone line; this is the slowest way to connect, but usually the least expensive per month.
- **Cable modem:** If your cable service has this available, it is a fast, direct connection.

---

*Note that modems can easily be damaged by electrical storms in your area. Make sure your dial-up phone line is protected (along with your other home office equipment) with surge protectors and UPS devices.

- **DSL (Digital Subscriber Line):** Offered by many local telephone companies, DSL uses parts of your phone line not used by your voice service. You have to be located relatively close to your telephone company's central office.
- **ISDN (Integrated Services Digital Network):** Not as fast as DSL but is more widely available.
- **Other options:** Include WebTV (a new device using a regular telephone jack), wireless, and satellite.

Printer

Invest in a good color inkjet printer. Print quality is measured in dots per inch (dpi). The higher the dpi the better print quality. You can purchase special papers to print photos, pictures, and some graphics. Laser printers are faster, but generally are more expensive. Two sources for printers: <www.epson.com>, <www.hp.com>.

Scanner

Scanners are very affordable and enable you to place images and photos into your computer text files. Flatbed scanners are generally the easiest to use.

SOFTWARE

A collection of your core applications should be installed on your computer: a home-office suite, word processor, accounting program, scheduler, database, spreadsheet, contact manager, and other business-related software, including industry-specific programs, shipping, inventory control, and credit card processing.

If you are building your Web site yourself,* you can also use a Web page editor ("Web page authoring tools"); graphics

---

*Learning Hypertext Markup Language (HTML), the universal coding language that is used to format Web pages, will enable you to enhance and customize your site, even if you use Web page creation software or a free Web page service.

software to help you draw or edit images; and/or storefront software that can help tutor you in the creation of your Web business and its online presence.

Browser

You will need either Microsoft *Explorer* or Netscape *Communicator* to display Internet documents. You can purchase these browsers or download them free from the Internet.

OTHER OFFICE EQUIPMENT

Telecommunications Equipment

You should have at least two working phone lines in your home, with maybe a third dedicated to your fax and/or modem. Voice mail with your phone company or your cellular phone sounds more professional than many "tinny-sounding" answering machines. Use a headset if you use the phone frequently, to prevent neck strain.

Fax (Facsimile)

You can purchase a separate unit or have a fax modem or software installed so that you can transmit faxes from your computer.

Digital Camera

Many people are bypassing scanners and using digital cameras to store images directly to a disk and then transmitting these images directly online.

Video Capture Devices

These are a combination of software and hardware that allows you to select images from your video camera and display them on your Web site.

Multifunctional devices

If you cannot afford all of this equipment, you may want to consider a multi-function device that combines a fax, copier, printer, and scanner.

RELATED RESOURCES

Books

Sign up for e-mail notification about the latest titles in Amazon.com's Computers and Internet section <www.amazon.com/computers>

Internet Sites

<www.atyouroffice.com> atyourOffice.com; Office supply site, including ergonomic accessories for computers

<www.bizrate.com>; <www.dealtime.com>; <www.computers.com>; Shopping bots to help you comparison shop

<www.cnet.com> CNET, Inc.; A leading source of information and services relating to computers and technology

<www.getspeed.com>; Helps you find what high speed Internet services are available to you

<www.igoergo.com> Neutral Posture Ergonomics, Inc.; Ergonomic chairs

<www.maxpatchink.com> MaxPatch Ink Supplies; Offers high quality Inkjet refill kits and cartridges for printers

<www.smalloffice.com>; The site of *Home Office Computing* and *Small Business Computing* magazines, with regular reviews of equipment and technology

<www.softwarespectrum.com/intouch/feedback.htm>; *In Touch*, "a Web magazine of technology solutions," spon-

sored by Software Spectrum (a global business-to-business software services provider) of technology solutions, with features on software industry developments and trends

<www.webshopper.com> Webshopper; Site for technology and computer equipment

Web Authoring Software

Macromedia *DreamWeaver* <www.macromedia.com/soft ware/dreamweaver> can be customized using HTML, JavaScript, and XML

Microsoft *Front Page 2000* <www.microsoft.com/frontpage>; a web site creation and management tool

Adobe *GoLine* <www.zones.com.sg/adobe-golive.htm>; Web publishing tool for Mac or compatibles

SPAM Eater Pro by High Mountain Software <www.hms .com/default.asp>; Helps block SPAM e-mail

Internet Service Provider (ISP)

Whatever type of Internet connection you select, you will have to use an ISP (a business that provides Internet access to individuals and businesses). You can go with a dial-up service provided by a local ISP or with a commercial one such as AOL, MindSpring.com, or others. Besides a dial-up connection, you may need to explore faster connection options such as an ISDN line, DSL, Network Connection (used primarily by big companies like Amazon.com and uses fiber optic cables), satellite, or wireless.

Some companies provide free basic Internet access, such as <www.juno.com>, <http://netzero.net>, <www.altavista .com>, and others, but you will have to put up with having advertisement bars—some large, some small—and you may or may not need to click on an advertisement every so often to stay connected.

You also have to select a server (the computer that maintains your Web site). Here are four choices:

1. ISP: Will house your site on one of its servers along with Web sites of other businesses and groups.
2. Commerce Service Provider (CSP): Will provide the infrastructure for your e-commerce, offering different price packages for the number of items you are selling and for the number of transactions taking place.
3. Dedicated server: A server at your ISP dedicated solely to your Web site, called a "co-location," but you will need to hire a system administrator to maintain your server distantly.
4. Your own dedicated server: A much more expensive option, but you may need one to handle the traffic if your business site grows substantially.

Many new online entrepreneurs will choose the easier option of using either their dial-up connections with a local ISP or a low-cost or free online CSP to host their Web sites.

Comparing ISPs

A local or national ISP will vary in its business services and costs. Make sure you review the offerings of more than one ISP to compare their terms *before* signing any contract. Here are some offerings you will want to consider:

*   **Direct access to the Internet:** A PPP (point-to-point protocol) account.
*   **Access to the World Wide Web:** Know if the dial-up service is nationwide or just local or regional.
*   **E-mail accounts:** Know how many e-mail accounts you can have and if there are additional fees, so you are able to filter your e-mail messages from clients/customers.

- **Tech support:** Limited or 24/7? Free or pay? Of course, you will want as much ready support as possible to decrease the length of time of any interruption of service to your online customers.

- **Megabytes of disk space:** You will want sufficient space for all your business's web pages.

- **Compatibility:** Your Web authoring software will need to be compatible with your connection (ISDN, cable, other).

- **Backup service:** This is important to provide continuing customer service if your server goes down.

- **Sufficient bandwidth:** The bandwidth must be sufficient to support your Web site's traffic.

- **Contract service terms:** Familiarize yourself with the terms of the contract you have with your ISP—the minimum length of time; any penalties for early cancellation; and any other clauses, before signing an agreement.

- **Web site support services:** For additional charges, some ISPs offer web design assistance.

- **Number of Web sites sharing the server:** Too many other Web sites on the same server may result in slower access to your Web site for your customers.

- **Secure transactions:** If you plan to take credit card payments, you will want an ISP/Web hosting service that offers a secure server to protect that confidential customer data. This security protection may or may not be included in your ISP's hosting package.

Weigh all of these considerations carefully, and if you can, talk with some of the online business owners of each category to get an idea of which type of Web host is the best for your business to start online.

COMMERCE SERVICE PROVIDERS (CSP)

Some CSPs offer free Web hosting services, such as Angel Fire <www.angelfire.com>, Yahoo! GeoCities <www.geocities.com>,

BigStep <www.bigstep.com>, and others. One advantage of starting with a free commerce service provider is that it is free (of course, you will have to have a connection to the Internet to go online). Nita Jackson's disability left her with little funds, so she started her site, Organize Tips, on a free server (see her profile in this chapter). Starting this way, you do not need to make a major investment in hardware and software. As mentioned before, some women start with just a simple Web page on a member-community site as a place to start showcasing their businesses and to also test market responses from online visitors.

Ragan Hughs has started three online businesses with a free commerce service provider, Bigstep.com. When asked what advantages using such a service gives her, she says, "Using a service like Bigstep.com to build your online business has so many advantages for a woman trying to use the Internet for business and/or self-promotion that there are almost too many to list! The biggies are: Bigstep.com is a free service, so it definitely helps lower your start-up costs; the Bigstep.com interface makes it ridiculously easy to produce very professional looking Web pages/sites very quickly; and Bigstep.com's business affiliations offer many networking/ promotion resources (you can even use Bigstep.com to submit your site to all the major search engines)."

Comparing CSPs

Some disadvantages of a free CSP are that you will have to accept commercial third-party advertising and these free services often provide minimal service, very limited functionality, and may not be able to handle your business's needs. Some are especially friendly toward small businesses, while others charge for commercial purposes. Only you will be able to decide which one(s) are best for your purposes.

There are also commercial Commerce Service Providers that charge fees and provide more extensive services. Before deciding on a particular CSP you'll want to consider the following:

- **Commerce:** Does the site permit you to have a for-profit online business?
- **Design and Hosting:** Does the site offer both design-your-own features as well as hosting?
- **Domain Name:** Do they offer a domain registration service? If you already have a domain name, can you use it?
- **Megabytes of available disk space:** How many Web site pages can you have?
- **Store setup fee:** What are the basic fees to open your online store and are there extra fees for increased customer activity?
- **Monthly leasing cost:** Are these costs within your monthly operating expenses budget?
- **Pricing plan levels:** Are there affordable packages for small companies?
- **Size of store:** Is there a limit to the number of items you can offer for sale?
- **Design template:** Can you customize your site or will all the Web sites with this host have the same "look?"
- **Item search:** Will your items be displayed so customers can easily find them?
- **Site promotion/Search engine submission:** Does the host include any promotions to help advertise your site?
- **Merchant account:** Do you have to sign up with their merchant account or can you use yours if you already have one? Note that, to accept payments from some credit card companies, you have to make arrangements directly with the companies themselves.
- **Setup fee:** Again, compare hosts' basic application charges to set up an account.
- **Charge per transaction:** What is the charge per number of transactions (often a percentage of each transaction)?

BUSINESS PROFILE: Ragan Hughs, Hand-Painted Furniture and Clothing for Kids

What is your Internet venture?

SavvyMoms.com <www.savvymoms.com>, PipperSnaps <www.pippersnaps.com>, and The Baby Bee <www.thebabybee.com>.

Is it solely an Internet business?

All of my businesses are solely Internet businesses.

When was the business started?

PipperSnaps started in August of 1999, SavvyMoms.com started in February of 2000, and The Baby Bee was fully launched June 30, 2000.

How did you originate the idea for your site?

The idea for PipperSnaps (hand-painted children's furniture) came from my desire to work at home so that I could stay home with my newborn son and still contribute income to my family. So many people wanted to know how I started my own business on the Internet with very little money that I wrote a guide for other moms. The huge and unexpected success of my guide spawned the idea for SavvyMoms.com, "An Online Community for Moms in Biz @ Home." The Baby Bee is an additional e-store where I will be retailing my self-designed exclusive line of baby (0–24 months) clothing.

- **Security for transactions:** What security is offered to allow for secure order forms?
- **Fraud-protection service:** Does the host verify credit card information for you?
- **Shipping and tax:** Who handles these—you? The host? An independent shipping service?
- **Customer reports:** Does the host offer reports on visitors and traffic on your site?

Some of the more popular CSPs are Yahoo! Stores <store.yahoo.com>, iCat Commerce Online <www.icat.com>, which

Do you have a vision statement for your Web site?

My vision statement for all of my sites would have to be "The only thing standing between you and a successful e-business is your willingness to go for it!"

How did you finance your start-up?

I have financed the start-ups of all three of my sites with my own personal funds (actually, the money my husband and I received from our wedding two years ago . . . shhh, don't tell!).

What resource helped you the most?

The best resources for ideas/inspiration/support/guidance that I have found are iVillage.com and my local SBA.

Can you offer any tips for creating a successful Web site?

My number 1 tip is to, at a minimum, learn the very basics of HTML so that you can perform updates/maintenance on your site when necessary without having to rely on anyone else. My number 2 tip is to perfect your customer service skills!

Ragan Hughs, author of
The SavvyMoms.com Work@Home Biz Guide.

also offer Web creation packages; and those offered by companies such as Dell's "DellEWorks" <www.dellshopstarter .com> and IBM's* "IBM Small Business WebConnections <www.ibm.com/smallbusiness>, offering several commercial e-commerce programs for companies, including a "Web Starter Kit," for smaller businesses. IBM also has *HomePage Creator* for e-business that provides you with the tools to create, publish, and maintain a Web site and online store from your browser.

---

*IBM also has a section for women business owners at <www.ibm.com/ smallbusiness/women>.

BUSINESS PROFILE: Nita Jackson, Time-Saving Tips

What is your Internet venture ?
  Organize Tips <www.organizetips.com>.

Is it solely an Internet business?
  Solely Internet.

When was the business started?
  November 30, 1997.

How did you originate the idea for your site?
  Personal need.

How did you finance your start-up?
  Honestly, I had a zero budget since I am handicapped. I started on a free server. I was just very patient!

What resource helped you the most?
  Que's publication called *HTML Web Publishing.*

Can you offer any tips for creating a successful Web site?
  Work, network, work some more. Work like it's a job. I found that if I'm not there every day working, I do not get paid!

Do you have any additional comments?
  A lot of patience and prayer for favors works wonders!

Nita Jackson; free planners, organizers;
free software for home, office, wedding,
pregnancy, holiday and budget.

With a CSP, you can leave the technical problems with them; it is an inexpensive way to get a store up and running quickly; and it can help you handle purchasing processes. On the downside, your site may look like all the others the CSP hosts, or the CSP may not be able to handle all your store's operations.

DIRECT CONNECTION

If your business is an already-established offline business with many products and services, or your Internet business expands beyond your wildest dreams, you may want to consider purchasing your own servers and installing the software applications of your choice. As previously mentioned, this involves hiring a system administrator to maintain the site and the hiring of other employees. Costs can run hundreds or thousands of dollars per month, but if your customer traffic demands it, then it will be the best option for you.

When Aliza Pilar Sherman of EVIVA.NET was asked at what point should a woman decide to have her own server for her Internet business, she said:

> Back in 1995, my personal Web site became so popular that my Internet Service Provider kept taking it offline because it was overloading their servers (and because I didn't want to pay the monthly fee for a commercial site). When my business grew out of my apartment, we bought a Web server because we were getting into the business of Web design and Web hosting. The benefit of having a server—which was solely for the benefit of the business and services we provided—was being able to host my own Web site. But I wouldn't recommend anyone buying their own server and keeping it on site. There are many businesses now set up to offer that service, and if Web hosting and tech support is not your core competency, it is a waste of time and money to do it yourself.

RELATED RESOURCES

Internet Sites

<www.getspeed.com> High Speed Internet Access; Helps you determine what high speed services are available in your area—DSL, cable modems, high-speed wireless, and satellite access

BUSINESS PROFILE: Aliza Pilar Sherman, Bilingual
Network and Marketplace

What is your Internet venture?

EVIVA.NET <www.eviva.net>, "Power for the Aspiring Latina—
Poder para la Latina con Aspiraciones." The first bilingual online
network and marketplace for Latina professionals and business
owners.

Is it solely an Internet business?

EVIVA.NET is 75 percent online and 25 percent offline with real-
world learning events held across the country.

When was the business started?

EVIVA.NET was officially started January 2000.

How did you originate the idea for your site?

EVIVA.NET came out of over 10 years online and evolving from
my first Internet ventures, Cybergrrl, Inc. and Webgrrls International. I was looking for a more global market to serve via the
Web and also for an underserved demographic of women who
could benefit from going online. A good friend was also looking for
a new opportunity, so we combined forces and formed
EVIVA.NET.

How did you finance your start-up?

So far, EVIVA.NET has been funded by my business partner and by
my own funds. We are currently seeking our seed round of financing from angel investors.

<www.hostsearch.com> HostSearch.com; Tools for helping
to find a Web host

<www.hostindex.com> HostIndex; A Web hosting directory

Your Business Plan

No matter how you intend to use the Internet to promote your
business, a business plan is a must. A business plan is a writ-

What resource helped you the most?

Right now, I'm writing a book about women and venture capital because I couldn't find a book that addressed the myriad of emotions and issues I'm facing as I go out to get millions of dollars for my venture. I've used the Garage.com newsletters, the Springboard 2000 Web site, and the SBA for some leads to suitable money sources.

Can you offer any tips for creating a successful Web site?

I'm a firm believer in using grassroots strategies for building a real buzz around a Web site and to allow visitors to participate in the growth of the site. Also, I believe in starting small and growing quickly rather than starting big and failing miserably!

Do you have any additional comments?

Even though I've been online for 11 years and was the first woman to start an online marketing and publishing company over five years ago, I still am facing challenges when seeking capital for my new company because the industry changes so quickly. Staying focused is key.

Aliza Pilar Sherman, the original Cybergrrl, founder of Webgrrls International and co-president of EVIVA.NET, author of Cybergrrl!: A Woman's Guide to the World Wide Web *and* Cybergrrl @ Work: Tips and Inspiration for the Professional You.

ten description of your proposed business's operations and goals. Starting a business without a plan is like constructing a house without a blueprint. It may get built, but the foundation may not be stable enough to support it. Also, if you are going to seek any financing for growth and expansion, your business plan will be demanded and closely examined by any potential investors and/or lenders.

Here are some major components of a business plan:

- **Executive summary:** A business plan summary, and the most important part, because it explains the concept and purpose.

- **Mission statement:** Your reasons for your business's existence and how it will serve its customers.

- **Business description:** What exactly it is that you will be selling; what makes these products or services stand out from your competition.

- **Business operations:** This section provides specific details of how you will deliver your products and/or services; the key personnel (including you) involved and how their experience and background can contribute to your business success.

- **Business goals:** Short- and long-term objectives as well as some of the steps you will take to achieve these goals.

- **Marketing plan:** Demographics of your target customers and your marketing strategies, pricing, and advertising plans.

- **Sales projections:** Data based on the results of your market analysis and test marketing.

- **Financing and a financial plan:** A listing of your start-up costs, a cash flow statement, a profit and loss statement, and a break-even analysis, the point at which you project your business's income will equal your expenses, after which you will be making profits.

With many online start-ups competing for financing, here are four tips to make your business plan get noticed:

1. Have your business plan reviewed and endorsed by a respected expert or executive in your business's industry.

2. Be honest, and do not inflate your projected revenue numbers.

3. Be as specific as possible in each section of your plan, and be ready to answer every question imaginable about your business.

4. Include examples of how your online business will stand out from the many Web sites already in existence.

A business plan need only be a few pages in length, but it should be reviewed periodically and modified accordingly as your business's growth dictates.

Determining Start-Up Costs

Web sites can cost many thousands and even millions of dollars to start up. As you will read, though, most of the women profiled in this book were able to start out with relatively modest funds. Naturally, start-up costs will vary with each business's online goals. Include one-time expenses such as purchasing equipment and experts' fees as well as projected marketing costs. Various books and software programs for writing business plans have excellent worksheets to help you determine your total costs and projected business income.

Deborah McNaughton, author of *All About Credit* and *The Insider's Guide to Managing Your Credit,* says in figuring your projected business income, "Be realistic on what your income should generate. Do not overextend your credit and let your household suffer while trying to set up an office at home."

The important points to remember are:

- Do not underestimate your total costs.
- It usually takes longer than you expect (remember Murphy's Law) to begin making a profit with your online business.

Market Research: Finding Your Niche

The Internet is a great tool for doing market research for your online idea and for finding your best niche market. Here are some ways to do this:

BUSINESS PROFILE: Deborah McNaughton, Professional
Credit Counselor and Author

What is your Internet venture?

Professional Credit Counselors; Financial Victory.com <www
.financialvictory.com>.

Is it solely an Internet business?

A service business with an online site.

When was the business started?

February 2000.

How did you originate the idea for your site?

Requests from the public. I wanted to expand my business through
advertising products, services, and offering business opportunities
for Credit Consulting Businesses, and new monthly newsletter
Financial Victory.

How did you finance your start-up?

Through business.

- Purchase information from research firms or online databases.
- If you already have a Web site, offer online polls or surveys.*
- Barter information by offering contests.
- Create an e-mail newsletter and invite the recipients to participate in a survey.

If your marketing research was thorough, the results
should tell you the following:

- Who your best target customers are—their profiles and demographics.

---

*Privacy is an important issue with many people, so it is best to reassure
any survey participants that you will not give out their information to any
other source.

What resource helped you the most?

A friend who worked for Pixelon (my server) showed me all the things I could do with my site.

Can you offer any tips for creating a successful Web site?

Make sure the public is aware you are there. Link with other sites. Network with all your contacts. Advertise who you are.

Do you have any additional comments?

Having a Web site makes it easier to access me and for an individual to learn more about my background, services, and my products. I'm interviewed on numerous radio talk shows, and the listeners can immediately go to my Web site to view my products and services. It has been a great resource to introduce my monthly newsletter, *Financial Victory.*

Deborah McNaughton, author of All About Credit *and* The Insiders Guide to Managing Your Credit.

- What your customers' needs are.
- How they will access your Web site.
- What prices they are willing to pay for your product or service.
- If there is any online (or offline) competition.
- If the Internet is the right place to market your product or service.

In fact, the right market research will help you determine if you should go from here to start an online business or if the Internet is the best place to market your product, services, or you!

Marketing Plan

Once your market research has revealed your best potential customers, you will need to concentrate on marketing the services and/or products that those customers want most to help meet their needs. The best way to do that is to form your actual marketing plan with the following components.

DESIGN AND DELIVER

This is a crucial part of your marketing plan. You will list your marketing objectives and begin to design a promotional strategy for each one. List as many low-cost promotional ideas as you can—talks, flyers, demonstrations, press releases, teaching a class, hyperlinks, articles—that you can use to achieve each marketing goal. This can be the fun part, being creative and thinking of usual and unusual ways to get your customers' attention.

MARKETING TIMETABLE

Draw up a marketing timetable to schedule the steps, and get started in enough time to complete your goals.

EMPHASIZE THE BENEFITS

Customers—be they consumers or businesses—want to know how your product or service will benefit them in terms of time or money (or both). The challenge, then, is to communicate in your promotions how you can do this better than your competitors.

SALES AND PROFITS

Jeffrey Dobkin <www.dobkin.com>, marketing expert, says, "You've got to have sales and profits in the plan—no sales, nobody eats; no profits, nobody eats for long. These two items must be addressed from day one of the new business. If you can dial in sales and profits from the 'get go,' you're going to be successful and everything else will fall into place."

FIND YOUR BUSINESS'S BEST POSITION

Positioning in the marketplace means making your product or services stand out from similar products or services existing on- or offline. You can do this with a catch phrase or slogan, name, or a special identity of your product or service—such as a computer expert's "The home business's computer consultant," or a handmade soapmaker's, "Natural soaps, for simple skin care."

MAKE CUSTOMERS YOUR PARTNERS

Futurists say the customers of the future will be more educated and expect more from whom they purchase items and/or services. To succeed, customers will want to know they can trust you and that you will be there if they have a problem—possibly an ongoing relationship or partnership in which you and your customer work together to fulfill their needs.

JOIN FORCES WITH COMPETITORS

Do not be afraid of the benefits of joining forces with other business owners. This includes competitors in your same industry. You can combine your strengths while each serving a different niche.

USE THE INTERNET TO HELP CORNER YOUR MARKET

You can provide customers with information, free sample downloads, feedback opportunities, and order placement. Remember to think of a worldwide market.

MAKE A MARKETING PLAN FOR NOW AND FOR THE FUTURE

Keep abreast of the latest developments in your industry and consumer buying trends—especially those predicted in the next few years. If you do not, you risk losing new customers, and even your loyal ones, if they feel your operations are outdated.

Marketing is an ongoing (daily) process of testing and evaluating your methods, based on your sales and customers' responses. The key to a successful marketing plan is to balance your current endeavors with goals that can adjust for future growth—and develop your business's own unique entity that will attract a steady flow of customers to produce a successful and thriving business.

RELATED RESOURCES
Books

Online Business Planning: How to Create a Better Business Plan Using the Internet, Including a Complete, Up-to-Date Resource Guide by Robert T. Gorman (Franklin Lakes, NJ: Career Press, 1999)

Uncommon Marketing Techniques by Jeffrey Dobkin (Merion Station, PA: The Danielle Adams Publishing Co., 1998)

Internet Sites

<www.artofselfpromotion.com>; The site of *The Art of Self-Promotion,* a quarterly print newsletter featuring free, invaluable information and easy-to-use marketing tools for entrepreneurs, small business owners, and freelancers by Ilise Benun (profiled in chapter 4); Also offers e-zine, *Quick Online Marketing Tips*

<www.bizplanit.com> Business Plans Right Now; A consulting firm with good tips on business-plan basics

<www.business-plan.com>; Site of business plan expert/author Linda Pinson; Offers business-plan books and software

<www.businessplans.org> The Center for Business Planning;
Resources and information to assist entrepreneurs in
every aspect of planning a business

<www.yudkin.com/marketing.htm>; Tips by marketing
expert Dr. Marcia Yudkin

Software

BizPlanBuilder Interactive by Jian <www.jian.com>

Business PlanPro by Palo Alto Software
<www.pasware.com>

Financing Your Online Venture

Finding money for start-ups and business expansion is a challenge for most entrepreneurs, and in the past, has often been difficult for women. However, because women-owned businesses have continued to grow faster than the general economy for more than the past decade (according to NFWBO statistics), women have been recognized by both investors and lenders as a stable force in the economy of the United States and many other countries.

TRADITIONAL FINANCING

Traditional financing includes:

Debt Financing

- **Short-term:** Full repayment in less than one year.
- **Long-term:** Repayment terms are arranged for more than one year.

Equity Financing

- Money given to fund a business in exchange for a share of business ownership.

Other Commonly Used Funding Sources

- **Short-term credit card financing:** In the past, when women were turned down for loans, many used credit cards for start-up financing. If you decide to use credit cards, shop for the lowest rates and pay off the balance before the interest rates increase.
- **Home equity:** Borrowing against the equity in one's home is permitted in all states except Texas. Just make sure you pay back the loan, or you could lose your home.
- **Personal assets:** Antiques, jewelry, and other personal items of worth are sold for cash.
- **Borrowing from policies, plans:** Drawing from insurance policies, pension plans, stocks, or securities have funded many a start-up. Before you borrow, though, be clear about the payback terms and any penalties.
- **Banks:** Traditionally, banks have approved small business loans or have extended a credit line—a short-term business loan on which you pay interest only on the total drawn.
- **Family and friends:** If you borrow from your family or friends, have a signed contract with repayment terms.
- **Personal savings:** Money saved from extra jobs or from your regular pay, gifts, and inheritances can all be put toward a business start-up. The less debt you start with, the better your chances for obtaining a loan later on for expansion, and the less interest you'll spend on any loans you do have.

Nontraditional Financing

When traditional funding sources are not available, entrepreneurs can be quite creative in finding money. Here are some of those ways:

- **Customers:** You may be able to get customers to provide deposits, prepay, or pay in installments, or you can give customers a discount if they pay in full when an order is delivered or a service completed.

- **Suppliers:** They may agree to accept payment in 90 days instead of 30.
- **Factoring:** Accounts receivable (money owed you by customers) are sold to a third party called a factor, which pays you a percentage of your invoices.
- **Trade finance:** If you are an importer or exporter, you may be able to take advantage of trade finance, a type of lending against purchase orders.
- **Partnerships:** A partner can be an investor in your business with 50 percent ownership.
- **Contests, grants:** If your business qualifies, government grants may be awarded to businesses that contribute to their communities' development, job potential, or education. Sometimes you can find in business publications advertised contests in which money is awarded to start-up companies. Gale Research publishes *Grants on Disc* and *Awards, Honors, and Prizes*.

Venture Capital

According to VentureOne <www.ventureone.com>, in 1999, $36.5 billion was invested in venture-backed companies. Though the larger percentage of these venture capital funds has been given to men-owned Internet businesses, women entrepreneurs have also been recipients; Courtney Rosen, founder of eHow.com <www.ehow.com>, a site that explains thousands of basic tasks; and Laurie McCartney, founder and CEO of eStyle.com <www.estyle.com>, are just two examples.

Venture capital financing provides a small, privately held business with a large amount of cash in exchange for part ownership. The venture capital partner may become very involved with the business's operations. Though much has been heard about venture capital funding for e-commerce start-ups, the reality is that only a few who apply for this funding actually receive it.

Here are just a few of the characteristics that venture capitalists want to see in a prospective company:

- Significant returns over a relatively short time period.
- A definite "edge" over competitors.
- Adequate access to existing distribution channels.
- Potential for significant growth and profits in the next several years.
- A strong management team, character, and commitment.

Each venture capital company or investor will have its own criteria that borrowers have to meet. Before you approach a venture capital firm, experts also advise that you should:

- Consult with an attorney, accountant, and other advisors familiar with venture capital arrangements.
- Research and make a listing of prospective investors that match your needs and company profile.
- Prepare a complete and well-documented proposal, including a comprehensive business plan.

In your venture capital search, business experts especially caution you to:

- Avoid investors who want a money guarantee on their investment should the venture fail. It is a risk for you both.
- Avoid any person or firm that requires you to give them money in the beginning. Check out any company's background, too, and get references to see if they are truly legitimate.
- Avoid wasting valuable management time if your business is not a good candidate for venture capital funding. Neglecting your business's daily operations may lead to business failure!

Jennifer Vallee (profiled in chapter 8) of British Columbia, Canada, president and CEO of Pallaslearning, a virtual learning center, says, "I think that many start-ups are spoiled by the millions they receive from venture capitalists. When we didn't have enough capital to pay course developers upfront, we devised a unique royalties-upon-sales model that everyone enjoyed because of our volume. When we didn't have a marketing budget, we secured major alliances that drove membership through the roof. Don't fall into the trap of big money. You lose all resourcefulness."

RELATED RESOURCES

Associations

Associations and their staff do not "match" companies who are seeking financing with venture capitalists. It is recommended you do your own research about venture capital companies that interest you and approach them directly with your ideas.

Forum for Women Entrepreneurs <www.fwe.org>; An organization cofounded by Denise Brosseau, whose mission is to provide access to funding and connections to fellow entrepreneurs; Co-sponsored Springboard 2000 <www.springboard2000.org>, the first all-women venture-capital forum, which gave 25 women-owned firms the chance to present their business plans to investors

The National Venture Capital Association <www.nvca.org>; Educational and networking opportunities for people who wish to learn more about equity investment

Books

Fundamentals of Venture Capital by Joseph W. Bartlett (New York: Madison Books, 1999)

Pratt's Guide to Venture Capital Sources by Stanley E. Pratt, editor (Newark, NJ: Venture Economics, 2000)

Zero Gravity: Riding Venture Capital from High-Tech Start-Up to Breakout IPO by Steve Harmon, John Doerr (Princeton, NJ: Bloomberg Press, 1999)

Internet Sites

<www.businessfinance.com> America's Business Fund Directory

<www.financehub.com> FinanceHub; Venture capital on the Web; Includes articles, database of investors with links to venture firms

<www.startupbiz.com> StartUpbiz.com; Includes a number of relevant links to investment capital sources and to leading venture capital firms

<www.vfinance.com> Venture Capital Resource Library; Bookstore, glossary of terms, news

ADDITIONAL FUNDING RESOURCES

Angel Investors

An "Angel investor" is a wealthy individual who seeks to invest her money in the early development stages of a company. "Angel groups" are informal or formal private investors groups that help to fund businesses that are too small to attract professional venture capital. These "angels" do not usually require a large piece of your company in exchange for their money.

One resource is the ACE-Net, the Access ("Angel") to Capital Electronic Network <http://ace-net.sr.unh.edu>, a Web-based service sponsored by the Office of Advocacy, U.S. Small Business Administration (SBA), which helps angel investors and small businesses looking for early stage financing find one another. A fee is charged, and companies must register their offering with the appropriate federal and state securities trading agencies as well as submit a Small Corporate Offering (SCOR) form for approval to be listed.

Small Business Investment Companies (SBICs)

Government-affiliated investment programs that help companies—locally, statewide, or federally—in which venture capital firms may augment their own funds with federal funds and leverage their investment in qualified investee companies, such as venture capital firms licensed by the U.S. Small Business Administration (SBA), to provide either long-term debt or equity financing to qualified small businesses. According to an SBIC fund director, an SBIC's average investment in a company is $1.5 million (compared to the average investment of $9 million dollars by other venture capital firms), and are located more in smaller towns and rural areas of the United States.

There are now several SBICs that are SBA-backed women-owned venture capital companies. However, please note that these private equity firms are for already established businesses in later stages:

- Capital Across America <www.capitalacrossamerica.org>, based in Nashville, Tennessee; Whitney Johns Martin, founder.
- Women's Growth Capital Fund <www.womensgrowth capital.org>, Washington, D.C.; Patty Abramson, founder.
- Viridian Capital <www.viridian-capital.com>, San Francisco, California; Willa E. Seldon and Christine B. Cordaro, cofounders.

For information about SBICs, contact your nearest SBA office, or visit <www.nasbic.org>.

RELATED RESOURCES

Books

Angel Financing: How to Find and Invest in Private Equity
     by Gerald A. Benjamin and Joel Margulis (New York:
     John Wiley & Sons, 1999)

Internet Sites

<www.womenangels.net> Women Angels.net; An all-female
     angel fund

Bartering

A barter exchange, in which member business owners trade
products or services, is still a taxable sale or income (keep careful tax records). When Susan Breslow Sardone (profiled in
chapter 7), a professional copywriter at Writing That Sells
<www.writingthatsells.com>, was asked for one solution she
used to save on expenses of a Web site start-up, she said, "I
solved that problem with one of my sites by trading services
with a graphic designer who already has her own site. We're
going to metatag and submit her site pages to search engines,
and she's going to design our logo."

Research any bartering exchange before joining to see how
the other business operates, how long they have been in business. Ask businesspersons who use the exchanges for their
opinions.

One Web site you may want to investigate is LassoBucks
<www.lassobucks.com>, a Web site on which entrepreneurs
can swap products and services with other businesses via an
Internet-based record-keeping system. It advertises itself as the
"leading online next-generation barter" system. Others you
might investigate: Barter Buys Online <www.barterbuys.com>;
I-Barter <www.i-barter.com>; and Ubarter <www.ubarter

.com>. A national, nonprofit organization of barter clubs and members is the National Association of Trade Exchanges <www.nate.org>.

Government Funding

Federal   The U.S. Small Business Administration has a number of ongoing loan programs to help fund small businesses' start-up and growth that are too comprehensive to be listed here. For more information, you can start with the SBA telephone number, 1-800-UASK-SBA (1-800-827-5722) or go to their Web site <www.sba.gov> to find an SBA office nearest to you. Note: The SBA also has an e-mail-based question and answer service <www.sba.gov/answerdesk.html>. Other federally funded offices that may be located in your area to assist you with loan information include:

- Small Business Development Centers <www.sba.gov/SBDC>; Usually located at a university.
- SCORE <www.score.org>; Retired executives that offer business counseling. Also offers e-mail counseling.
- Women's Business Development Centers <www.onlinewbc.org>; Offices located around the country with the sole purpose of helping women entrepreneurs. Their Web site offers extensive business start-up and expansion information, including e-commerce, for women entrepreneurs.

The Web sites of these federal organizations have many articles and information on starting a business and e-business and general business management.

State   Contact your primary state government agency that provides one-stop guidance on financial programs and services offered to small businesses, including minority/women's opportunities at the state level. If you are unsure of which agency or agencies to contact, ask your local state representative or senator.

Local   Contact your local business groups and associations for any existing entrepreneurship support programs. Check also to see if your local and/or county government has business funding programs. Local foundations, colleges, and local schools often have programs to help entrepreneurs with start-up and funding information.

Associations and Organizations

Associations such as the National Association of Women Business Owners <www.nawbo.org>, Women Incorporated <www.womeninc.com>, and nonprofit organizations like the newly formed "Count Me In" program <www.count-me-in.org>, which provides women across America with loans of $500 to $10,000 to start or expand their businesses, are assisting women in obtaining financing.

RELATED RESOURCES

Internet Sites

<www.livecapital.com> Live Capital.com; An Internet-based loan center, including SBA-backed loans

<www.websitefinancing.com> Websitefinancing.com; "A leading provider of financing options for income-producing Web sites and software"

Promoting Your Web Site

Whether you have just a simple Web site for your business consisting of a few pages describing your products and/or services or a Web site that is more complex with articles, forums, chats with guest experts, and other features, there is no guarantee that potential customers will find it among the millions of other existing Web sites. Building traffic to your site, and making sure people will return to it over and over again, requires a variety of dedicated marketing efforts on your part. This chapter is presented to assist you in discovering the most effective promotional methods for getting your site noticed and, hopefully, with profitable results.

Netiquette

Just because the Internet is sometimes called the "Wild, Wild Web" does not mean you can do or say anything you want when you're using it. There are laws we must follow, and there is also "netiquette"—a set of rules of conduct that Internet users are expected to follow. With millions of people online, there are bound to be conflicts and disagreements; different groups will have different ideas as to what is and is not acceptable behavior. (An excellent book on this topic is *Netiquette,* by Virginia Shea. Unfortunately the book is out-of-print, but you may be able to find copies in your local public library, or an online bookstore may be able to obtain a copy for you.) Following are some business netiquette guidelines:

- Do not post blatant ads to mailing lists and newsgroups. An alternative is to answer questions about your business and participate in the discussion with information or your own questions. You may offer information on a topic related to your business's products or services on your Web site's home page instead of directly advertising them. Put your Web site's URL in your "signature" (see definition later in this chapter); this will inform people of your site and give them the option of viewing it if they so choose.

- Do not use inappropriate language or derogatory comments (flaming) in online discussions or e-mail unless it is acceptable in that group.

- Do not type in ALL CAPITALS. On the Internet that is considered "shouting," and usually is characteristic of SPAM (unsolicited e-mail sent for advertising purposes).

- Do not forward deceptive or pyramid schemes or scams.

- Spell check your e-mail before you send it, and review it for grammatical errors.

- Ask permission before you send anyone attachments. Too many destructive viruses are sent this way!

- Respond to one person, not an entire mailing list, and conversely, if you are sending the same e-mail carbon copy to a mailing list, do it so that no other person's e-mail address will be read. You can do this if your e-mail client has the field *bcc, blind carbon copy.* The addresses entered in the *bcc* field do *not* appear in the message you are sending to an individual recipient. Conversely, when you enter addresses in the *cc* field, the recipient will see the other entered addresses. Just be sure you know which one you are using. For most promotional purposes, for example, like e-mail press releases, it is better to take time to know the name of the person who should receive your e-mail, rather than sending out bulk messages and irritating unknown recipients for whom your news has no relevancy.

- Read FAQs sections on Web sites completely before you send an e-mail question.
- Make sure the newsgroups to whom you post information will be interested in your information and expertise.
- Remember, if your e-mail is not something everyone could read, then do not write and send it, because it can go anywhere in "cyberspace"!

Better Business Bureau's "Code of Online Business Practices"

At the writing of this book, the Better Business Bureau (BBB) Program was soliciting comments for the final version of its "Code of Online Business Practices," which the BBB said "will be the newest self-regulation tool developed by the BBB system to provide Internet businesses with a well-respected means to foster consumer trust and confidence on the Web." They hoped the final version of these online business guidelines would be released by mid-2000. To read this code, visit the BBB site <www.bbbonline.org>.

- Develop a set of your own online business ethics, just as you would with an offline business—be honest with your customers and clients.

There are other guidelines, but generally, if you treat others with respect, the same way you would wish to be treated (the "Golden Rule" does apply!), you will be practicing good netiquette. When asked the following question: "In your opinion, what are one or two basic 'netiquette' principles that online entrepreneurs should follow?" Sandra Kinsler of Woman Motorist.com answered, "You are not anonymous. Be as polite and patient online as you would be in person. Fools abound. Just because others are rude does not give you license to do the same. Being nasty is dangerous as it makes one a target for vengeful hackers."

Netiquette is a set of unwritten, online behavior guidelines whose purpose is to foster respect towards all those who use the Internet for either personal or business use and communications. If everyone abides by these guidelines, the World Wide Web just might evolve into maybe not a perfect "world" but one that can offer unlimited positive opportunities for all individuals, organizations, and businesses.

RELATED RESOURCES

Internet Sites

<www.thirdage.com> Third Age.com; Has a "Business Netiquette" guide you can read on its site

Traditional Versus Internet Advertising and Marketing Techniques

With so many Web sites already existing, you will have to conduct daily, active marketing—first to attract people to your site and then to have them return again and again. Business experts recommend you try a variety of marketing and advertising strategies to find the most successful methods to attract site visitors. You may not be able to spend millions of dollars, as some new Web sites did for Super Bowl television commercials, but you can still find affordable and effective ways both on- and offline to let potential clients and customers know about and come to your Web site.

Here are some Internet marketing principles to keep in mind:

- Devise a marketing plan specifically for your Web site—with goals and the steps you need to take to achieve them.

- Web advertising differs from print advertising in that it not only tells people you have something for sale, it can provide them with in-depth information about your products and services to help in their buying decisions.

- Be patient, diligent, and persistent with your Web site's marketing efforts. The Internet is vast, and it will take time for you to build your site; for your site to be indexed on the search engines with whom you register; for potential clients to discover your site; for customers to trust in ordering from you; and to build and maintain your online business overall.

- With ads bombarding consumers and businesses from all types of media, people are skeptical about product and service claims. You will have to prove to your customers that your business is legitimate and worthy of their time and money.

- Keep your Web site ahead of your competition's by updating it regularly with news your customers can use and by staying informed with trends in your industry.

- Use your money wisely to get the most for your promotional dollars. Try as many free and low-cost methods (discussed later in this chapter) as you can for your site. As your budget permits, you may want to pay for major

BUSINESS PROFILE: Sandra Kinsler, Magazine Publisher and Radio Show Producer

What is your Internet venture?

CyberAd Media, Inc., publishers of: WomanMotorist.com <www .womanmotorist.com>, RoadTestOnline.com; producers of *Road Test Radio Magazine*.

Is it solely an Internet business?

The business began as a Web-only magazine publishing company. Our intent was to create consumer editorial publications online and then migrate them to traditional media such as books, radio and television shows, magazines (where applicable), and quarterlies. We now have two e-zines and one radio show with a third e-zine due to roll out by midsummer.

When was the business started?

September 1995.

How did you originate the idea for your site?

My husband, Brian Leshon, and I were doing PR and photographic work in the auto racing industry. We learned that automakers and automotive aftermarket products companies had no problem finding outlets to communicate marketing messages to men. With respect to women, they were struggling. I had a background in media management and distribution and had been watching the Internet show signs of commercializing, and Brian was familiar with publishing. Between the two of us we had the skills to start a publication and saw the opportunity to provide the first widely accepted women's consumer automotive publication.

How did you finance your start-up?

We were a self financed start-up. We used savings, but mostly we worked other jobs while we were starting and until we landed our first advertising clients.

What resource helped you the most?

We're pioneers. When we started there wasn't much to rely on. There weren't even many books on HTML coding at that time.

We're self-taught and relied on the few Web sites—mostly developed by universities—for coding information. In fact, I've been teaching Internet Marketing at the University of California, Santa Barbara for four years. And that was the first course of its kind taught in the United States that we know of.

Can you offer any tips for creating a successful Web site?

1. Know whom you are trying to reach—demographics. If you don't know whom you are going to be talking to, you can't plan a site.
2. Planning. Know what content you need, where it is going to come from, and how to organize it so that the intended audience will be comfortable using it.
3. Research. Know the market you plan to work in. If you are going to fund the project with advertising sales, it is critical to know how that industry works and what the standards and benchmarks are for being able to justify sales.
4. Be patient. Things take longer than you hope. Make sure you can survive financially during a three- to five-year start-up.
5. Don't over-commit. It's easy to have too much work and spend too much money. Prioritize tasks and content. A site doesn't have to have everything on it that you hope for at the start. It can grow over time and still be successful.

Do you have any additional comments?

Owning a business is both gratifying and frustrating. We work with people every day who benefit from what we do while acting as if they are doing us a favor by talking to us. Let bad behavior roll off your back—don't take it personally.

Sandra Kinsler, president, CyberAd Media, Inc;
editor-in-chief and copublisher of WomanMotorist.com;
managing editor and copublisher, RoadTestOnline.com.

Advertising Regulations Online and Offline

- The Better Business Bureau <www.bbb.org>. Besides the Better Business Bureau's "BBBOnLine Code of Online Business Practices" <www.bbbonline.org>, there are regulations that you must adhere to in your advertising—on- and offline. Again, at the BBB's site, their Council of Better Business Bureaus (CBBB) offers the following:

  CBBB's Children's Advertising Review Unit (CARU): CARU's Self-Regulatory Guidelines for Children's Advertising

  Subscriptions to *Do's & Don'ts in Advertising*, containing monthly supplemental advertising updates on new and existing federal regulations and guides as well as numerous industry codes and guides

  "Code of Advertising"; Basic advertising standards

- The Federal Trade Commission (FTC) <www.ftc .gov>, 600 Pennsylvania Avenue N.W., Washington, D.C. 20580. The FTC periodically joins with other law enforcement agencies to monitor the Internet for potentially false or deceptive online advertising claims. To help you avoid any advertis-

search engine's keywords, which can help increase traffic of the best potential customers for your business.
- Know that not everyone "plays fair" on the Wild, Wild Web, and that if you have a good response to your site, somebody will copy your text or metatags to try to divert some of your traffic to their site.

ing infractions, you can write the FTC or visit their
site's "Business Guidance" section. If you advertise on the Internet, many of the same regulations
that apply to offline advertising apply as well to
online ads. These include prohibiting:

Unfair or deceptive advertising

Disclaimers

Demonstrations of products

Refunds

Advertising to children

Protecting consumer's privacy online

Business opportunities: Franchises; multilevel
marketing (MLM)

Other: Mail and telephone orders, jewelry selling,
Internet auctions, Web scams, selling internationally, and other important compliance
information

It is your responsibility to know these guidelines,
rules, and regulations before you begin advertising on
the Internet, in addition to staying current with any
changes in these laws.

- Outstanding customer service to a focused group of
customers and clients will help ensure a Web business's
success.
- A Web site must advertise, provide product and service
information, and learn about its customers' preferences all
with the customer's consent.

- Introduce Web site visitors to other "friends" on the Web —areas that relate to your site.
- Use a combination of both on- and offline marketing methods to increase site visitors, plus always be on the outlook for new methods to try.

With Internet marketing, it will be a challenge for you just to get the attention of potential customers. Once that happens, your success will depend on what you offer them and how you meet their needs with your products and services.

Differences and Similarities of Traditional and Internet Marketing

When Ilise Benun, a self-promotion specialist, was asked the following question: "What marketing advantage does the Internet give a business over the traditional marketing avenues?" she answered, "To me, the incredible thing about the Web is that it allows people to find out about you anonymously, to get a sense of who you are and what you're offering without contacting you first. This saves a lot of time for everyone."

Some other similarities and differences between traditional and Internet advertising:

Similarity: People do not have time to listen to long commercials in offline media, nor will they wait for long downloads

Difference: People will read longer articles in print than online, where they are reluctant to scroll through long pages of text or graphics

Similarity: Good customer service will foster faithful customers and good "word- or Web-of-mouth" about your business

Difference: If you make a mistake with an offline customer, they may give you a second chance. With the Internet, your competition is only a "click" away.

Similarity: Your promotional materials offline and Web site online should look professional, no matter how small your business

Advertising is just one of many marketing tools, but if you don't concentrate on the types of advertising that work best for your site, you will be wasting time and money your business cannot afford to lose.

RELATED RESOURCES
Books

101 Ways to Promote Yourself: Tricks of the Trade for Taking Charge of Your Own Success by Raleigh Pinskey (New York: Avon Books, 1997)

Deep Branding on the Internet by Marc Braunstein and Ned Levine (Roseville, CA: Prima Communications, 2000)

Self Promotion Online by Ilise Benun (Cincinnati: North Light Books, 2001)

Internet Sites

<www.ideabook.com>; General marketing and design tips by Chuck Green

<www.marketingtips.com> The Internet Marketing Center; Marketing newsletter and home study course, "The Insider Secrets to Marketing Your Business on the Internet"

BUSINESS PROFILE: Ilise Benun, Self-Promotion Specialist

What is your Internet venture?

The Art of Self Promotion <www.artofselfpromotion.com>; "Manageable Marketing for the Self-Employed."

Is it solely an Internet business?

It's a publishing and consulting company, and the Web site offers samples of the material and details about services offered.

When was the business started?

1990.

How did you originate the idea for your site?

It was obvious to me that I'd need a Web site for my quarterly newsletter so that people who wanted a sample issue could go directly online to see it.

How did you finance your start-up?

There wasn't much overhead at the beginning of my consulting business, and whatever expenses I had and couldn't cover, I put on my credit card, which I was, fortunately, able to pay off shortly thereafter.

How to Get Listed on the Major Search Engines

Search engines are computer software programs, usually located on a public computer network, that find information in response to a question or statement you enter in its submit box/area. Some of the more popular and well-known search engines are Alta Vista <www.altavista.com>, Excite <www .excite.com>, HotBot <www.hotbot.com>, and Yahoo! <www .yahoo.com>. Some of the search engines, like Yahoo!, offer a variety of news, shopping, and even e-commerce set-ups, while Google.com <www.google.com> (one of my favorites) is exclusively a search engine.

What resource helped you the most?

My best resources have been other business owners, and mostly women. Early on, I started a local group of women business owners, and we'd meet monthly to discuss the different issues and challenges we were facing. That was a huge help, and continues to be, though we no longer meet as a group.

Can you offer any tips for creating a successful Web site?

Provide useful content to those you consider your prospects and clients, and invest your time and energy in linking to and from other complementary sites rather than on search engine rankings.

Ilise Benun, author of Self Promotion Online *and director of Hoboken, New Jersey–based* Creative Marketing & Management.

Statistics demonstrate that a majority of Internet users go to a search engine first when seeking information. Registering your Web site on these search engines is an effective and low-cost way of generating publicity for your site.

Evelyn Salvador, owner of Desktop Publishing Plus <www.designerresumes.com>, says a tip for having a successful Web site is to "use as many keywords as possible so the search engines pick up your site through various search topics."

When Shannan Hearne, President of Success Promotions <www.successpromotions.com> (who has made a "commitment to giving time and resources back to women via the Internet") was asked, "Do you have a tip for an online entrepreneur for increasing traffic to their sites?" she answered:

Three of the most important things to consider when planning a site are the elements that will achieve high rankings in the search engines—because these three things are what the different search engines use to index and rank your site: they are content, keywords, and metatags. You can't leave them to chance. You really must think about them and utilize them in ways to directly relate to your site's purpose and message.

The content of the page has to be relevant to the entire page, or some search engines will bar the site from listing, and other search engines will list it in entirely incorrect categories.

The keywords are used when actually submitting a site to the search engines for spidering and indexing, and they also must be completely relevant to your site.

Finally, the metatags are "keywords" that are embedded into the HTML code of your Web site. The metatags tell some of the search engines what your site is about and what types of Internet searches should include your site in the results. For all three—content, keywords, and metatags— remember that synonyms and misspellings are good! You want to tell the search engines everything you possibly can about your Web site so they, in turn, can tell people and drive traffic. While search engines aren't the only way that you will drive traffic to your Web site, most studies credit the search engines with generating between 60 and 80 percent of the average site's total visitors. So they are an important part.

You can register your Web site yourself:

- By going to each search engine and submitting your site as instructed.
- By purchasing and using submission software like Web Position Gold <www.webposition.com>, Submit Wolf <www.submitwolf.com>, or SoftSpider <www.softspider .com>.

- By using a submission service like Submit It! <www
  .submit-it.com>, which will charge you a fee for registering
  your site with a certain number of search engines.
- By using a free service like Register It <www.registerit
  .com>.

You should also know the difference between a search
engine and a directory. Search engines create their listings automatically with the use of "spiders or "crawlers" that index
your site based on the keywords and phrases you enter, and
index all the pages in your Web site. Directories, like Yahoo!,
employ individuals who review your site to decide if they will
accept it to be included based on the description you submit
manually. No promises are given that your site will be
included.

Here are some other ways to maximize search engine
publicity:

- Periodically update your pages' metatags and related information, so your rankings stay high in the top listings of
  the major search engines when some other person regis-
  ters keywords similar to yours.
- Sue Harris (profiled in chapter 5), the owner of Scandia
  International, which publishes and distributes The Consignment Workbook (see consignment.org for more details), says, "Try to pick a site name word that will be
  general. When I first purchased my site, consignment.org,
  the site came up in the top 10 in every search engine. Now
  I'm number 63 on Netscape, and heaven only knows where
  else on the other ones. I recently paid for some company
  to try to get me to the top of all the lists, $90 for six
  months of maintenance, but was disappointed in the
  results. I think the site owner needs to upgrade and update
  the site every month and fill in the request on each site to
  be reconsidered for better placement."

BUSINESS PROFILE: Shannan Hearne, Site Branding Services

What is your Internet venture?

Success Promotions, Internet marketing and site branding service for business people online <www.successpromotions.com>.

Is it solely an Internet business?

This business revolves around the Internet obviously, but I still have a fair amount of offline contact with clients.

When was the business started?

September 1997.

How did you originate the idea for your site?

I was having a hard time finding a pre-packaged business that both suited me and wasn't already saturated in my area. So I gravitated toward using my marketing and Internet experience to start a service-oriented business that would meet the needs of all those other e-business owners, knowing that my target market would be large and would continue to grow.

How did you finance your start-up?

Success Promotions was started completely on a shoestring. I learned most of my marketing secrets by building my own business online without spending hefty sums on advertising and marketing. Even the software in use today as a part of the promotions work done for clients wasn't purchased until the business was generating its own revenue.

- Search engines and directories will differ in how they evaluate your site's submission, and you should familiarize yourself with the criteria each uses to ensure a high ranking.
- Pay attention to your title tag, which usually is selected as being the most important for its keywords.
- Strive to stay high in the top 10 or 20 listings, as most people do not look beyond these for information.

What resource helped you the most?

The Internet marketing arena has grown greatly since I jumped in with both feet. When I started, the few other people in the same field were unreachable, unwilling to offer help or mentoring, or offering it through their own personal success manuals for more money that I was willing to invest initially. My biggest help came from a group of online working moms located at <www.moms network.com>. This group of phenomenal women definitely motivated me into success.

Can you offer any tips for creating a successful Web site?

The Internet is not a field of dreams; just because you build it does not mean that people will come. You have to create a site with useful information of interest to your potential customers and then market the site in such a way that those potential customers looking for information such as you offer can find you.

Do you have any additional comments?

The Internet may very well be both the last and the greatest level playing field on which women can compete with men. Additionally, it allows women to work from wherever they choose and to some extent, whenever they choose. Isn't that perhaps the most important thing?

Shannan Hearne specializes in helping people build their e-businesses, in addition to providing promotion services. Her site contains tips, tools, and resources for building a high level of traffic to a Web site.

Check with the directories and search engines with whom you have registered for your listing verification, and resubmit your site whenever major modifications have been made to it.

Registering with search engines is not a guarantee that you will get a dramatic traffic increase to your site, but is it an important marketing tool that can possibly lead new customers to come for a visit and stay!

RELATED RESOURCES

Internet Sites

<www.howtointernet.com> HowToInternet.com; Internet marketing information; How to write copy for the net; Tips and pointers on search engine optimization and Web consulting

<www.searchenginewatch.com> Search Engine Watch; Covers search engine submission and registration topics in its "Search Engine Submission Tips" (formerly called "A Webmaster's Guide to Search Engines"); Covers ways to add a search engine to your Web site

Software

Traffic Builder by Intelliquis <www.intelliquis.com>; Web site and submission to search engines

Internet Research on Potential Customers

As was discussed previously, you need to conduct thorough research to make sure customers exist for your product or service and to decide if your idea is feasible and affordable enough to justify your starting this venture. Combining the resources of the Internet itself and offline methods of research, you can find out much of the information you need.

OFFLINE RESOURCES

Primary Research (direct contact to consumers and business owners): Direct mail questionnaires, telephone interviews, in-person interviews, responses to print ads

Secondary Research: Commercial, educational, and public sources (government agencies, chambers of commerce,

public and college libraries and institutions), media sales
departments, business newspapers and trade publications

ONLINE RESOURCES

Primary Research: Message boards, chats responses to online
classified ads, newsgroups

Secondary Research: Research firms and online database services, search engines, company profiles, online sites featuring e-commerce news, online publications

Once you have collected the data, you will need to analyze it and use the results to aid you in forming a business
strategy to reach your focus customers.

RELATED RESOURCES
Books

*Millennium Intelligence: Understanding and Conducting Com-
petitive Intelligence in the Digital Age* by Jerry P. Miller,
editor (Medford, NJ: Information Today Inc., 2000)

Internet Sites

<www.cyberatlas.com> Cyberatlas; Statistical information
about the Internet

<www.deja.com> Deja.com; Permits you to originate a per-
sonalized page from which you can join all Usenet
groups; Do not SPAM or blatantly advertise, or you will
be unwelcome

U S. Department of Labor

<www.researchbuzz.com> Research Buzz; Internet research
articles, news, hints, and sources to help you use the
Internet as a research medium

<www.emarketer.com> eMarketer; Internet market research firm

<www.estats.com> eStats; Provides accurate data on Internet
   facts and figures

Analyzing Your Competitors

You could be lucky and start an entirely new type of Internet
business site and not have any competition, but more than
likely, there already is competition to your site's idea. You will
want to:

1. Determine who they are.
2. Determine what they *are* and *are not* providing to their
    customers.

OFFLINE

Primary: Conduct surveys at consumer trade shows and
   events, give away free samples and ask for feedback;
   Pose as a customer and order something from your
   competition; Ask your customers directly if they have
   patronized a competitor's Web site and their opinion
   of the experience

Secondary: Study competitors' advertisements and promotional materials for their offerings; Read any news publications in your industry for feature news and stories
   about your competitors' business success or lack of it

ONLINE

Primary: Order something or call in an order to evaluate
   their customer service; Talk to suppliers for any news
   about competitors; Monitor Usenet posts for comments
   and to ask what commercial sites they visit frequently
   and why; Monitor competitors' sites for message boards
   and chats that may have some posts for complaints;

Subscribe to any e-mail newsletters your competitors offer

Secondary: Monitor search engines for recently updated Web sites and new articles put out by your competitors. Create a comparison chart between your site and a competitor's and ask someone to objectively rate your site with the others.

When Anne Holland, CEO of MarketingSherpa.com, was asked how one can use the Internet to do research in analyzing competitors, she said, "You can use the news and research sources, such as Hoovers.com and Powerize.com to research companies as effectively as you used to be able to research them in the Library. But most of all you should sign up for their site newsletter, member list, or buyer file. That's the best way of learning how they interact with their customers/visitors and what they have planned going forward. I'm constantly shocked at how many marketers and business owners have not signed up for their competitors' newsletters!"

Periodically, review your competitors' sites to see what changes or additions have been made, but do not let it obsess you. Oftentimes, customers will shop at more than one site for like items, so there is usually room for the competition. Just concentrate on doing what you do best and offering superior customer service; that's a combination that any competitor will have a hard time beating!

RELATED RESOURCES

Internet Sites

<http://cnnfn.cnn.com/markets/multex> CNNFN; Search tool that will provide you with the URL of any company if you enter in the stock symbol or name of a business

BUSINESS PROFILE: Anne Holland, Resources for
                          Dot-Com Marketers

What is your Internet Venture?

MarketingSherpa.com, <www.marketingsherpa.com>; practical
news and tips for Internet Marketers.

Is it solely an Internet business?

Currently only Internet.

When was the business started?

January 2000.

How did you originate the idea for your site?

I wanted to create something for Internet marketers because that's
what I know best. So I went to trade shows, to email discussion
groups, and also individually interviewed a lot of people in person
and asked them, "What do you need that the other Internet marketing and advertising news and information sites aren't giving
you?" Basically, I asked people to whine! They told me what they
really needed and wanted, and then I set out to build it.

Do you have a "vision statement" for your Web site?

MarketingSherpa's goal is to be the most hands-on, practical, fun,
and beloved resource for dot com marketers, Internet specialists
at offline companies, and related agencies and service firms.

<www.hoover.com> Hoover.com; Gives basic company infor-
    mation and more in-depth to members who pay a mem-
    bership fee

<www.howtointernet.com> HowToInternet.com; Internet
    marketing information, how to write copy for the Net,
    tips and pointers on search engine optimization and Web
    consulting

<www.ProfitInfo.com> Internet Marketing Goldmine by
Marty Foley

How did you finance your start-up?

Personal savings, friends and family investments.

What resource helped you the most?

Networking with other Netpreneurs to learn what I needed to do and how to do it.

Can you offer any tips for creating a successful Web site?

Think about your visitor, what they want to see and how they'd like to see it. Forget about yourself.

Do you have any additional comments?

If you are doing this to get rich quick, forget it. This is about loving and serving your marketplace as well as you possibly can. And if the profits come, that's nice too.

Anne Holland, CEO and publisher of
MarketingSherpa.com and founder of
DotComWomen e-mail discussion group
<www.egroups.com>.

Building Traffic to Your Site

You have most likely read the saying, "You may build it (your Web site), but will they (your customers) come?" in Internet marketing articles many times. It is true that you will need to:

1. Make potential customers aware of your site's presence.
2. Convince them to return repeatedly.

This can be quite a task considering that in "E-Life," a *Newsweek* special issue published in Spring 2000, it was reported that at that time there were an estimated 12 million existing Web sites, with the domain-name-registry service Network Solutions adding a new "dot-com" every five seconds! However, every new business needs to establish itself and make itself known to customers, so this is nothing new for an entrepreneur. What is new are the Internet's technological "twists" to old marketing tools and the presentations of new ones to help your business connect with customers around the world. Following are some commonly used promotions and tips.

PRESS RELEASES

Press releases are announcements of a new business, promotion, or other newsworthy event (such as introducing a new business, a business alliance, a new product, or a new contract; appearing on media; holding a seminar; publishing a book or research findings).

Tips for Press Releases

- **Basic Principles:** A press release should contain just the facts: answers to Who? What? When? Where? Why? and How?; and your contact information (telephone number, URL, e-mail address); it should read like a "mini" article and not like an ad or a sales brochure. Note: Many editors still prefer press releases sent through the regular mail.
- **Internet "slant":** Keep it short in length (four or five paragraphs); use your subject line to capture interest (avoid the use of the word Free or all CAPITALS, which SPAMmers use); personalize the release to each editor and make sure it is a subject that they cover; post and archive your releases on your site; do not send as an attachment.

When Shannon Kinnard, president of Idea Station, an e-mail marketing agency in Atlanta, was asked if she had a tip for sending a business press release via e-mail, she said, "Do not just send one unrequested. Use Profnet.com, Businesswire .com, or InternetWire.com and let them send a paragraph about your release to the reporters who request it. Then, when your release is requested, you can send it to the press via e-mail."

RELATED RESOURCES

Internet Sites

<www.businesswire.com> Business Wire

<www.internetwire.com> Internet Wire

<www.netrageousresults.com/pr> The NETrageous Publicity Resource Center; Publicity tips

<www.profnet.com> Profnet

<www.xpress.com> Xpress Press News Service; Article: "How to Write a Press Release for E-mail Distribution"

CHAT GUESTS

Chats (short for Internet Relay Chat) are real-time online discussions that you can host on your site with invited guests, or use to talk to your customers for feedback or technical support; or you can be a guest on a related site frequented by your potential customers.

Chat Tips

Use chat programs that do not require your customers to have special client software; encourage chat guests to provide helpful information, not advertising, to chat participants; archive the transcripts of any scheduled chats for viewers who missed them; use transcripts to garner new FAQs; have a posted

BUSINESS PROFILE: Shannan Kinnard, E-Mail
Marketing Specialist

What is your Internet venture?

Idea Station, <www.ideastation.com>.

Is it solely an Internet business?

It is an online business primarily, but if it were an offline business
I'd be doing print newsletters instead of email newsletters, which
is what I do now.

When was the business started?

January 1, 1998. (Guess what my New Year's resolution was that
year!)

How did you originate the idea for your site?

I wanted to be a full-time writer and had done email newsletters
at a past job and someone remembered me months later. I started
out thinking I would just write for magazines, but the money was
sporadic. I decided that the annuity income from doing email
newsletters would be more stable than simply writing for magazines and there was a market opportunity for this service.

policy for rules of conduct in your chats—no solicitations, or
profanity, or potentially libelous statements. Costs and maintenance may be prohibitive for new online start-ups.

RELATED RESOURCES

Internet Sites

<www.chatspace.com> ChatSpace

<www.eshare.com>; Expressions Interaction Suite of eShare
    Technologies, Inc.

<www.ichat.com>; iChat Rooms, Message Boards

<www.talkcity.com> Talk City

Do you have a "vision statement" for your Web site?
To offer quality information, resources and services for marketing with email.

How did you finance your start-up?
Personal savings, credit cards and a loan from my sweet fiancée (boyfriend at the time).

What resource helped you the most?
Another author who was a client of mine at the time.

Can you offer any tips for creating a successful Web site?
Quality information. Clear writing and a dedication to frequent updating.

*Shannon Kinnard is president of Idea Station
and author of* Marketing With Email

BANNERS

Banners are visual advertising bars that broadcast your business. They often have animated features to catch potential customers' attention and questions to entice them to click on the ad to lead them to your Web site. You will usually pay by the number of impressions, and can rotate two or three different banners to test their effectiveness.

Banner Tips

Banners can help to create a brand for your business in the minds of your potential customers, but can be costly for the newbie business owner to purchase. If you use them on your site, make sure they do not take your viewer away from your site for good or get overused. If you accept banner ads on your site for added revenue, be prepared to handle the extra work this will require you or someone else to do.

When Lesley Spencer, founder and director of Home-Based Working Moms, was asked if she had a tip how an online entrepreneur can get sponsors or make the best use of banners on her Web site, she said, "First, create a site with current, updated content and good design that will attract repeat visitors. Research some of the online advertising agencies who will sell banner space for you in exchange for a percentage of the advertising revenue. Or consider joining with similar, but not competitive, businesses who cater to the same market and hire an ad rep to sell banner space for all of the sites."

RELATED RESOURCES

Internet Sites

These offer the opportunity for member businesses to freely exchange ads.

<www.bcentral.com> LinkExchange Banner Network

<www.smartage.com> SmartAge.com

Software

The Banner Generator by Prescient Code Solutions
    <www.code.com/creations/banner>; For creating your
    own simple text-only banner

Headline Studio by Metacreations
    <www.metacreations.com>; Web banner formation with
    video effects

Paint Shop Pro by Jasc Software, Inc. <www.jasc.com>;
    Banner software creation program

Affiliate Programs: "Working Both Ways"

Affiliate (sometimes called "associate") programs let you promote your site on other sites with your logo or graphic ad. A customer visiting the site posting your ad can click on your ad to go to your site. If this results in a purchase, you pay a predetermined commission to that affiliate. This works for you, too, when you become an "affiliate partner," and sell other sites' goods, such as books with Amazon.com's program. Sometimes affiliates are paid by the advertiser every time someone just clicks onto the advertiser's site.

Affiliate Tips

Make sure all the sites you have or are connected to are compatible with and relevant to your site's products and services and offer your customers security and privacy. Check payment percentages and schedules. Do not overload your site with too many reselling programs. Customers want information and help more than hard sales. If you are the affiliate, offer a steady and meaningful commission with a minimum payout.

Related Resources

Internet Sites

These are examples of affiliate marketing programs.

<www.absoluteauthority.com> Absolute Authority

<www.affinia.com> Affinia.com

<www.befree.com> BeFree

<www.linkshare.com> LinkShare.com

<www.nexchange.com> Nexchange

BUSINESS PROFILE: Lesley Spencer, Resources for Home-Based Working Moms

What is your Internet venture?

Home-Based Working Moms (HBWM) <www.hbwm.com> is a great resource for moms working at home and those wanting to—providing great information, networking, tools, support, a monthly (print) newsletter, member's listserve, panel of experts, member's business showcase on the Web, online membership directory, and more.

Is it solely an Internet business?

We operate through the Internet and do not have a retail site.

When was the business started?

The association was founded in December 1995. Our Web site was launched in July 1997.

How did you originate the idea for your site?

It began with my own need for networking, support, and information as a home-based working mom and grew as I learned of the demand and need from other HBWMs.

How did you finance your start-up?

Personal savings.

When asked if she had a tip on how to start using affiliates to promote your site, Susie Glennan of The Busy Woman's Daily Planner <www.thebusywoman.com>, said, "Make it fun, make it easy, and tell them how to best utilize the affiliate program."

NEW INFORMATION

Business Web sites and print media need articles that will both inform and entertain their customers. When you provide them with articles based on your experiences and/or expertise, they will give you a credit or tagline in which you can list the URL of your Web site.

What resource helped you the most?

Other moms that I met online. SCORE <www.score.org>. Books: *101 Best Home-Based Business for Women* by Priscilla Huff, *Working from Home* by Paul and Sarah Edwards <www.pauland sarah.com>.

Can you offer any tips for creating a successful Web site?

Have a genuine interest in helping people. It shows in your product or service and in your attitude. And as a bonus, you are likely to get referrals. Get feedback from visitors and customers and see how and where you can improve. Continually look for ways to market your Web site. Give people what they want.

Do you have any additional comments?

Find a business that you truly love. Only then will you find true success.

Lesley Spencer, M.Sc., founder and director,
Home-Based Working Moms, "The association that helps
bring working moms closer to their children." Free e-News,
e-mail: hbwmoms-e-news-subscribe@egroups.com.

Article Tips

Review the online site, or samples of the publication on- or offline, to make sure that your site and information are appropriate for their audience and vice versa, and that you get an idea of the style of writing for that site or publication. If you do not have the time to write an article, offer a quick tip with a signature that will list your site. How-to articles on your site or for others are especially needed.

Internet slant: In writing for Web site readership, pay attention to word length, and organize your information in highlights or bullets, which work well for viewing on a monitor; add some related information and a couple of links to

---

BUSINESS PROFILE: Susie Glennan, Products
for Busy Women

What is your Internet venture?

The Busy Woman's Daily Planner <www.thebusywoman.com>,
"Purses, Planners and Other Specialty Products for Busy Women."

Is it solely an Internet business?

About 50/50.

When was the business started?

Sometime in 1991—the previous owner designed and developed
it. Then I purchased the company on April 1, 1999.

How did you originate the idea for your site?

I kept thinking of how hard it was for me to look for something,
find it, see it, and purchase it. So I tried to make my site easy to navigate and purchase from. Then people wanted my articles, so I put
those up as well.

---

additional information (unless the site's editor wants the site
visitor to stay within the pages of her site).

RELATED RESOURCES

Books

*Writing for New Media: The Essential Guide to Writing for
    Interactive Media, CD-Roms and the Web* by Andrew
    Bonime, Ken C. Pohlman (contributor), (New York:
    Wiley, 1997)

When Shane Brodock, a certified professional virtual assistant (VA), was asked why she decided to include articles on
her site, <www.AskShane.com>, she said, "I think that many

How did you finance your start-up?

I went on the premise that I could get a woman-owned business loan, had my husband cosigning, and still couldn't get a loan on that basis. Then I spoke with my old bank and they looked at my credit, let my husband cosign, and gave me the personal loan in three days!

What resource helped you the most?

Other entrepreneurs.

Can you offer any tips for creating a successful Web site?

Keeping up on it, getting feedback from others, changing it often enough to make people want to come back and see what's new.

Do you have any additional comments?

It's a 24-hour-a-day job that needs constant attention.

Susie Glennan, "What getting organized is all about." Subscribe to our monthly newsletter. E-mail: thebusywomantips-subscribe@onelist.com.

people feel more secure about doing business with someone on the Internet when they see that the 'print media' acknowledges an online business."

USE OF SIGNATURES

A signature file is a text message that is automatically added to your message by newsgroup and mail software programs.

Signature Tips

Your signature file is an "electronic business card" and can include your business name, URL, contact information, a slogan, and even the latest product or service you are offering.

BUSINESS PROFILE: Shane Brodock, Professional
                    Virtual Assistant for Authors,
                    Entertainers, and Public Speakers

What is your Internet venture?

AskShane.com, <www.askshane.com>, "Working Solo Doesn't Have to Mean Working Alone."

Is it solely an Internet business?

Internet business.

When was the business started?

January 1998.

How did you originate the idea for your site?

Initially it started as a Web brochure for marketing purposes. As my business grew, I realized that I needed more—a place for clients to learn more about me and my services, as well as a place they could go to for great resources.

How did you finance your start-up?

Personal savings.

It can be a good way to let people know about your business site without hard selling. Modify your signature according to the interests of the people to whom your messages are being sent. Debra Koontz Traverso adds something different every time she sends off an e-mail or letter. She says, "I never got into a branded signature because I do not want folks with whom I communicate several times in a short period of time to feel as though they are being bombarded with my 'advertising,' if you will."

Sample Signatures

Following are sample signatures from two of the women profiled in this book:

What resource helped you the most?

Books: *Outsmarting Goliath* by Debra Koontz Traverso, *Working Solo* by Terry Lonier; Organizations: Assist University, SCORE (both locally and their Web site), WriteDirections.com (for writing classes).

Can you offer any tips for creating a successful Web site?

Remember who you are creating the Web site for. It needs to be designed with your ideal customer/client in mind.

Do you have any additional comments?

Find a group of advisors (mentors) to advise and support you when you need it. There were several times I was stuck and they helped me get back on track. Define your target market, then invite several people from this group to take a look at your Web site, and listen to their comments.

Shane Brodock, Certified Professional Virtual Assistant.

Debra Koontz Traverso,
> co-president, www.WriteDirections.com,
> author of *Outsmarting Goliath* (Bloomberg Press, 2000)
> mail to: Debra@OutsmartingGoliath.com
> "The place to optimize your small-business image"
> (phone number here)

Shane Brodock, Virtual Assistant

> "You Can Do Anything, You Just Can't Do Everything."
> For more information, contact me (phone number here)
> mailto: shane@askshane.com
> (www.askshane.com)

RELATED RESOURCE

Internet Sites

<www.coolsig.com> CoolSig; Samples of many signature
   lines for your review

HYPERLINKS

Also called a "link," a hyperlink is a listing of one Web site's
URL on another site's page, usually to provide related information. A user can click on the hyperlink to move immediately
to the second site.

Hyperlink Tips

Create a separate page for links, and ask permission from the
owners of sites with whom you wish to link, stating how the
relationship would be mutually beneficial. Make the links
noticeable and readable on your screen. Include both recipro-
cal and one-way links to resources that are helpful to your
site's visitors and customers. If you'd rather not have visitors
leave your site, just list the Web addresses of the sites you think
would best suit your target audience. Regularly check the links
listed to ensure they are still "active" and not "dead."

RELATED RESOURCES

Internet Sites

<www.link-box.com> Link-Box Link Exchange; Allows you
   to trade text ads instead of banners for free

E-MAIL MARKETING WITHOUT SPAM

E-mail marketing involves sending e-mail to customers to
announce promotions or to provide information. E-mail to
your customers reminds them of your business, encourages

them to respond, and can provide them with information that will help them in their businesses or personal lives.

Adrienne Press, marketing expert at NetCreations, Inc., a New York provider of opt-in e-mail marketing services, says, "E-mail marketing is more effective because of its intimacy aspect as well as being a faster, better way of doing direct marketing, with a 5 to 15 percent response as opposed to an average of 1 percent return from postal direct mailings and only 0.7 percent from Web banners."

E-Mail Marketing Tips

- Make use of autoresponders, e-mail addresses that are configured to respond automatically to a request for information so that every potential customer receives a reply.
- Use permission marketing—providing "opt-in" sections on your Web site inviting people to (voluntarily) enter their e-mail or home/business addresses in order to receive more information about your products or services, or to subscribe to an e-mail newsletter. They are giving you permission to send them e-mails in which you can provide information to help sell your products or services. Do not forget to have your "Privacy Policy" stated on your site saying how you will use or not use any data that is provided to you by any individuals who sign-up—and make sure you follow that policy! Just stay away from unsolicited e-mail. No SPAMming allowed!
- Always provide a way for people to "unsubscribe" to any regular e-mails or e-zines. Jim and Nikko McGoldrick, who author romance books under the pen name, "May McGoldrick," have a mailing list garnered from their readers who have requested updates about the couple's latest books. At the end of these promotional e-mails they have a personal message to any readers who may wish to

BUSINESS PROFILE: Rosalind Resnick, E-Mail Marketing Services

What is your Internet venture?

NetCreations, Inc. <www.netcreations.com>, a 100 percent opt-in e-mail marketing company, specializing in e-mail address list management, brokerage, and delivery. Our PostMasterDirect.com service gives marketers a better, faster, and smarter way to reach shoppers on the Web.

Is it solely an Internet business?

Solely an Internet business.

When was the business started?

March 1995 by Rosalind Resnick, a business journalist, and Ryan Scott, a computer programmer. (An IPO in November 1999, no venture capital).

How did you originate the idea for your site?

We created several Web sites, including one for Web masters that had a sign-up form for more information. When we saw the resulting list of interested persons, this gave us the idea of the possibility of renting that list. The response to the list was so good, we decided that this might be a service that we could sell to other businesses.

How did you finance your start-up?

Our business was started with $1,000 of personal funds; we reinvested the profits back into the business's operations to where it has grown today.

What resource helped you the most?

Our circulation director was very important in helping us understand the direct marketing terms and how it could be transferred to an e-mail application.

"opt-out" of their mailing list: "P.S. Please let us know if you would like to be removed from our mailing list. Our feelings won't be hurt, and we promise not to name a villain after you." Nikko and Jim McGoldrick (May McGoldrick's home page: www.maymcgoldrick.net).

Do you have any additional comments?

We started our company with a strong business model and have been able to use the advantages of Internet affiliations—we work with some 260 sites as list partners. We provide them with another option to offer on their sites, and we help them build their e-mail lists as well as guide them in their e-mail marketing by testing links and subject lines and monitoring the returns. Then we split the rental income of those lists with our partners, giving them another revenue stream.

We are an ethical company in that we give the "power" to the consumers to opt in or opt out as they choose. We receive their permission twice: when they initially sign up and then when we send a confirmation to their e-mail addresses asking them to verify that they requested the information. If any individuals do not respond to our confirmation request, then their e-mail addresses do not become part of that database. This helps us compile strong lists of the most qualified recipients.

We protect the privacy of those who "opt in" in that no company who rents our lists ever sees the e-mail addresses of those who do sign-up. We do the mailings. Our lists are category-driven, not demographic-driven, which also results in a list of people who more interested in receiving the information than other general lists.

Rosalind Resnick, cofounder, CEO,
Net Creations, Inc.
<www.netcreations.com>.

- Use only simple text in ASCII format, write a compelling subject line, keep wide margins in your paragraphs, and list the most important information first. Select the e-mail messages that bring you the best response.

RELATED RESOURCES

Books

Marketing with Email: A Spam-Free Guide to Increasing Awareness, Building Loyalty, and Increasing Sales by Using the Internet's Most Powerful Tool, 2nd ed. by Shannon Kinnard (Gulf Breeze, FL: Maximum Press, 2000)

Permission Marketing: Turning Strangers into Friends and Friends into Customers by Seth Godin (New York: Simon & Schuster, 1999)

Poor Richard's Email by Chris Pirillo (Lakewood, CO: Top Floor Publishing, 2000)

Software

Eudora Pro <www.eudora.com>; E-mail software and related products

MS Outlook <www.microsoft.com/outlook/>; E-mail software, managing and organizing office e-mail and personal information

Mailloop <www.mailloop.com>; Software with capabilities to automate e-mail tasks

Pegasus <www.pegasus.usa.com>; PC e-mail system; Internet mail server products

E-NEWSLETTERS AND E-ZINES

For pennies, you can provide an e-mail newsletter that contains good articles, leads, a classified advertising section, an announcement area, and descriptions of your products and services. It can also be in the form of an e-zine that appears regularly on your Web site. It can be one of the most effective methods for promoting your Web site and your business's products and services.

When Anne Holland of MarketingSherpa.com was asked, "How can an e-zine or e-mail newsletter benefit an online business?" she said, "Four biggies: One, it serves as a reminder to people to come back to your site. Two, it serves as a viral marketing tool (something they can easily pass along to their friends so they too will visit the site). Three, it serves as an additional bearer of advertising either for your products or for paid advertisers. And four, if you're smart, it also serves as a method for you to gather targeted names which you can use for surveys and in other ways to better understand and serve your marketplace."

E-Zine Tips

Choose a name that synopsizes what your e-publication is about; decide its format; use it to return customers to your site for more in-depth articles and product information; offer information that subscribers can use; and include instructions for removing one's name from your e-newsletter list. Depending how extensive your mailing list is, check with your ISP whether you can send out a mailing-list publication and whether there is a limit on the number of e-mails they can handle. If your subscriber list grows, you can outsource the mailing through a list-server service.

RELATED RESOURCES

Internet Sites

<http://ezinesuccess.com>; "Your Information Center for Learning How to Profit from Ezines"

<www.incor.com> INCOR Entrepreneur Center; business resources, including a listserver for your own newsletter

> ### Business Profile: Packy Boukis, Certified Wedding Consultant
>
> **What is your Internet venture?**
>
> Only You Wedding and Event Consulting <www.cleveland.com/onlyyou>.
>
> **Is it solely an Internet business?**
>
> It is a service business with an online site.
>
> **When was the business started?**
>
> January 1997.
>
> **How did you originate the idea for your site?**
>
> I researched other wedding consulting sites as well as other sites that were well-designed. In addition, I consulted with Web developers and bartered my expertise in wedding forums in exchange for the Web site.
>
> **How did you finance your start-up?**
>
> No borrowed money was used to finance my business. As contracts were signed with couples, I purchased office equipment.

<www.skylist.net> SKYLIST.net; A professional listserver service

Classified Ads

Classified ads can be a very affordable way to advertise your Web site on others' Web sites and in e-zines and e-mail newsletters, or you can offer to charge others to list their ads in your e-mail newsletter.

Classified Ad Tips

Obviously, make sure your target customers are readers of the e-publications or visitors of the sites where you advertise, and

What resource helped you the most?

My association, June Wedding, Inc., was instrumental in jump-starting my business. Wedding books promoting my association ultimately helped me also. Being involved on the national level was very beneficial.

Can you offer any tips for creating a successful Web site?

An interactive Web site is interesting and encourages people to return to your site. Message boards and chat provide the vehicle to do this.

Do you have any additional comments?

Large Web sites often offer the opportunity to register your Web site for free. There are many wedding Web sites that encourage experts to write articles for their Web sites.

Packy Boukis, Only You Wedding
and Event Consulting.

ask to see a copy of the e-publication before you pay anything. Avoid being the last ad posted in the publication, because many people never finish reading it to the end. Look for sites offering free classified ads.

RELATED RESOURCES

Internet Sites

<http://classifieds.excite.com> Excite Classifieds; One of a number of classified advertising sites

<www.infojump.com> Info Jump; An online directory of e-zines that allow you to search for a publication in a specific subject area

OTHER WAYS TO INCREASE TRAFFIC

- **Announcement sites:** You can read about new Web sites, pages, articles, and resources. The postings appear for only a short time, but they are archived.
- **Award sites:** You can submit your site for consideration and possible recognition.
- **Directories:** You have to register your Web site with them and they will review your application to decide if your Web site is appropriate to be listed or not. Packy Boukis, a wedding consultant from Cleveland, Ohio, <www.cleveland.com/onlyyou> says, "I recommend registering in the directories that are provided by online services such as AOL. The media will oftentimes use these as resources for contacting experts in their field."
- **Partnering:** These are strategic alliances formed to help both parties gain something together that they could not alone. Potential partners could be suppliers, customers, or competitors who would complement and add value to your products and services and bring to them additional revenue streams and publicity.
- **Contests:** Offering giveaways and contests can help spread word-of-mouth or a "buzz" among Internet groups. Make sure you are following all required guidelines. (See the FTC site <www.ftc.gov>.)

Nikoo and Jim McGoldrick (a.k.a. May McGoldrick) <www.maymcgoldrick.net> are coauthors of historical romance novels set in Scotland (*Flame, The Dreamer, The Firebrand,* and others) and also of the nonfiction book *Marriage of Minds: Collaborative Fiction Writing.* He is a college English professor, she is an engineer, and they are the parents of two sons. In using the Internet to publicize their novels they say:

Having a Web page allows us to connect directly with so many readers that we normally would not be able to reach, . . . mailing costs being what they are. That page also allows readers to find us easily with questions and comments and suggestions. Without that page, a reader living in rural Australia would have to go to added expense and several extra steps to reach us—writing to our publisher, waiting for an answer, writing to us. Now, the effort is minimal and the result is immediate! As a result, we hear from readers from all over the world nearly every day.

In addition, we can offer promotional items without using a publicist. For example, as we write this, we are running a monthly promotional giveaway on our Web page to raise awareness of the trilogy of novels and the nonfiction book on writing that we have coming out this year. There are a number of sites that serve as "contest info centers" where we put up a notice of our contest and leave a link to our site."

Marianne M. Szymanski also suggests using contests to draw people to your site, as you will read in her profile.

- **Communities and newsgroups, mailing lists, Usenet:** You cannot enter solicitations in these forums or you will be kicked out because of bad "netiquette," but you can participate in discussions, provide information about the topics being discussed, and mention your Web site if so asked or if the opportunity presents itself.

  Or you might want to offer a forum on your site to encourage your site's patrons to discuss topics related to your expertise. For example, Lisa Schmeckpeper (see her profile in chapter 6), an Internet marketing specialist, offers a forum on her site, LRS Marketing <www.lrsmarketing.com>, called "Critic's Corner" (CC), which is an online Web site review community. "Visitors can get friendly

---

BUSINESS PROFILE: Marianne Szymanski, Toy Researcher

What is your Internet venture?

ToyTips.com (www.toytips.com) is a site dedicated to providing research on toys that have been tested through The Toy Research Institute to communicate results and findings on the best toys based on skill development.

Is it solely an Internet business?

Toy Tips is a publishing and research company that distributes *Toy Tips Magazine* annually and online. Retail clients buy our magazine and distribute it in their stores.

When was the business started?

1991.

How did you originate the idea for your site?

It became a marketing tool for *Toy Tips Magazine* in 1993. We were a content provider for abc.com and toysrus.com.

How did you finance your start-up?

Personal funds.

What was the best resource that helped you?

Mentors.

Can you offer tips for a successful Web site?

Update content, have a comment area and respond immediately. Offer contests (we had a Curad Design-Your-Own Bandage contest) and provide links to relevant areas of interest.

Marianne M. Szymanski, President and
Founder of Toy Tips Inc. and ToyTips.com.

---

advice via a Web site review discussion board or by applying for a free review and the chance to be featured in the *Website Success Monthly* newsletter <www.website successmonthly.com>," says Schmeckpeper. She continues, "The free service is open to amateur webmasters only. Professionals must pay a small fee to have their sites viewed by our volunteer staff. Anyone (professional or amateur) is welcome to post on our discussion board where our moderators keep any negative posts off the board. Our rules of 'No harsh attacks or comments,' is followed by 99 percent of our posters, and we catch the other 1 percent quickly and remove the offending post."

Schmeckpeper concludes, "I find the number 1 benefit of having the CC forum is the return traffic. Having something truly interactive and immediately helpful is the best way to get people to return time and time again. And if they did not remember the site name or its URL after the first visit, they will definitely remember it after the second or third or fourth. When it comes time to recommend a site to a friend, they are much more likely to recommend your site because they remember you."

If you do decide to create a message board or chat service, Internet experts suggest that your site first have a significant amount of traffic to warrant it and that you actively manage it like Schmeckpeper does, to minimize angry postings. (See Terms of Use, in chapter 2.)

- **Viral marketing:** This is a type of online word-of-mouth publicity in which your site's visitors or customers can e-mail your site's articles to others or refer other customers to you when you offer them a special offer or discount in return.

- **Web rings:** These are groups of sites with similar interests that refer people to one another for free. If you participate, you have to promote the Web ring itself and associated affiliates.

RELATED RESOURCES

Internet Sites

<www.liszt.com/news> Liszt; Mailing list directory

<www.refdesk.com> Refdesk.com; Newsgroups, Web forums, mailing lists

<www.ringsurf.com> Ring Surf; Many listings of possible
   rings; Lets you start your own Web ring free

<www.webring.com> Web Ring

Of course, even if your Web business is solely an online
business, you can promote it offline by writing books and
articles, giving presentations, appearing on radio and TV
programs, teaching courses, doing talks, and conducting workshops at trade shows and conferences; and by using promotional materials—business cards, brochures, promotional
gifts, magnetic car signs, T-shirts, and anything else that could
bring your site to the attention of potential customers.

Georganne Fiumara (profiled in chapter 2), founder of
Mothers' Home Business Network and creator of Home
WorkingMom.com <www.homeworkingmom.com>, says one
of the offline tactics she uses to have mothers find out about
her site is to "mail postcards with HomeWorkingMom.com's
logo in color on the front. We also seek publicity in newspapers, magazines, and books."

Maximizing a combination of on- and offline "active"
marketing methods will help to draw potential customers to
your site. Market-test any advertising first to see if it is worth
your time and advertising dollars. Analyze the results of your
promotional methods, and of course repeat the ones with the
best customer responses often. Once people come to your site,
if you make a good impression with your site's design, offerings, and customer treatment, they will "reward" you with
their regularity and creating a solid base on which to establish
and grow your business.

RELATED RESOURCES

Books

101 Ways to Promote Your Web Site by Susan Sweeney (Gulf
   Breeze, FL: Maximum Press, 1999)

303 Marketing Tips Guaranteed to Boost Your Business (Irvine, CA: Entrepreneur Media, Inc., 1999)

Dan Janal's Guide to Marketing on the Internet: Getting People to Visit, Buy and Become Customers for Life by Daniel S. Janal (New York: John Wiley & Sons, 2000)

The Digital Estate: Strategies for Competing, Surviving, and Thriving in an Internetworked World; and Net Future: The 7 Cybertrends That Will Drive Your Business, Create New Wealth, and Define Your Future by Chuck Martin <www.netfutureinstitute.com>

Hyper Wars: 11 Strategies for Survival and Profit in the Era of Online Business by Bruce Judson <www.GrowYour Profits.com>; Judson's site offers (for a subscription fee) the e-mail newsletter *Bruce Judson's Grow Your Profits: Freebies Online for Business,* which is designed for small businesses and home-based workers

Internet Marketing Goldmine by Marty Foley <www.Profit Info.com>

Internet Sites

<www.bizweb2000.com> BizWeb2000; Owner Jim Daniels, author of *Insider Internet Marketing,* shares his Internet marketing experiences at the site and through his *BizWeb E-Gazette.* "Free help on building an Internet business that makes money . . ."

<www.eweekly.com> *E Commerce Weekly*; Internet marketing articles

<www.freepromo.cjb.net> Freepromo; Source for free web site promotion

<www.gmarketing.com>; Web site of marketing "guru" Jay Levison (author of the series of Guerrilla Marketing books)

<www.growyourprofits.com> Grow Your Profits; Bruce
   Judson's site, author of *Hyper Wars: 11 Strategies for
   Survival and Profit in the Era of Online Business*

<www.promotionworld.com> Promotion World; Web site
   promotion tips and advice

<www.sitesell.com> *Make Your Site SELL! (MYSS!),* an
   800-page digital guide to site-selling and traffic-building
   on the Web by Dr. Ken Evoy, Canadian physician and
   entrepreneur

<www.virtualpromote.com> Virtual Promote; e-commerce
   marketing tips and information

<www.webmarketeer.com> Web Marketeer; Helping compa-
   nies and individuals create marketing strategies

<www.williecrawford.com>; Willie Crawford's site, with an
   excellent marketing forum

<www.wilsonweb.com> "Web Marketing Today"; Dr. Ralph
   Wilson's "Internet premier marketing resource portal
   site"

Software

Internet Marketing Suite DBM <www.marketingsuite.com>;
   Free download of a collection of eight tools for site
   promotion

Customer Service

What builds customer confidence to purchase and/or do business with you over the Internet? This chapter discusses these important points about selling and delivering your products and services, and making sure visitors to your site will become faithful and regular customers.

Overcoming Customer Fears

Here are some factors that will help your customers overcome their fears:

Receive Certifications and Awards

There are a number of certificates of authenticity that verify your identification and pledge that your server uses encryption and is secure. This helps assure customers that you are legitimate. To apply to receive certification, fill out an application; the certification companies will check your background and other information before issuing you a certificate. These companies also assign identification numbers to customers that prove they are who they claim to be, to protect online companies from being

ripped-off. Two companies that offer this are VeriSign <www
.verisign.com>, and Thawte Consulting <www.thawte.com>.

Following are some additional organizations and companies that help build trust and confidence between consumers
and online business owners. You may want to have them
review your business's Web site so that you may post their
approvals and seals on your site:

- The Better Business Bureau's <www.bbb.org> BBBOnLine
  program <www.bbbonline.org>. If approved, you can
  place its seal on your site; when a visitor clicks on the seal,
  it will provide your business's profile.
- TRUSTe <www.etrust.com>. As a licensee, you must
  pledge to follow their principles regarding use of personal
  information and disclosure. There is a yearly fee.
- ePublicEye <www.epubliceye.com>. A service that allows
  customers to rate e-businesses for reliability and customer
  satisfaction. Application review is free.
- WebTrust <www.aicpa.org/webtrust/index.htm>. A program developed by the American Institute of Certified
  Public Accountants (AICPA) and the Canadian Institute of
  Chartered Accountants (CICA), which review your site to
  determine whether it meets their criteria.

Awards and other designations can help potential customers
take notice of you and encourage them to take a better look at
your site and its offerings. Before entering your site for an
award consideration, study the award criteria to make sure
your site is ready for a review. It makes sense, too, to apply for
awards that are related to the topic or subject of your Web site.

When Jennifer Dugan was asked, "How did your receiving the HIPP award help build confidence of potential customers visiting your site?" she answered, "HIPP stands for
'Home Income Producing Parents,' and it means so much to
me that I have been recognized. Other HIPPs refer people to

me, and my name is out there. It lets people know that I am a parent that made the choice to work hard at having a home business so I could have my children home with me."

Know Your Product

Provide complete and accurate information about your product and services. Provide charts, samples of your work, and examples that show your products and services as outstanding from others. This is the place to share your knowledge, help your customers resolve their problems, and give them the tools to adjust your products or services to their specific needs.

Provide Testimonials

Customer letters, e-mails, and postings to online forums can all provide testimonials from your customers. You can include a page solely for their positive comments, or highlight a few on your home page or other strategic places on your site. Just make sure you ask permission to use them before posting, and select comments that talk about different aspects of your business. Put up new ones as they come in, and do not be afraid to post letters from customers who had a complaint and were satisfied with your resolution.

Tell About You

When you consult with a doctor or lawyer or other professional, you usually see all their diplomas and degrees hung about their offices. This helps to assure you that the person is qualified to help you. You can help your customers gain confidence in you by posting on your site an "About Us" section providing details of your qualifications, experience, your business' mission and vision, and even personal information if it is relevant to your business or if you want your customers to get to know you a little better.

BUSINESS PROFILE: Jennifer Dugan, Travel Agency

What is your Internet venture?

Dugan's Travels <www.onlineagency.com/duganstravels>.

Is it solely an Internet business?

It is both an Internet and local business. Local business is the most promising for me, but the Internet has helped me find all my agents.

When was the business started?

September 1997.

How did you originate the idea for your site?

The Web site company specializes in only travel agencies—and I was able to build it myself.

How did you finance your start-up?

I used what money I had to get started. I did not get a loan because there was little start-up cost involved.

What resource helped you the most?

OSSN (outside sales support network) for the travel portion, and on the business side of things other moms working at home that I met on the Internet. I also took a class at the local college on starting a home business. I got my hands on anything I could about home businesses.

Can you offer any tips for creating a successful Web site?

Let people know it is out there. Use it as a tool like a business card. Update it regularly and check your e-mail often. Too many people have e-mail and never check it.

POST A PRIVACY POLICY

The Internet is still a scary place for many people who are wary about sharing any personal information online. This is one of the ongoing issues with e-commerce these days. Having an

Do you have any additional comments?

I am an ordinary mom who wanted to be at home with my children and also have a career. I knew I could do what I did at work at home also. And I have made it happen for me. I don't make millions but I make enough to be at home. Every day I work to make my business the best it can be. Mainly, I want to get out the word that people can start a successful travel agency and even those who don't know travel can do so. I have 34 agents who work with me now. I help them run their businesses. Most of my agents had no experience prior to joining my agency. With a lot of help and hands-on experience they are really giving customers what they want.

I started my small business back in September of 1997 when I decided I couldn't work and be away from my baby. So I took what I did each day at the office and brought it home. Then I began to realize how many others wanted to do what I was doing. I decided that I could help others and build my business at the same time. I kept costs down for those who wanted to work with me, and we have been steadily growing the business. It may sound sappy but every day it makes me feel so good that the women (and a few men) I have working with me are successful because of what I help them with. I was alone when I decided to become a home-business owner. I really thought I couldn't do it. But then I just decided I was going to make it happen and it is now.

Jennifer Dugan, Dugan's Travels
<www.onlineagency.com/duganstravels>.

established privacy policy should be part of every commercial Web site. Posting yours on your site will help allay potential customers' fears about purchasing items from your store or supplying you with information.

Guarantee Satisfaction

With your products, pledge to offer a guarantee of satisfaction with all your orders, and make it easy to return a product, receive a refund, or get a replacement.

Establish a Brand

Getting potential customers to recognize that your brand of product and/or services stands for quality and good service will help them save time, because they will choose your business over other less well-known businesses.

Give Added Value

Knowing what is important to your customers—saving money; finding solutions to their problems; helping them reach their goals and objectives—will help you better evaluate the price your customers will spend for your products or services. List the benefits of using your business, so that your customers will choose to do business with you rather than a competitor.

Provide Great Customer Service

You have probably heard, "The customer is always right." I heard a woman business owner say, "Even if the customer is wrong, she is right." No matter whether your business is on- or offline or if you are a professional with clients, satisfying your customers is the only way to ensure your business's longevity and success. Here are some additional tips to ensure that you gain your customers trust and they will return again and again:

- Be accessible to your customers, with e-mails, your business address, telephone and fax numbers, the name of a person they can ask for help. Merry Schiff, HRS, founder of the National Electronic Biller's Alliance <www.nebazone .com> says:

> I do 100 percent of my business on the Net. I stopped advertising three years ago. My "trick/tip" is to stay online. I stay online all the time and answer my e-mail immediately. I think that's the trick. People say, "Oh my gosh, I never expected a response back so quickly," but to me that is business. If they are going to give me money, how else do I tell people that I am good at what I do or that I am going to take care of them, if I don't prove it before they ever give me their money!? Thus my one tip for Internet business success: "Commit to being at your computer all day, and answering e-mail."

If need be, use different topic-specific e-mail addresses to separate the questions. You can use something like Microsoft *Outlook*'s filters to direct the e-mails to the right address.

- Respond promptly to any customer inquiries. If you cannot answer immediately, use an autoresponder to acknowledge the e-mail and list the hours that someone will be available to answer questions or give feedback. Post hours and telephone numbers that a customer can use to speak to you or a sales representative—provide the human touch.
- Create an FAQ page based on your customers' actual questions, not what you think they want to know.
- Follow up on sales and service to get feedback, and to let customers know you care about their satisfaction.
- Use regular e-newsletters to offer tips, new offers, discounts, and rewards and to keep in touch with regular customers.
- Offer toll-free numbers and home delivery of your products.

- Treat each customer as if she is your only customer. If possible, personalize your product offerings to your regular customers based on their previous purchasing records.

- Get help. If you are overwhelmed with customer service demands, you may want to consider outsourcing part or all of these duties with a call-management company like PeopleSupport <www.peoplesupport.com>.

- Prevent complaints. Test-market your site by having a friend or family member go online and order something via your site, or use your online services. Then use their feedback to anticipate any problems. Take the time to do it right from the start!

- Use complaints. If you make a mistake, contact the customer as soon as possible and offer your guarantee or ask how you can resolve the problem. Use a feedback service like PlanetFeedback <www.planetfeedback.com> for responding to customers who offer comments about you or your company. Use complaints to identify and solve real problems.

PROVIDE INTERACTIVE AND SELF-SERVICE OPTIONS

Time is one commodity that many people are short of these days, so offering self-service or interactive eCRM (electronic customer relationship management) options for ordering will help your customers order quickly and return often for repeat business. Provide adequate information about your products and easy navigation tools to start, shop, and complete their transaction from beginning to end, such as easy-to-fill-in forms for orders or questions. In addition to automated e-mail and e-mail response, an increasing number of online businesses are adding real-time, live chat, VoIP (voice over Internet Protocol) and other ways to quickly respond to customers' questions and concerns. Quick-time responses keep customers interested and less likely to click on a competitor's site.

While having a beautifully designed Web site is important to your business, customers—on- or offline—care most about the service you give them. Giving them your best the first time they order or do business with you will help ensure that it will not be the last time they come to your site for business!

Related Resources
Books

Customer Service on the Internet: Building Relationships, Increasing Loyalty, and Staying Competitive by Jim Sterne (New York: John Wiley & Sons, 2000)

Customers.com: How to Create a Profitable Business Strategy for the Internet and Beyond by Patricia B. Seybold and Ronni Marshak (New York: Times Books, 1998)

Internet Sites

These sites offer eCRM technology for your site.

<www.eshare.com> eshare NetAgent; Providing interaction site capabilities

<www.liveperson.com> LivePerson; Online sales and customer service solutions

<www.quintus.com> Quintus; Managment of Internet customer interaction

Secrets to Selling Online
Products

Besides customized personal customer service, convenience, and quickness, consumers buying products from online businesses want good prices. They expect it all—a challenge that sole business owners will have to meet to compete on the Web. Before you sell any products online, see if other products like yours are being sold online. It will be hard to compete with larger companies that are selling the same items. If the item you wish to sell is not being sold online, ask yourself "Why?" and whether it is feasible for you to do so. Finding a niche, like selling materials related to a hobby, is one of the best ways to get started. Some items sell better online, like e-books, music, software programs and technology, designs, and information, because they do not have to be shipped.

Mary Risman of Bark and Fly <www.barkandfly.com> pet products says her tip for gaining repeat customers for your products is to "treat your clients well and bring them a good price."

A Few More Selling Tips

- **Price discounts and low prices:** Online buying trends are proving that shoppers are expecting good value and prices.
- **Quick response:** Amazon.com generally delivers their books within a few days. They also send prompt e-mails to confirm their customers' orders. People who order online also expect prompt confirmation of their orders and delivery, so have all the ordering and shipping details worked out before you open your online "doors."
- **Availability:** QVC does a daily inventory of their stock so that they do not disappoint their customers. Build your store slowly and according to your customers' demands. It is better to sell a few items well than to create havoc and disorganization by trying to sell too many that you cannot keep in stock.

Service Businesses

Service-oriented businesses can also use the Internet to help them promote their offerings. When asked if she had any tips

BUSINESS PROFILE: Mary Risman, Pet Sitting and Pet Products

What is your Internet venture?

Bark and Fly Designs <www.barkandfly.com>.

Is it solely an Internet business?

Yes it is an Internet business.

When was the business started?

Our pet sitting took place in 1993; this site took place in 1998 with our online pet products.

How did you originate the idea for your site?

One of our clients approached us with the idea of promoting our two businesses.

How did you finance your start-up?

We did a barter arrangement.

What resource helped you the most?

Pet sitting for profit helped us out in the pet sitting end of it, and then we decided to design pet products by seeing what was out there.

Can you offer any tips for creating a successful Web site?

Know what you want and who you want your Web site to target.

Mary Risman, owner of Bark and Fly Designs, lives in Toronto.

for selling professional services and courses online, Terri Levine said, "At Comprehensive Coaching U, we sell training courses, and at Comprehensive Coaching we sell coaching services; and for both, the tip is to allow people a way to try on the services and see if they enjoy them. We provide complimentary coaching sessions and also trial coaching classes so people get the experience of coaching. This method brings us business every week consistently and with ease."

BUSINESS PROFILE: Debra Haas, Policy Consultant

What is your Internet venture?

Haas Policy Consulting, Inc. <www.haaspolicy.com>.

Is it solely an Internet business?

It is not an Internet business. HPC, Inc is a consulting business; however the Web site is a great way to provide people with information about my clients, the work I do, and references.

When was the business started?

HPC, Inc was incorporated in May 1998, and the Web site was established in October 1999.

How did you originate the idea for your site?

My site is based on information I provide to prospective clients in a summary document. The Web site also includes links to my clients and other areas of interest, and testimonial statements from clients.

Do you have a "vision statement" for your Web site?

I have an introductory statement on the index or home page which provides a brief description of my business. It reads: "Haas Policy Consulting, Inc. is a public policy consulting firm specializing in issues related to public education and school finance. Based in Austin, Texas, Haas Policy Consulting, Inc., provides services to both public and private sector clients.

"Haas Policy Consulting, Inc. provides research and analytical services to clients in state government, local school districts, and the private sector in the areas of public education and school finance. Areas of expertise include budgeting, fiscal analysis, program evaluation, and teacher salary, recruitment and retention issues.

Here are some ways that service businesses use the Internet for promotion:

- Save valuable production time by posting answers to oft-repeated questions on their Web sites, explaining their services, prices, qualifications, and other operations and procedures.

"Haas Policy Consulting, Inc. is certified as a 'Historically Underutilized Business (HUB) by the State of Texas General Services Commission."

How did you finance your start-up?

My business was financed with personal savings, all of which I was able to recoup within a year. My significant costs were:

- Attorney and filing fees for incorporation: $1,500
- Accountant fees for incorporation and setting up books: $500
- Laptop computer and high-end printer: $4,000
- Office furniture and supplies: $750

What resource helped you the most?

I found that talking to other small consulting businesses was very helpful. In the process of setting up my own business I developed a network of people with small businesses who referred me to bankers, accountants, and lawyers. I also found several resources on the Web to be quite useful—these included: iVillage (www.ivillage.com), Home Based Working Moms (www.hbwm.com), the Online Women's Business Center sponsored by the Small Business Administration (www.onlinewbc.org).

Can you offer any tips for creating a successful Web site?

Don't overdo it! A Web site that loads quickly and is informative is very important. If your site is too cluttered or takes too long to load, people may move on without looking at the whole site. Try to provide a good introduction on the home page, and make sure you provide a form or Web address for feedback.

Debra S. Haas, Haas Policy Consulting, Inc.
<www.haaspolicy.com>.

- Promote customer interaction with service feedback, surveys, polls, and other opt-in opportunities to gather customers' opinions.
- Include client endorsements and previous job experiences.
- Provide useful information clients can use. Regularly updating their news and tips will encourage return visits.

BUSINESS PROFILE: Terri Levine, Business Coach
Training Program

What is your Internet venture?

Comprehensive Coaching and Comprehensive Coaching U <www
.comprehensivecoachingu .com>: A coach training program
for professionals who want to be professional coaches or for managers in business to learn coaching skills; <www.comprehensive-
coaching.com>: A coaching company for business and personal
coaching.

Is it solely an Internet business?

Comprehensive Coaching U is an Internet business and was started
in July 1999. Comprehensive Coaching is not solely an Internet
business and was started in November 1988.

How did you originate the idea for your site?

For Comprehensive Coaching U, I just thought up the site late one
night after about 50 people approached me and said, "Train me to
be a coach like you." For Comprehensive Coaching, I came up with
the site idea after visiting hundreds of sites on the Web.

How did you finance your start-up?

Personal savings—all me!

- Take advantage of market exchanges or expert sites that
  bring buyers and sellers of services together, such as BizBuyer
  <www.bizbuyer.com>, EXP.com <www.exp.com>, Expert
  Central <www.expertcentral.com>, or AskMe <www.askme
  .com>.

SELF-PROMOTERS

Speakers, authors, comedians, musicians, photographers,
clothing designers, and other well-known figures are creating
Web sites featuring their books, tours, speaking engagements,
and other offerings. Examples are Libby Elgin <www.elgin
pix.com>, wildlife photographer, women's clothing designer;

What resource helped you the most?

The book, *The E-Myth Revisited* by Michael Gerber; my coach; my Web designer.

Can you offer any tips for creating a successful Web site?

Update it regularly; make it fun; reflect you and who you are versus what you do. I get so much feedback on my race car and have gotten hired because they want 'the race car lady' to coach them.

Do you have any additional comments?

I have made substantial income and met people from around the world with my Internet businesses, and I love marketing to masses of people instead of one at a time. It is fun, lucrative, and takes me new places and introduces me to new opportunities. It's a whole new world and I am enjoying the journey.

Terri Levine, M.S., founder and managing partner.
For a free newsletter, e-mail: CoachesCorner On@lists.webva-
lence.com.

Paula Hian <www.paulahian.com>; and author Peter Bowerman with the Web site for his book, *The Well-Fed Writer* <www.wellfedwriter.com>. Chrissy Carroll, wife and manager of comedian/cartoonist Jimmy Carroll <http://members.tripod .com/jimmycarroll>, created and uses her husband's site to list tour dates, his books, his CD, the dates of the comedy clubs she manages, and photos of his cartoons. Chrissy Carroll says it was (and is) time-consuming to create and maintain a self-promotion Web site, and she is looking to hire a Web master so she can concentrate on other promotions; however, she says having a Web site has saved her time and the expense of mailings to her husband's fans.

RELATED RESOURCES

Internet Sites

<www.elance.com> Elance.com; Bid on jobs in all kinds of fields

<www.freeagent.com> Freeagent.com; Support services for freelancers

<www.freejob.com> FreeJob; Bid on posted assignments

<www.Guru.com> Guru.com; Freelancers, consultants, career advice

RETAIL STORES

If your business is primarily offline, the Internet provides a new sales channel and can foster sales through existing channels by increasing brand awareness of your products. The Internet has not yet replaced the in-store experience, and probably never will completely, because people like to be able to see the size, texture, and feel of items before they do any purchasing. A retailer can use the Internet in additional ways:

- To give store hours and location.
- To link to other complementary stores and sites.
- To notify regular customers of sales events and new product lines.
- To get improvement feedback.
- To network with others in your industry for on- and offline tips.

When Daphne Harris, owner of Red Rose Vintage Clothing store <www.rrnspace.com> in Indianapolis (profiled in chapter 6) was asked, "How can the Internet help women business owners who have 'brick-and-mortar' shops like yours?" she says:

The Internet is an excellent medium for reaching new customers—at the relatively low cost (especially if you design it yourself) of setting up a site. It's worth it just as an advertisement even if you don't actually sell merchandise through your site. I'm surprised and pleased with the number of customers who come in the door of our brick-and-mortar shop having found us through our Web site. It's still a new way to shop and do business, but as people grow more comfortable with the technology, it's becoming a rapidly growing sector of the market. It's ideal for my type of business, as I have items that are not readily available in all parts of the country, but I think it would help most any type of business. The more different ways someone can find your business the better!

Some other tips for using a Web site to help your "real" store or business:

- Try to obtain the same domain name as your business name, like Bert Schwarz did (profile following) with her store, Bucks Trading Post, <www.buckstradingpost.com>.
- Plan how you are going to integrate the customer service of your store or business and its Web site: More product information? Answering FAQs? Having a real-time customer chat?
- Coordinate your color schemes, logos, slogans, and other recognized features of your real store with your Web site.
- Plan to use your Web site in ways your real store cannot: including a personal history of you and your store; adding a map to your store; providing links to sources of related information; or any other highlights that can enhance the shopping experience of your customer in either your virtual or your real store.
- Use your online site to feature outstanding employees and to hire additional ones as your business grows.

BUSINESS PROFILE: Bert Schwarz, Collectibles,
Country Laces, and Curtains

What is your Internet venture?

Bucks Trading Post <www.buckstradingpost.com>.

Is it solely an Internet business?

It is a retail business with an online site selling antiques and collectibles, lace curtains, mantel scarves, mats, and runners.

When was the business started?

Web site launched (with shopping cart) November 1999.

How did you originate the idea for your site?

I already sold lace curtains and other items from my store through mail order and thought that having a Web site would be another way for both my established customers and new customers to view and order my product lines and new items being offered for sale.

How did you finance your start-up?

I financed the Web site with my shop's sales and am using any profits from my Web site to upgrade and maintain it.

What resource helped you the most?

My Web designer and then the woman Internet marketing specialist he hired to help his customers with promoting the Web sites he designed. The magazine *E-Commerce* was also helpful.

WHOLESALING

You may want to resell items made by others—that is, buy wholesale and sell retail online. You need to obtain a resale permit or resale tax number from your home state (you collect state sales tax from items sold to residents in your state). You also need to charge the sales tax rate for the state from which the purchase is made (where your customer lives). A resource for items and information is the site <www.whole salecentral.com>.

Can you offer any tips for creating a successful Web site?

Setting up a business Web site has been a whole learning experience. At first, my Web site was just an advertising tool for me, just like taking an ad out in a newspaper or magazine, and did not really generate any extra business. Then, I added a shopping cart to my Web site to actually sell products. I use Miva Merchant, the host for my site, and they have a free shopping cart to sell an unlimited number of products, which is included in their hosting fee.

I really believe that once I do some concentrated promotions I will have more sales. In my opinion, I do not think a store will get very many new customers from people just looking through search engines. I think that most people buying on the Internet already know the company, know what they are looking for, and buy it through a referral.

I decided to pay an extra $100 to have a secure certificate, so when somebody goes onto the site, they see that the certificate is in my name. I think this, too, has helped to increase the number of people ordering online over my site, because they know and trust me.

Bert Schwarz, owner, Bucks Trading Post

RELATED RESOURCES

Books

Web Rules: How the Internet is Changing the Way Consumers Make Choices by Tom Murphy (Chicago: Dearborn Trade, 2000)

Internet Sites

<www.fsb.com> Fortune Small Business; Offers a regular Web site success tips and columns by Web experts

Processing Orders

Your store can be as simple as an e-commerce site that posts a product list or a graphic with a sales e-mail address beside it, or a sophisticated one-transaction processing, or anywhere in-between.

Make buying easy. Have a simple, fast-loading Web site that the majority of potential customers can view easily using their browsers and basic PC programs. Carefully orchestrate the ordering process in a logical order so that your customers can add to their individual shopping carts as they shop through your site. An e-business site consists of five basic components:

1. Your catalog of items.
2. Your shopping cart to collect the customer's purchases.
3. Secure transactions using encrypted or secure credit card processing. Ensure that any information you receive from customers is secure and that you have a privacy policy posted on your site regarding the use of any information that you gather from your site's visitors/customers and that you adhere to your stated policy!
4. Order processing (totaling costs—including taxes and shipping; charging customers' credit cards).
5. Fulfillment of orders (getting the products to your customers).

YOUR CATALOG

Some hosting services offer simple software tools to assist you in creating online catalogs, or you can use simple software to design your own or have your Web designer assist you with a more complex catalog software design package. An online catalog will save you mailing and printing costs, and you can add animations, three-dimensional photos and illustrations, voice-overs, and other technological techniques. Depending on the number of items involved, you will need to procure an illustration, graphic, or photo of each item and write the ad copy for each, as well as determine your pricing.

YOUR SHOPPING CART

Bert Schwarz says, "With a retail business, if you have many products, a shopping cart program needs to be there. Do not expect people to see your home page and come to your store, or e-mail or call you for a catalog or download this order form, etc. I just never had much business through my Web site this way. Maybe some others did, but I did not."

Web sales began with simple HTML order forms that were on different pages from their item descriptions. Next, there were price lists and secure order forms, but sites did not include a shopping cart program. Customers would complete the order form and send it in via e-mail or "snail mail." Next came electronic shopping carts, which allow customers to browse through a store's catalog and place items to purchase in a virtual shopping cart. When the customer is finished shopping, she clicks a "check out" link that shows the items she selected, at which point she can remove any items not wanted. Her total price, including shipping, taxes, and any other costs, is calculated by the software and is posted. Some shopping carts also provide inventory management capabilities.

Now there is "storefront" or "store-building" software that includes shopping cart capabilities and allows you to change your products' listings and conduct other e-commerce solutions. The larger your store, of course, the more sophisticated and expensive your requirements will be. You also have to ask your ISP what software their server will work with. Experts advise you to be wary of Web hosts and the free shopping carts they might offer, which are often limited in their support. It is best to look for Web hosts that offer shopping cart programs as part of a total online commerce service package. In other words, when you first start out, often a more affordable solution is to pay for a turnkey operation that will provide you with everything you need to start an online store.

Small-to-medium merchants can purchase storefront software as stand-alone products or, for a monthly fee, from an ISP such as OpenMarket's *E-Business Suite* <www.openmarket .com>, ShopSite <www.shopsite.com>, or *Miva Merchant* <www.miva.com>, whose resellers often bundle other services such as Web hosting and Web design.

The more sophisticated programs used by mid-sized to large stores can range in price from $5,000 to $20,000 and up. Popular e-commerce solutions include those offered by IBM's *Solutions for E-Commerce* <www.ibm.com> and Microsoft's *Servers* <www.microsoft.com>. These programs consist of a Web server, a database server, one or more application servers, and an assortment of tools used to build and maintain an online store. Much larger companies, of course, use powerful software and applications that cost thousands of dollars.

The choice of the right e-commerce solution, of course, will depend on your financial resources and the size of the store you want or need. Consult with Web commerce experts before you spend any significant amount of money. An excellent source of Internet commerce information is the site Wilson Web <www.wilsonweb.com>, which also offers a free marketing newsletter, "Web Marketing Today," and Web Commerce Today (by subscription), and covers selling products online.

Your Order Form

In the past, creating a form for customer feedback or ordering required that you write or edit CGI (Common Gateway Interface), a computer script that processes information submitted by customers on your site into a readable format that was e-mailed to you or in a text file. Computer programmers or Web masters wrote these scripts, but with the Web page programs like Macromedia *Dreamweaver* <www.macromedia.com/software/dreamweaver>, Microsoft *FrontPage* <www.microsoft.com/frontpage>, and others, you can create forms and the scripts that will transform the entered data for you.

You can also use the services of companies like MnetWeb Services <www.mnetweb.com> and FormSite.com <www.formsite.com> to help you build a form for your site.

Your forms should be easy to understand and follow and offer a confirmation of their order or form submission. Your forms should include the following: customers' names, addresses, phone numbers, e-mail addresses; ordered items; choice of delivery methods; customer ID or account number; order confirmation number; payment options, and—if they use credit cards—the type of card, number, and expiration date. Also provide your contact information—e-mails, telephone numbers, and addresses—so customers can contact you if they have questions about their orders.

INTERNATIONAL ORDERS

From the time your Web site goes up, you will be in a global market. Handling any international sales will require you to deal with the following:

- Forms: Foreign shipments require customs forms for shipping and handling.
- Telephone numbers: Contact your long distance carrier about toll-free international numbers.
- Validating international credit card numbers: You may have to contact your merchant services for the international bank numbers.

- Communications via spoken language, e-mail, and order forms: You may need to use a translation service or one of the Web sites offering free translation of phrases.
- Other payment options: Specify options of payment—in U.S. funds? You could post, "Payments by money orders or checks must be in U.S. dollars and drawn on a U.S. bank."
- International laws: Some items may not be exported or imported.

RELATED RESOURCES

Agencies

U.S. Department of Commerce's Trade Information Center (TEC), 1-800-USA-TRADE (1-800-872-8723) <www .ita.doc.gov/td/tic>; *Export Programs Guide* to federal export help and ordering information for the book, *A Basic Guide to Exporting* by the Department of Commerce (1-800-631-3098)

U.S. Small Business Development Centers: Look in your local phone directory for an office near you or visit <www.sba.gov/SBDC>

Books

Creating Stores on the Web, 2nd ed., by Ben Sawyer, Dave Greely, and Joe Cataudell (Berkeley, CA: Peachpit Press, 2000)

Internet Sites

<www.aestiva.com> AESTIVA, LLC; *Aestiva HTML/OS* shopping software offering a selection of shopping cart designs. For information: sales@aestiva.com>

<www.answermenow.com> Answer Me Now, Inc.; Customer service assistance; Provides interactive technology to help

your customers gain information about your products using video, graphics, animation, slideshows, live camera, and textchat

<www.sba.gov/oit> U.S. Small Business Administration's Office of International Trade; Links to offices, publications, trade events, and other resources for first-time exporters

<http://ecommerce.internet.com> Electronic Commerce Guide; Resources and tools, reviews

<www.humanclick.com> Human-Click; Free live-chat product to help you deal with customer requests

<www.ifront.com> Internet Frontier, Inc.; Storefront design

<www.miva.com> Miva Merchant; Offers a browser-based storefront development and management system

<www.sba.gov/oit/info/guide-to-exporting>, online publication of *Breaking into the Trade Game* (or order a free copy by calling 1-800-827-5722)

SECURITY ISSUES

Privacy is one of the biggest concerns of online shoppers. Because people value their personal information, they are reluctant to give it out unless they know how it will or will not be used. Many commercial sites use permission-based marketing (asking personal details in exchange for something free in return or an entry in a contest for a product) before collecting your information; other "opt-out" sites instead collect your personal details until you stop them.

Privacy

The U.S. and other countries' governments are urging all sites to post privacy policies. As mentioned before, the Federal

Trade Commission's site <www.ftc.gov> has various documents that can be downloaded or ordered, like "Consumer
Privacy in the Online Marketplace," "Protecting Consumers
Online," "How to Comply with the Children's Online Privacy
Protection Rule," and other important and informative brochures.* They recommend that your privacy policy be linked
to your home page and do the following:

- Be worded clearly and concisely.
- Describe exactly how personal information will or will not
  be used. Once you have issued this, you cannot use information from your site's users otherwise.
- Inform visitors how they can "opt out" of giving information; or how they can modify it if they so choose.
- Be approved by your lawyer or legal advisors looking over
  your policy, so that it adheres to the laws of the states and
  countries in which you conduct business and sales.

View other sites' privacy policies to get some ideas. One
business Web site has on its "Policies" page the following: Their
use of customer information (promised never to give out); their
refund policy; their secure server affirmation statement; infor-

---

*At the time this book was being written, a new standards project called
the Platform for Privacy Preferences (P3P) was being tested. P3P sets a person's browser to specify that she does not want her name or e-mail address
given out to third parties. If she comes across a site that does collect this
information, an alarm will sound.

The Federal Trade Commission offers a guide, "How to Comply with
the Children's Online Privacy Protection Act" which became effective April
21, 2000. The FTC says, "If you operate a commercial Web site or an online
service directed to children under 13 that collects personal information from
children or if you operate a general audience Web site and have actual knowledge that it collects personal information from children, you must comply
with the Children's Online Privacy Protection Act."

There are several factors the FTC will consider to determine whether a
Web site is directed to children. For more information, write to FTC, Washington, DC 20580; call (202) 326-2222; or visit their Web site <www.ftc.gov>.

mation about credit cards accepted as payment and other payment options; shipping and handling information; and contact "for more information"—numbers, address, e-mail.

Once you give out information over the Internet, there is no guarantee that it will stay private, even when promised, so if you do not want something divulged, never give it out.

RELATED RESOURCE

Internet Sites

<http://privacy.net> The Consumer Information Organization; Offers information about online privacy issues

<www.epic.org> The Electronic Privacy Information Center; Offers more information on online privacy

Viruses

In order not to inadvertently spread computer viruses to your customers (or vice-versa), you must make use of programs and other systems that protect against such "invasions." It may just be impossible to protect your hard- and software from all present and future computer viruses. Viruses are designed to disrupt or damage programs. Two examples are "worms" (viruses that are spread from computer to computer using shared services) and "Trojans" (computer viruses that you must open to activate). However, you can take precautions to protect your equipment and data:

- Use personal firewalls (software regulating who can get into a network from outside it using a modem or router (a device that connects any number of LANS—local area networks). Personal firewalls protect your system from unauthorized entry and control over your system; if the system is entered, the firewalls attempt to prevent the information from being sent back to the hacker or intruder who sent it.

- Realize that virus protection software is meant to protect you against viruses that already are known. To protect your computer and its programs, update your present protection with the updates as they are issued, and scan your files for possible new invading viruses once or twice every day.
- Never open an e-mail attachment unless you:

  1. Know the sender.
  2. Were expecting the attachment.

  Even so, the "I love you" virus attached itself to e-mails already stored in address outboxes and was sent with a person's name as sender. When workers came into their offices, they saw a familiar e-mail sender with the subject line, "I love you"; as soon as they clicked on the attachment, the virus was released and spread to other unsuspecting computer users, costing companies thousands of dollars to restore their computers and in lost work time.

- Keep current about the latest viruses and hacker attacks by reading an e-commerce or computer publication regularly. You can also visit sites that update this news daily: <www.hackernews.com> or <www.securityfocus.com>. Also, network with others in your industry for their feedback and recommendations on these protection devices and strategies.
- Do not have all your systems open at the same time, leaving everything vulnerable to an attack.
- Before you sign on with an ISP, ask them what security procedures they have in place.
- Some experts recommend that you have a second computer that will never be connected to the Internet on which to keep your important and confidential files.

- Consider taking advantage of antivirus companies that are now offering to be application service providers (ASP). The companies deliver 24-hour antivirus protection and intrusion detection over the Internet to subscribers. Some examples are Network Associates Inc.'s <www.nai.com> new company, called myCIO.com, and Trend Micro, <www .antivirus.com> which has partnered with phone, Web hosting, and ISPs to offer antivirus protection at the network level.

RELATED RESOURCES

Books

Defending Your Digital Assets Against Hackers, Crackers, Spies, and Thieves by Randal K. Nichols, et.al. (New York: McGraw Hill, 1999)

Internet Sites

<www.antivirus.com/free_tools/default.asp>; *HouseCall* by Trend Micro; Free antivirus tools

<www.mcafee.com> McAfee.com; *Personal Firewall;* Subscription fee

<www.symantec.com/nis> Symantec; *Norton Internet Security 2000;* Subscription fee

<www.watchguard.com> WatchGuard Technologies; *WatchGuard SOHO;* Plug-in application designed to protect Digital Subscriber Lines (DSLs), Integrated Services Digital Network (ISDN), and cable modem connections to the Internet

<www.zonelabs.com> ZoneAlarm; Free for individuals and a fee for businesses

TAXES

A majority of available storefront software programs can sum up the total taxes a customer needs to pay when they complete their orders. Or you can use a tax table if you need to calculate taxes in your city or state (your accountant can recommend or supply you with one). A recommended program for figuring exact present U.S. and Canadian taxes is TaxWare's *Sales/Use Tax System* <www.taxware.com>; there are also some inexpensive shareware sales tax programs you can download.

ACCOUNTING SOFTWARE

A virtual business presents the challenge of integrating online ordering numbers into your accounting and fulfillment systems. You will see an improvement and increase in the better development of e-business accounting as more businesses go online. Two examples of currently available programs that import customer ordering information are Peachtree Software's <www.peachtree.com> *PeachtreeLink,* which can be integrated into Peachtree Complete Accounting program; and Mercantec's <www.mercantec.com> *SoftCart,* which can import orders into Intuit's <www.intuit.com> *QuickBooks.* Find a program that works for your business, but stay alert for the new e-business accounting programs that are sure to be introduced as Internet selling increases.

CREDIT CARDS

When Georganne Fiumara (profiled in "Introduction"), founder of Mothers' Home Business Network and creator of HomeWorkingMom.com, was asked, "How does a woman who wants to sell items on her site get an account to accept credit cards from customers?" she says, "We did a lot of research on this topic and found many scams. Eventually we chose ECHO—Electronic Clearing House—as our merchant account provider of choice. They are a very honest company and provide good, low-cost options for beginners. For more information, see our special report on this topic at: <www .homeworkingmom.com/echo>."

Web sales are showing that more people will purchase an item from an online store if they can order using their credit cards. Judith Dacey, C.P.A. (see her profile in chapter 1) of Small Business Resources, Inc. <www.easyas123.com>, says,

> You need to find a competitively priced credit card processor because Web sales means Web credit. Look for three things:
>
> 1. A low percentage fee, such as 2.04 percent for Visa/ Master Card (American Express and Discover are always more).
> 2. A small transaction fee, like 25 cents per each transaction.
> 3. A processor that credits your bank account with the full transaction amount and debits the processing fee separately each month. Otherwise, matching their deposits against your charges will be instant virtual frustration.

If you do not already have a merchant account—a set-up with a bank that allows your business to accept credit cards— you will need to apply for this. Without a merchant account, you will only be able to accept payment mailed to you in the form of money orders, certified checks, checks paid in advance, or C.O.D.s. Depending on how you plan to clear your transactions, you may or may not need to purchase processing software or hardware.

To process credit card orders, you will need a "secure server" (a server that operates software that encrypts all transmitted information from your customer's browser) to host your site, to ensure that your customers' credit information is safeguarded. As mentioned in the beginning of this chapter, you can gain the confidence of consumers who want to purchase online by obtaining an electronic certificate that verifies your identity and guarantees that your server is secure or uses encryption to protect information. Two sources of these are Thawte Digital Certificate Services <http://thawte.com> and VeriSign Internet Trust Services <www.verisign.com>.

Locally, you can find a merchant service company in the business section of your telephone directory under "Credit Card and Other Credit Plans"; you will be interviewed about your business and have a background check. Banks may still be leery about giving accounts to businesses that do not have brick-and-mortar storefronts, so if you have a sales record from your business and a firm business plan, these may help. If you cannot get a merchant service company locally, talk to other online entrepreneurs for recommendations, and shop around for the best ones for you. Web hosts usually have associations with banks that specialize in Internet payment options.

Payment processing software enables encrypted data of customers' credit card information to be verified as it is sent over the servers and returns in just a few seconds to approve or decline the customer's purchase. After approval, funds are automatically transferred to your bank account.

You can opt to use vendors that enable you to offer real-time credit card processing on your site. Real-time transactions require a secure socket layer (SSL) or SET (secure electronic transaction—a recognized universal standard presently being developed to ensure secure transactions the world over). If you use these vendors, make sure they work with the bank that you use for merchant card status. Some of these include Authorize .Net <www.authorizenet.com>, CyberCash <http://cybercash .com>, and VeriSign Payment services (formerly Signio) <www .verisign.com/payment>.

You are also vulnerable to credit card scams and fraudulent use of credit cards. To avoid credit card scams, beware of unscrupulous ISOs (independent sales organizations that are links between merchants and the banks and the processing companies). These companies offer very low or discount rates to small Web businesses and then raise fees and overcharge for software after the businesses are signed up. Ask for references, and be skeptical if anyone offers you a deal that is unusually good.

Note customers who make large orders but with no specific sizes or colors, won't verify the addresses, or use free e-mail accounts for ordering; or if you suspect a child or teenager is using their parent's card for toys or games. If in doubt, call the telephone number of the cardholder. Never automatically process an order without all the information you need. Post some FAQs about your security measures and some tips about preventing illegal use of one's credit card. Check the Internet Fraud Watch's site <www.fraud.org/internet/intset.htm> for periodic news and tips on how to prevent online fraud.

As more people buy and sell via the Internet, the development of secure, private, standard automated payment systems that can be used worldwide will be needed to protect all parties involved in the virtual exchange of money for products and services.

Accepting credit cards online will most likely increase your orders, but make sure you do your preliminary research as to which payment method will be best for your online business transactions.

RELATED RESOURCES

Internet Sites

The following sites provide information/articles about accepting credit cards online.

<www.amercanexpress.com> American Express

<www.ccnow.com> CCNOW, Inc.; "A full-service electronic commerce solution for small businesses and individuals"

<www.mastercard.com/business/merchant/ecomm.html#top> MasterCard Business Merchant Center

<www.mhbn.com/echo>; Page on Mother's Home Business Network's Web site that describes Electronic Clearing House's credit card transaction methods

<www.savingsdirect.com> Savings Direct; Click on "Accept credit cards," for information about E-Commerce Exchange, a real-time transaction processing system

<www.wellsfargo.com> Wells Fargo Bank

<www.whg.org>; the site of the Web Host Guild, which urges its members to provide the best possible security and reliability in conjunction with the needs of the customer

OTHER PAYMENT OPTIONS

Judith Dacey says, "The best price I've found for MO/TO (mail order/telephone order: without the physical credit card) is through the Costco Membership Program with the Nova Credit Card Processing company."

Other payment options include:

- **Electronic checks:** Customers enter their bank account information and a check is processed electronically.
- **Smart cards:** These enable the holders to use the e-cash or digital verification to complete online transactions.
- **Computer or phone:** You can have customers fill out all the ordering information and selection and the first several

numbers of their cards, and then use a toll-free number to supply the other numbers and to verify their orders. Some sites have systems enabling purchases to be billed to customers' telephone bills instead of their credit cards.

As this book is being written, the growth of e-commerce is giving rise to more companies that offer and handle online payment alternatives for both merchants and individuals that are convenient, reliable, and often have lower transaction fees. Two of the companies offering alternative options are Beenz <www.beenz.com> and Flooz <www.flooz.com>. Always research carefully *before* entering into any business relationship or contract with either credit-card or alternative payment companies to ensure you and your customers' do not become victims of Internet fraud.

DELIVERING YOUR PRODUCTS

Once they've ordered your products, of course customers will want prompt fulfillment and delivery of their items. This process involves packing; shipping (obtain shipping accounts with the companies that handle your deliveries); filling out paperwork, paying special attention to international regulations; handling customer inquiries about their orders; invoicing or billing; and getting customer feedback on the entire purchasing process. Here are some tips:

- If you offer free shipping with orders, specify geographical limits or you could lose money shipping items all over the world. You can offer regular international customers discounts instead.
- Confirm all orders via e-mail—personally or using autoresponders—or any other method that will state order details, shipping date, and how customers can check the status of their orders.

- Provide links on your site to the shipping companies that you use so customers can track their packages.

- Compare shipping costs to get the best rates. Use online services like InterShipper <www.intershipper.net> and others to keep shipping costs down and give your customers better prices.

- Follow the Federal Trade Commission (FTC) rules regarding mail order and notification if an original shipment date can not be met: "Selling on the Internet: Prompt Delivery Rules Alert." These rules stipulate how to notify a customer if you cannot deliver a package on time; it is just good customer service to do this as soon as you suspect a problem. Notify your customer and give them the option of waiting or receiving a refund, a replacement, and so on. If you do not provide good service, especially when there is a problem, you will probably never have them as a customer again. (For more information, write to FTC, Washington, DC 20580; call 202-326-2222; or visit their Web site <www.ftc.gov>.)

- Keep careful and accurate records of all orders sent and notices of any delays or cancellations sent to your customers for FTC inspection should they ask to see them.

- Give customers a selection of delivery options. Provide tables of shipping methods and costs to help them make a choice.

- If you use a fulfillment company to handle your packaging and deliveries, be sure they are reliable.

- Ask for customer feedback to improve your fulfillment processes and to let your customers know that you care about them and their opinions.

When Sue Harris, author of *The Consignment Workbook* and owner of the company that publishes and distributes it was asked, "How do you deliver your books?" Harris answered, "Via priority mail from the post office."

BUSINESS PROFILE: Sue Harris, Author and Publisher

What is your Internet venture?

Scandia International, publishing company selling *The Consignment Workbook,* at <www.consignment.org>.

Is it solely an Internet business?

Internet business, plus my book is listed in Books in Print, which generates orders from Amazon .com, Barnes & Noble, Borders, etc.

When was the business started?

1998.

How did you originate the idea for your site?

Wanted better exposure for *The Consignment Workbook.*

How did you finance your start-up?

Personal savings.

What resource helped you the most?

Books helped us start our consignment business, books helped me start the publishing business, and my son set up my Web site, but I would have paid to have that done anyway, if he didn't know how.

Do you have any additional comments?

If I can do it, anyone can.

Sue Harris is the author of The Consignment Workbook *and owner of Scandia International, which publishes and distributes* The Consignment Workbook.

RELATED RESOURCES

Internet Sites

<www.airborne.com> Airborne Express; "Distribution Solutions for Business," including Internet shipping

<www.teldir.com> International telephone directories' index

<www.dhl.com> DHL; Worldwide Express

<www.fedex.com> FedEx; Check costs, track packages, pick up orders; Also "FedEx e-Business Tools"

<www.usps.gov> U.S. Postal Service; Rate calculator, tracking of express mail, zip codes, and more

Software

Harvey Software, Inc. <www.harveysoft.com>; E-commerce software products handling Web/Email management; shipping

HelpDesk by Simply Amazing Software <www.helpdeskpro .net>; Uses *Filemaker Pro* to help with tracking, logging, and customer service inquiries

Intershop Online <www.intershop.com>; "Seller Enablement Solutions"; Store software with inventory management

The Invoice Store by Software Store Products, Inc. <www .softstore.com>; Customer tracking, invoicing, other features

Web Site Survival Tactics

Once your Web site has been designed, hosted, posted, announced to the world, and begins to get its first visitors, you'll need to observe and analyze people's opinions and reactions to your site. This analysis is vital to your site's existence; it allows you to fine-tune and improve the site's effectiveness in helping to grow your business and/or your self-promotions. Having a static Web site is like trying to sail a boat in a calm sea. It may look beautiful sitting there, but you will never reach your destination unless there is a stirring of wind to get you moving. You need to keep your site active and moving, so you and your business can achieve your goals.

Monitoring Your Site

Following are some techniques you can implement to monitor and evaluate your site's activity and effectiveness.

OFFLINE TECHNIQUES

- Get feedback from your target customers—the people most likely to use your goods or services—with post cards inviting them to look at your site.

- Ask friends and relatives who are connected online for their opinions.
- Follow up selected orders with personal phone calls to get customers' opinions about your site.
- Depending on your budget, hire a "usability lab" run by an Internet consulting company to run a series of tests on your Web site to test its effectiveness in various categories.
- Give talks and presentations at conferences, trade shows, and events; pass out business brochures, with your site's URL, that ask questions concerning your site. You may have to entice responses with a discount coupon or a contest entry; brochures can be mailed back to you (postage paid).
- If you have an established offline business, include a Web site evaluation with your follow-up customer service evaluations and thank you's.

ONLINE TECHNIQUES

- Use tracking software or if your budget permits, tracking services (see Related Resources). The term *tracking* (or reporting) refers to analyzing and measuring the traffic (the people who visit your Web site): what pages they visit at your site most often, how long they stay at your site, if they return, and other ways they might use your site. This is important feedback about your Web site, it's design, and effectiveness.
- If you use tracking software, your ISP or hosting company may have to install it for you on one of its servers. If the host does not permit this, you can buy tracking software that does not need to be installed on a server.
- Check periodically yourself or pay to have a service monitor your site's rankings in the top search engines.
- Add a search engine to your site to see what information your site's visitors are searching for most often.

- Access your Web site using different browser programs to see how it looks with each version.
- Use online customer polls and surveys with direct comments or multiple choice selections.
- Have a spot placed on your home page inviting site visitors to comment about your site.
- Invite others from Web rings, online business associates, and others to visit your site for feedback on it.
- Sponsor a giveaway or contest to encourage response to questions about your site's usability.
- Offer several e-mail addresses and options for customers to enter the appropriate responses. You can devote an entire Web page for customer feedback. You can set up separate e-mail addresses for different kinds of feedback: for more information about products/services, to add questions to your FAQs, to express their opinions about your service or product, for orders or special orders, or to contact you or another person in your business. Remember to acknowledge all e-mails as promptly as possible. If you can offer some incentive such as a discount or a contest entry for taking the time to give you feedback, you may find a higher percentage of responses.
- Use a "real-chat" program to talk directly with site visitors and potential customers to answer questions and to ask about their needs.

Lisa Schmeckpeper, an Internet marketing specialist, has a "friendly" online Web site review community/forum on her site: The Critic's Corner (CC). She offers this advice for getting the "right" kind of helpful feedback:

Getting feedback can sometimes be easy but getting the right kind of helpful feedback is the trick. I've found that when people ask their friends and family or even close business associates they don't get the honest truth. We never want to hurt the people we know so we usually sugarcoat whatever advice we give. That kind of feedback doesn't help when you are trying to improve upon your Web site in this highly competitive world.

On the opposite end of the scale, if you ask strangers or post in most public forums you can sometimes get advice in a less-than-friendly manner. I've seen people call site owners stupid, dumb, and other colorful phrases just because they had common site errors. Nobody wants their name or reputation drug through the mud in this way so many people shy away from asking for help in that type of forum and find they have nowhere to turn for true help.

For this reason, Schmeckpeper created her Critic's Corner, to help people get honest (but not cruel) feedback about their Web sites. She continues:

> From the feedback we have received about this community and the thousands of site owners we have helped, I'd say this is the safest place to get "real advice." The next best place is actually your own personal circle of business associates. I occasionally ask a select few in my circle for their honest opinion, and they give it to me.
>
> I think getting the right answers lies in asking the question the right way. Don't say, "Hey visit my new page and let me know what you think. I spent hours on it and think I've got the next Yahoo.com." No friend is going to want to burst your bubble when you ask for advice that way. Saying something like: "As you know, I really value your opinion and keen sense of insight. I've created a new site and I'd really appreciate it if you could take a look at it for me and give me any advice for improvements."
>
> Now you've complemented them and told them exactly what type of feedback you are looking for. It makes it clear that you aren't fishing for compliments but actually looking for advice.

BUSINESS PROFILE: Lisa Schmeckpeper, Internet Marketing Specialist

What is your Internet venture?

LRS Marketing <www.lrsmarketing.com>. We help small and medium-sized businesses develop their Web presence. Everything from Web site design to hosting and marketing.

Is it solely an Internet business?

It is 100 percent online.

When was the business started?

December 1996.

How did you originate the idea for your site?

I saw the Internet developing and wanted to help new businesses become a part of it.

How did you finance your start-up?

Personal savings. It wasn't until our second year that we were profitable.

What resource helped you the most?

I've also found guidance in various discussion groups and member-based sites for marketers.

> *Lisa Schmeckpeper of LRS Marketing,*
> *"The Internet Marketing Specialists."*

Analyzing Your Data

You will want to analyze this data to evaluate your site's role in your overall marketing of your business and to evaluate the effectiveness of your site itself in fostering your business's growth. Pay particular attention to

- The total number of daily site visits and page views.
- The navigation paths visitors take through your site—which pages are most often viewed.

- Online and offline answers to polls, questionnaires, and chat responses.
- Visitor responses from banner ads, affiliate programs, or links from other sites.
- Money you are saving because of your Web site (issuing an online catalog as opposed to mailing one, for example).
- Customer letters, testimonials, and other comments directed to you.
- The ways customers are ordering from your site.
- Any new business revenues attributed to your site's presence.
- Results of tracking your on- and offline advertisements.
- Responses from your promotions.
- Words that were used most often in searches, to use in your metatags.

When Bert Schwarz, owner of the "brick-and-mortar" shop, Bucks Trading Post <www.buckstradingpost.com>, was asked how she uses customer feedback on her Web site, she says:

> On the end of the Web site order form, I have a question: "How did you find my Web site?" At first I had customers write their answers to this question in a box on my site, but now I have specific answers they can check, such as "From Country Sampler magazine? From a search engine? From a link? Or from my mailings or promotional materials?" The results of this poll have revealed that a majority of people are finding my site through Country Sampler magazine's site, which posts my (print) magazine ad that has my Web site's address in my contact information. So, I am finding that the combination of offline and online promotions is the most effective way to increase my sales. I am hoping my site will be ready and busy by the start of the year's holiday shopping season.

Comparing Results to Goals

Use the evaluation or the results of your feedback to check whether you are moving toward the goals you set in your Web site's original business plan and to help you modify or change direction in the following ways:

- **Increase sales:** To change your ads to target an unexpected (and lucrative) customer group that demonstrated interest in your Web site.

- **Stay current:** To help you foresee a new trend in your industry that can modify your business's offerings.

- **Provide better customer communications:** To improve some aspect of your customer service.

- **Improve business management:** To decide how much inventory to carry in anticipation of demonstrated demand.

- **Reduce complaints:** To decide which Web pages need the most revision and regular updates.

Cookies

There has been some debate about whether or not to use "cookies" to track visitors who come to your site. A "cookie" is not a virus or "bug," but a special file that a site puts on your hard drive so that the next time you visit that site, it "remembers" you (when you visit Amazon.com, you are "greeted by name" if you have ordered something there before).

Cookies can be used to personalize your customer service and help customers save time by completing their forms in half the time. "To cookie or not: That is the cyber question!"

BUSINESS PROFILE: Leslie C. Wood, Writer

What is your Internet venture?

Writer4u <http://writer4u.com>.

Is it solely an Internet business?

It is a service business—I write for many publications and do corporate communications and technical writing. The site is used as an advertising and marketing vehicle for me to obtain new work and for clients to have a place where they can view samples of my work, as well as clients I have worked for and projects I have worked on. It has worked extremely well, as I get most of my work from my Web site.

When was the business started?

I did my first Web site three years ago. I started my writing and communications business about seven years ago.

How did you originate the idea for your site?

I am a very visual person so I spent weeks thinking about what I wanted and how I wanted it to look. Then I created an image in my head and from there developed a navigational chart (like an organizational chart), which acted as a map for the site. I wrote all the copy, did all the design, and all the HTML. It was a long, painful experience but well worth the blood, sweat, and tears—not to mention sleepless nights! Everyone should do a Web site; it's a great exercise in patience, stamina, creativity, and marketing!

- **Create new revenue streams:** To see which affiliates relay the most traffic to your site.
- **Cut back on customer assistance calls:** To upgrade the "flow" of your site so that visitors can easily and logically go from page to page and back again.

As you have read in the previous profiles of the women netpreneurs in this book, a Web site can help you achieve your goals and dreams of doing the work you love. Freelance writer Leslie C. Wood of Writer4U is no exception.

How did you finance your start-up?

"Personal savings and part-time jobs unrelated to the field of writing or communications. I did whatever I had to do to make my business succeed. I left a very well-paying, lucrative position to do this. But, it has always been my dream and I was determined to have it come true. It has, and I will tell you that I would not trade what I do for anything.

What resource helped you the most?

The best resource for me was my determination to succeed as a freelance writer. I didn't read any books or consult any consultants. I just jumped in feet first, figuring that I was either going to sink or swim in the process.

Can you offer any tips for creating a successful Web site?

Make it a part of you. Give it your personality. My Web site is very much who I am. I think it's that way because I did it myself. It's difficult for clients to know who you are when someone else did the copy writing. Have lots of samples of your work on your site. Give potential clients much information about yourself and your work, as this will allow them to make a fast decision as to whether or not you are what they are looking for.

Leslie C. Wood, freelance writer and communications
specialist, is based in Philadelphia.

RELATED RESOURCES

Internet Sites

The following sites provide tools for Internet site analysis.

<www.accesswatch.com> *AccessWatch;* Website traffic analysis software package

<www.hitbox.com> HitBox.com; Traffic analysis software tools

<www.mycomputer.com> MyComputer.com; "Small Business Website tools"

<www.vantagenet.com> Vantagenet.com; free tools to make
your Web site interactive with polls, guest books, forums
and more

<http://websitegarage.netscape.com> Web Site Garage;
"Services for maintaining and improving your Web site"

The following sites provide information on customer care
services and information.

<www.customersupportmgmt.com>; Online site of the print
publication, *Customer Support Management;* Also publishes *Source Book,* a directory of vendors that provide
customer support services

<www.cyberdialogue.com> Cyber Dialogue; an Internet cus-
tomer relationship management company; Check for fees

<www.isky.com> iSky; Multi-channel customer care service;
Check for fees

<www.webtrends.com> Web Trends; "Enterprise Solutions
for e-Business Intelligence and Visitor Relationship
Management"

Improving Your Web Site

Do you know how to "listen" to your customers? When Dottie
Gruhler, President and CEO of HerPlanet Network was asked,
"How do you learn from your visitors to improve your site?"
she said, "I receive an enormous amount of daily e-mails from
visitors." Your customers' needs and demands will guide you
in redesigning your site.

REDESIGNING TIPS

• Make one or two copies of your Web site on a hard drive
and portable zip drives in case your data is accidentally

destroyed and have one copy on which you can experiment with new designs or practice your design and updating skills.

- Redesign the pages periodically for a fresh look and/or to improve their usability as needed or suggested by customer feedback.

- Offer upgraded technology—like chat programs, video, audio, and other interactive content—but not to the point that it causes your customers' browsers to crash.

- "Spark" your site with new photos, graphics, colors, and other interactive add-ons or plug-ins—but keep them simple so as not to distract the customer from the real purpose of your site.

- Straighten up your site, getting rid of broken links, and optimizing your code to make it faster to load.

RELATED RESOURCES

Books

Web Pages That Suck: Learn Good Design by Looking at Bad Design by Vincent Flanders and Michael Willis (Alameda, CA: Sybex, 1998). Author Vincent Flanders' site <www.webpagesthatsuck.com> has examples of Web sites plus "Web Design Info & Resource Links"

CUSTOMER SURVEYS

As mentioned before, encourage customer feedback to improve your business—offer discounts, a contest, a giveaway to entice them to give you feedback. Remember to inform your customers what you plan to do (or not do) with any personal information you collect from them. Give them options to sign up or not. Here are some types of questions to ask in your surveys:

BUSINESS PROFILE: Dottie Gruhler, Women's Network

What is your Internet venture?

HerPlanet, Inc. Network <www.herplanet.com>.

Is it solely an Internet business?

Solely Internet.

When was the business started?

Last quarter of 1998.

How did you originate the idea for your site?

By talking with other women on the Web who were looking for more from the Web.

Do you have a "vision statement" for your Web site?

To provide more than an informational portal for women—to give them a place they can truly be involved and grow.

How did you finance your start-up?

Personal savings.

- How did they hear about your business?
- What types of ad gets them to respond the most?
- What influences them to buy from your site? Price? Service?
- Do they refer your business to others?
- What do they like/not like about your business?
- What can your business offer them that it does not presently offer?
- If they had a complaint, were they satisfied with your solution?

Give your regular customers discounts or free samples of new products or services for their honest opinions before you offer these on sale for your Web site. You have heard it many times before, but it is true: It costs twice as much to get a new

What resource helped you the most?

Mainly listening to other women on the Web—their needs and wants—and building that dream.

Can you offer any tips for creating a successful Web site?

1. Never give up.
2. Think outside the box. Don't just *dare* to be different—*strive* for it.

Do you have any additional comments?

The Web can be a difficult place, and a real misleading place for those trying to make it out here. Learn from as many different sources as possible—look for experience.

*Dottie Gruhler, president and
CEO, HerPlanet, Inc. Network*

customer as to keep a regular one, so look to keep those customers happy by listening to them often.

RELATED RESOURCES

Internet Sites

<www.humanclick.com> HumanClick; Enables you to chat in real time with those at your Web site and track visitors' use of your site's pages

<www.websitetrafficreport.com> Web Site Traffic Report; Free statistical reports about the keywords used by visitors to find your site, number of times each of your pages were accessed, and other important statistics

<www.zoomerang.com> Zoomerang; "Create surveys and get feedback"

Adjusting Objectives

Use the feedback from and the interaction with your customers, suppliers, and other visitors to take a second look at the objectives you originally set when starting out. Ask yourself the following questions to decide if you should modify your business's objectives:

- Am I focusing on a niche or spreading my business's offerings too thin to meet anyone's needs?
- How do customers say they are using my product or professional services?
- Has there been a repeated request for another product or service sideline that could add revenue to my business, while better serving my customers?
- Has my business been slow or nil? Or has it grown beyond all expectations?
- What other marketing strategies could I use to expand the business?

Review your business plan, marketing plan, and your overall business strategies to see if you need to rewrite your objectives and the steps you need to take to achieve them. Organize each day's activities around your objectives.

Web Business "Spin-Offs"

Many times an entrepreneur starts one business, only to find from customer inquiries, suggestions, and/or surveys, that another profitable sideline or "spin-off" is begun. For example, Ragan Hughs (profile in chapter 3) started her first Web site to advertise her hand-painted children's furniture. From this experience she wrote the guide for stay-at-home moms and sold it on an online auction site. It had such a good response that she started her Web site, SavvyMoms.com. She is now branching out for a third Web business—selling her self-designed baby clothes.

Business experts do suggest that you focus on one business at a time instead of heading into too many entrepreneurial directions, but you can still make note of repeated requests for a product or service by your customers which may just turn out to be a very profitable sideline venture in your future.

Rochelle B. Balch of RB Balch Associates <www.rbbalch .com> also started with one business and then, because of customer requests, has just started a Web sideline business, as you will read in her profile. Balch started her computer consulting business several years ago when she was downsized from her job. As a single mother (with a mortgage) she started her one-employee business from her home to grow to where it is today: a business generating several million dollars a year with over thirty employees.

You can develop successful business spin-offs from either off- or online businesses. Some examples are: self-publishing books, other publications; creating software related to your work; being a public speaker on a special topic or on your success in your industry; writing articles; starting a television cable show or radio program; becoming a consultant. Keep listening to your customers, and you might just hear a new sideline calling you.

Mistakes to Avoid

Your Web site is a visual "picture" of your business. Make sure it presents the best possible professional image. Here are some common Web site mistakes to avoid.

- A poorly designed site. You do not need to spend thousands on Web site design, but it should look professional and be easy to use. Start simply and upgrade your site as your business grows and you have more resources available

BUSINESS PROFILE: Rochelle B. Balch, Computer Consulting, Programming, and Support

What is your Internet venture?

RB Balch & Associates, Inc. <www.rbbalch.com>, a computer consulting firm providing custom programming and on-site PC small office support: and WebSiteDemos.com <www.website demos.com>, to create web sites online and let the small business owner self-publish the site.

Is it solely an Internet business?

For RB Balch, we use our site to generate consulting business. WebSiteDemos is an Internet-based business. Right now it still requires contacting us for finalization, but we are going to be about 80/20 Internet driven.

When was the business started?

RB BALCH: February, 1993; Websitedemos (WSD), about April, 2000.

How did you originate the idea for your site?

For WSD, after several of our RB Balch customers were asking what a web site could do for them, it was the logical thing to do— most do not have a clue where to start, so WSD was developed to walk them through the creation of what their site might look like.

Do you have a "vision statement" for your Web site?

Completely automated, self-contained self publishing of Web sites for small business owners and organizations.

to you. Try not to have too much too soon, and seek several opinions about it.

- Not having your own company domain name. Get your company's domain name; it is relatively inexpensive, and says to your customers that you are your own business, and not just office space in someone else's store.

- Not having a policy page or listings of your privacy statement, your security practices—a secure order form to

How did you finance your start-up?

My original company, RB Balch, was financed through personal savings. I took $5,000 and put it in a checking account and started up. I used a personal line of credit and an equity line on my house for payroll financing. I did not take a salary for about one year.

What resource helped you the most?

Networking with other business owners—especially other single women whose livelihoods depend on their businesses.

Can you offer any tips for creating a successful Web site?

Have an easy domain name, easy navigation, and a way to contact someone "live." As for the business itself, be prepared to advertise; do not think just being on the Web will self-promote the site. You must still market the site and the business.

Any additional comments?

Have an idea, develop it, plan it, write it, do it—go for it!

> *Rochelle Balch, president, RB Balch*
> *and WebSiteDemos.com, and author of*
> C-E-O & M-O-M: Same Time, Same Place.

accept credit cards, your return policies and guarantees, and anything else that can affect the confidence of your customers.

- Not taking advantage of the interaction technology the Internet affords. Keep in touch with your customers with e-mails and e-newsletters, and where applicable, provide them with tools to help them, such as online calculators, demos of products, and links to other helpful resources.

BUSINESS PROFILE: Daphne Harris, Vintage Clothing

What is your Internet venture?

Red Rose Vintage Clothing <www.rrnspace.com>.

Is it solely an Internet business?

I have a brick-and-mortar shop as well the Internet site. In terms of sales the shop probably does about two-thirds of the business right now, but it varies. Because each piece must be listed separately, it's time-consuming to add merchandise to the site, but I'm constantly trying to expand and enrich the site.

When was the business started?

September 1998.

How did you originate the idea for your site?

My business—selling vintage clothing—is a narrow niche market and it's very specialized. Since I sell one-of-a-kind items the Internet enabled me to expand outward nationally and internationally to reach the customers who may be specifically interested in a particular item. For example, people who live in small towns and are vintage clothing collectors and connoisseurs may not even have a vintage shop in their area, and traveling to a large city with several vintage clothing shops may not be feasible either. The Internet can bridge that gap and bring them things from all over the world from my shop and others that they would otherwise never get to see.

Lack of communication with customers will cause you to lose them to other markets.

- Not doing daily marketing to promote yourself or your site. The quality of your products, services, and customer service may be the best in your industry, but if you do not make a daily promotional effort to let potential customers know this, you will fall behind your competitors who will make this effort.

Do you have a "vision statement" for your Web site?

It's not explicitly stated on the site, but I do strive to present a constantly changing variety of the best of twentieth-century fashion.

How did you finance your start-up?

As I already had a shop of inventory, my set-up costs were limited to a digital camera (photos are essential to marketing my merchandise), creating room (which I did in my home), the computer, and software for the site. I created my own site without using a professional.

What resource helped you the most?

I would say books were quite helpful—I had a head start on running a business as I'd done so for many years, so it was merely a matter of mastering use of the computer and the camera and setting up a toll-free line for credit card orders. Also prompt courteous e-mails to customers are vital and finding a reliable ISP so that your site will be up and running at all times.

Do you have any additional comments?

For women with brick-and-mortar shops, it is worth having a Web site just as an advertisement—even if you don't actually sell merchandise through your site. The more different ways someone can find your business, the better.

Daphne Harris, Web mistress,
Red Rose Vintage Clothing.

Of course, you will make mistakes—but learn from them as well as from others' by reading and networking with other netpreneurs—and try not to repeat them.

RELATED RESOURCES
Internet Sites

<www.bigfoot.com> Big Foot; "Tools for the Internet"

Tips for Success

- Upgrade your site often—you can list when it was last updated—and consider having a "What's New?" section or page as a quick way to inform your faithful visitors of the latest happenings, changes, or new products and services. Daphne Harris, owner of Red Rose Vintage Clothing in Indianapolis, offers this tip for a successful Web site: "As far as having a retail site, I would say changing and updating it frequently is essential. People like to see new merchandise when they check in, and if they are seeing the same things all the time they won't come back."

- Watch that your site's colors do not obliterate your text and other important information.

- Periodically, try something new on your site—experiment with a new service, poll, or some other element that may add interest to your Web site.

- Keep up with technology to offer the best service for your customers and to improve your business's operations.

- Invite experts in your industry to submit articles and/or tips to provide a broader range of information for your customers.

- Periodically check the speed at which your site's pages load with different connections to ensure that all visitors can access them, whether they are connected via cable modem, dial-up, or another way.

- Be on the lookout for new marketing methods to test, new ways to improve customer service, and new ways to increase revenue—three essentials to Web site survival.

- Stay informed about the "Wild, Wild, Web." New research, technology, and trends are developing almost daily as the Internet business frontier progresses. Make it a daily ritual to read a variety of sources both on- and offline about Internet news, attend conferences, network with others in your industry and other Web site owners, and listen to what your customers—either consumers or other businesses—are demanding.

RELATED RESOURCES

Books

The Complete Website Upgrade and Maintenance Guide, 10th ed. and CD ROM ed. by Mark Minasi (Alameda, CA: Sybex, 1999)

Internet Sites

<www.lynda.com/hex.html> Lynda.com; Lists of color choices most browsers can read; Site of Lynda Weinman, author of Web graphic and design books, including *Creative Html Design.2* (Indianapolis: New Riders Publishing, 2000)

Keeping your Web site active at the same time as managing your business's operations can be time-consuming and overwhelming. Barter or hire experts to help you in areas that need bolstering, and a webmaster to help you update your site if it demands more updates and revisions than you can handle. Make a commitment to refine and maintain your Web site to keep it current, to maximize its possibilities and opportunities for enhancing your business and serving your customers, and to integrate it with your business's ongoing and future plans.

Increasing Your Business Profits on the Internet— Without a Web Site

Before you invest time and money in a business Web site, you can use the Internet for promoting your business and increasing your profits without a site of your own. Following are some options you may want to consider.

Virtual Malls and E-Marketplaces

A virtual or online mall is a group of online businesses listed in an index or directory; they are a kind of Web hosting service. In reality, you do have a Web site, but you are grouped together with other stores—just like in offline shopping malls. Large online malls like Yahoo! group the businesses in categories, while smaller ones can be listed on one home page. Advantages include the potential that customers who are visiting the mall may stop by to see what you have to offer; they also offer an easy way to set up and start operating your store.

To set up shop on a mall, you can either create your own Web site or use the utilities and page forms that some malls provide, transfer your files to the mall's Web site, and pay their monthly fees. The fees will depend on the services that you choose, and are often based on the number of items you have to sell. Malls can host different kinds of stores or stores in the same industry, as evidenced by craft malls and art galleries or theme-based malls like Terry Scopes's Town of Tumbleweed.

Terry Scopes, mayor/president of the Town of Tumbleweed, a virtual mall featuring unique Western goods, answers the question, "What advantages does a virtual mall or 'town' like yours give to women netpreneurs?" by saying, "It saves the cost of retail space, printing, and in many cases carrying the inventory (it's easy to drop-ship with e-commerce). The Internet is in its infancy, and I believe it offers as equal a 'business playing field' as there ever has been."

In answer to the question, "What should a woman know before she starts an online site like yours?" Scopes says, "She needs to educate herself about the technologies she'll be shopping for, as well as writing a detailed plan of all the functions she wants her Web site back end to perform, the design of the front end, and the navigability of her site. If she has existing software operational systems in her new site, make sure all this information is part of the bidding process for Web developers. She may find that it is more cost-effective to rebuild existing systems rather than integrating them with the new Web site systems."

Here are some tips to help you select a mall:

- Shop for the best combination of services and prices.
- Check to see if there is a requirement to post banner ads.

- Talk to other store owners for feedback on the mall (a good guideline to use with all of these options).
- After signing-up, track the activity and of course, the sales you generate from participating in the mall.

RELATED RESOURCES
Internet Sites

The following sites are mall stores.

<www.store.yahoo.com> Yahoo! Store; How to open a Yahoo! Store

<www.excitestores.com> ExciteStores; Become an ExciteStore merchant

Writing Web Content

With millions of existing Web sites to lure people, you'll need to pay special attention to your site's content—helpful information and guidance that will encourage your visitors to return often. If you enjoy writing and wish to share your experiences and expertise, many Web site owners will welcome your contributions in the form of tips and articles. Some sites will pay for articles from "guest experts," depending on their budgets and policies, while others will invite you to submit your tip sheets and sign off with a signature or tagline listing your e-mail address and business contact information.

If you can write good ad copy, you might also sell your services to Web designers and Internet marketing experts.

Some tips for writing for the Web:

- Keep articles short, with a few vital resources and helpful links. If you have more to offer, write it as an "e-booklet" that can be downloaded and sold like LaDonna Vick's computer book (see chapter 1).

BUSINESS PROFILE: Terry Scopes, Virtual Mayor of the
Town of Tumbleweed

What is your Internet venture?

Tumbleweed Trading, Inc. d.b.a. Town of Tumbleweed <www
.townoftumbleweed.com>.

Is it solely an Internet business?

Solely e-commerce.

When was the business started?

Online live: June 1999; Incorporated, May 1997.

How did you originate the idea for your site?

The original concept was for a year-round, self-contained, brick-
and-mortar destination site that offered a print catalog of participating merchant wares.

Do you have a "vision statement" for your Web site?

Town of Tumbleweed is an online virtual Old Western town offering unique, high-quality, Western goods dedicated to the timeless
values, legendary craftsmanship, and romantic lifestyle of the Great
American West.

How did you finance your start-up?

SBA loan, bank loan, UTFC Funding (Utah Technology Finance
Corporation), angel investors, personal savings.

- Check whether sites that are popular with your target customers have a "Write for Us" page with submission guidelines.
- Consider approaching sites that sell columns, like iSyn-
  dicate <www.isyndicate.com>, or self-syndicate your own.
- Writing for the Web, like writing for print, should include
  the essential who, what, when, why, where, and how
  points.
- Personalize Web content as you write, as though you were
  writing to one individual who needs your assistance.

What resource helped you the most?

Professional publications from the print catalog industry adapted by me to the e-commerce industry (there weren't any reliable statistics for e-commerce when I was writing my business plan). Our SBA contact at First Security Bank was our most important contact, financial educator, and supporter throughout the funding process.

Can you offer any tips for creating a successful Web site?

Allow more time than you anticipate for online testing (three to six months, depending on the complexity of your site). Have your marketing strategies in line and ready to go—but do not implement them until you're sure your Web site is working.

Do you have any additional comments?

When screening potential Web developers, make sure that the software systems they are using to build your site are generic—ensuring that your site is transferable. You may want to move to a different developer/hoster down the line, and if your site is too custom, moving becomes a very expensive proposition.

Terry Scopes, mayor/president of
Tumbleweed, "Go West on the Web."

- Put together an FAQ file based on your expertise or industry and make it available for posting on appropriate sites.

When Leslie C. Wood, freelance writer and communications specialist and owner of the Web site Writer4u <http://writer4u .com> (profiled in chapter 6), was asked if she had a tip for writing for the Web, she says, "Short, sweet, and to the point."

When Susan Breslow Sardone, a professional freelance copywriter and the principal of Writing That Sells <www .writingthatsells.com>, was asked the question, "Do you have

---

BUSINESS PROFILE: Susan Breslow Sardone, Professional
Copywriter and Web Site Publisher

What is your Internet venture?

Writing That Sells: <www.writingthatsells.com>. I also own the following URLS: DirectMailWriter.com <www.directmailwriter .com>; WebSiteWriter.com <www.WebSiteWriter.com>; and Idea person.com <www.Ideaperson.com>.

Is it solely an Internet business?

I provide a service—marketing communications—and the majority of my business continues to come through word of mouth. Thanks to my sites, though, I have gained new clients over the [Web] transom and also use the site as an online portfolio.

When was the business started?

1997.

How did you originate the idea for your site?

I wanted to create an interactive promotional tool and showcase for my existing business.

How did you finance your start-up?

Personal savings.

What resource helped you the most?

New York University's Multimedia Technology division. I studied for a certificate there and gained the tools to master the Web . . .

---

a tip on writing Web content for one's business Web site?" she says, "Make it brief, clear, and painless for the visitor. Try to include useful, non-promotional information as well. For example, I offer tips on 'How to Write a Newsletter.' "

Debra Traverso, copresident of WriteDirections.com, is yet another writer who is using the Internet to make profitable use of her writing ability and teaching background. She offers several good tips on creating good Web text content in her profile featured here, as well as this Web writing tip: "Make your text reveal benefits to the reader, not features you offer."

and evaluate the abilities of others who claimed to do the same. I also credit my husband, who is my webmaster and manages the technical and design aspects of the site.

Can you offer any tips for creating a successful Web site?

Make it fun to enter, easy to navigate, quick to load, and good to look at. Give visitors opportunities to contact you and stay in touch. And promote the site in all media you have access to (including, of course, search engines).

Do you have any additional comments?

I get responses to my site from all over the world, and it would be untenable for me to work with all these individuals. I'm still struggling with finding a way, though, to do business with these prospects. Perhaps I need another site that's a worldwide network of copywriters . . .

Susan Breslow Sardone is a professional freelance copywriter and the principal of Writing That Sells. She teaches Marketing Communications Writing at New York University, and is an Online Travel Guru @ Honeymoons from About.com <http://honeymoons.about.com>.

RELATED RESOURCES
Internet Sites

<www.epigraphics.com> EpigraphicsSoftware, Inc.; *Clip Words* software for assistance in writing ad copy text; View samples from the book

<www.HowToInternet.com>; Internet marketing information, including tips on how to write copy for the Net

<http://myks.sitesell.com/profits13.html>; Information on how to sell your knowledge with e-books (by Ken Evoy, M.D. and Monique Harris)

BUSINESS PROFILE: Debra Traverso, Writing Institute

What is your Internet venture?

WriteDirections.com <www.WriteDirections.com>. We are a virtual writing institute, offer more than 45 classes in various forms of writing, from overcoming writer's block, to writing a book proposal, to writing a winning news release, to book promotion. Our classes are taught in one-hour sessions over the phone, supplemented with e-mail handouts. Thus, our students get immediate answers to their questions, but don't have to leave their homes or offices to attend. We are made up of eight writing instructors who are also successful freelancers, authors, journalists, and business communication specialists.

Is it solely an Internet business?

About 75 percent Internet. Students register right at the site. However, we conduct workshops in person too, and work with corporate clients at their locations.

When was the business started?

March 1999.

How did you originate the idea for your site?

Actually, my business partner should take the credit. We were writers who met and formed a bond, then began to hold one another accountable for our writing and our business growth. Soon, we realized we wanted to be able to help a wider audience of writers. She started WriteDirections and within one month had talked me into helping her build it.

Joint Ventures and Marketing Co-ops

Several of the women interviewed for this book are either business partners, co-owners, or member partners in a larger online community like Women's Forum <www.womensforum.com>. Joining forces with other Web business owners or those business owners who have sites can help you combine your marketing ventures and work on projects together. For example,

How did you finance your start-up?

No loans. We used our own personal money.

What resource helped you the most?

I had owned a management consulting firm prior to this one for 10 years, and I write business books. My latest is *Outsmarting Goliath: How to Achieve Equal Footing with Companies That Are Bigger, Richer, Older and Better Known* (New York: Bloomberg Press, 2000), so I'm well versed in business operation. As for the writing expertise, I have a master's degree in journalism/public relations, but most of my expertise came after time in the trenches, countless rejection letters, hundreds of articles, several books, and through my experience as an adjunct faculty member at Harvard University, where I still teach.

Can you offer any tips for creating a successful Web site?

Be creative in your marketing efforts. Solicit and use testimonials. Continually list with search engines and directories. Offer a newsletter and build up a following. Keep your site tight and clean. Don't offer too many options for visitors to click away from your site. And, be the best at what you do. We try to offer 120 percent in each of our classes. As a result, we get many referrals.

> *Debra Traverso, copresident of WriteDirections.com*
> *and business journalist, teaches a one-hour course*
> *in writing effective Web copy called, "Winning*
> *Web Sites: Words Make the Difference."*

Rosalind Resnick's NetCreations, Inc. (see profile in chapter 4) works with other sites to gather opt-in mailing lists that they rent, and then share the revenue.

You can also join online buying groups to get better deals on supplies or equipment. Just make sure you have a signed agreement if money and responsibility is involved.

When Jennifer Dugan, of Dugan's Travels <www.online agency.com/duganstravels> (profiled in chapter 5), was asked,

"What advantages does partnering your site with Online Agency give your business?" she responded, "The main advantages for me is that the suppliers (cruise lines, tour companies, etc.) update their specials and I don't have to. I also can sell luggage, books, port passes, and other things through online agency.com and be paid a commission. They only deal with travel agencies so they know what I need. Plus I am in complete control over what my Web site looks like, and I can change things myself. I don't need to know HTML—it is 'fill-in-the-blanks.' "

RELATED RESOURCES

Books

Teaming Up: The Small Business Guide to Collaborating with Others to Boost Your Earnings and Expand Your Horizons by Paul and Sarah Edwards, and Rick Benzel, contributor (Los Angeles: J P Tarcher, 1997) <www.paul andsarah.com>

Internet Sites

<www.Shop2gether.com>; Negotiates discounts on business products and services for pools of buyers for educational institutions and small and mid-sized businesses

Video Conferencing, Chats, Radio Interviews

Many larger Web sites are using real-time, interactive tools and multimedia content to better serve their clients and customers by featuring expert chat guests, recorded and/or live radio interviews, video clips, and mini-conferences. The drawback, however, is that not all persons connected to the Internet will have the technology to participate in these multimedia events.

Find out by doing your own research and through industry resources and networking sources what sites invite guests, and find out the proper procedures to approach them for an interview. This will be another promotional avenue for you, especially if you conduct workshops or teach courses. You may also be able to teach an online course.

Debra Traverso of Write Directions.com invites authors to talk about their books with her teleclasses, and Jennifer Vallee of Pallaslearning <www.pallaslearning.com> (see profile in chapter 8) includes in her lifelong learning magazine a new section called, "What Are You Learning?" which contains interviews of women about their current learning paths. Pallaslearning also has online workshops hosted by invited guest experts.

Online Auctions

One retired woman (and grandmother of ten children) makes an average of $500 weekly selling collectibles she finds by scouring local garage sales, but before you start looking through those boxes in your attic, heed her tips:

- Take time to study the auction "houses" that interest you, their procedures, requirements, policies, and how they operate.
- See what sells—study their offerings and prices. E-Bay <www.ebay.com> sells a print publication that can help educate you to this way of selling.
- Photos, as well as good descriptions, definitely help to sell your items.
- It will take a good deal of time to do this successfully!

Two other tips:

1. You can use online auctions to test customer reaction and salability of your products before selling on your site (or even building a Web site).

2. To avoid auction scams, first read the FTC's <www.ftc.gov> guide, "Internet Auctions: A Guide to Buyers and Sellers."

Ann Graf <www.annetteonline.com>, author of the book, *How to Sell on E-Bay and Other On-Line Auctions*, revised (South Milwaukee, WI: Graf Publishing, 2000) offers these comments about using online auctions to promote a business:

I sell my book on the auctions and link it to my Web site. I also sell craft patterns, which I also link the auctions to. Currently, the link from the auctions brings in about 75 percent of my sales.

I use the auctions on a regular basis, depending on how much I want to list each week. Of course, the more I list on the auctions, the more I sell. On average, it's about $200–$300 a week and I list about 10–15 auctions a week.

To get started, it's just like a regular retail business with its ups and downs. You should find something you enjoy selling. For myself, I enjoy craft patterns, because it's what I know. That way when someone asks me a question, I can answer them honestly. The best thing is to go on one of the sites such as E-Bay and look around. See how to register and what others are selling.

It's a great outlet for women to sell their products, from baby clothes, gift baskets, crafts, jewelry, services, and more. Make sure the customers know how to reach you to find out about your other site, by linking your Web site or advertising where your shop is located in a banner ad on the auction. (You can check out my auctions by clicking on the E-Bay link on my Web site for examples.)

The tips I can provide you for online auctions are to be honest and treat your customers well. Your items will sell if you describe them well and show pictures. Do not lead anyone on, and answer all their questions to the best of your ability.

RELATED RESOURCES

Books

Complete Idiot's Guide to Online Auctions by Michael
   Miller (Indianapolis: Que Education & Training, 1999)

Internet Sites

These are just a few of many other sites with auctions.

<www.amazon.com> Amazon.com

<http://auctions.yahoo.com> Yahoo.com

<www.onsale.com>; The New Egghead.com

Newsgroups, Message Boards, Listservs

If you follow the netiquette and procedures of the online discussion groups of Usenet, AOL, and other online services, you
may find these to be another way to get new business, and
make some friends along the way. Message boards found on
various community sites can also help you with business questions. Listservs, also called mailing lists, are like message
boards, but you communicate with others of similar interests
using your e-mail.

Some tips:

- Study the groups for awhile to see if they will permit you
  to post your signature with your input.
- Take time to help others as a way to establish yourself as
  someone knowledgeable and willing to share your tips.
- Read the terms of use and FAQs of these groups to ensure
  that you follow acceptable use.

RELATED RESOURCES

Internet Sites

<www.ivillage.com/work/index.html>; iVillage.com's Work from Home page has articles, chats, and a number of work-from-home topical message boards

<www.liszt.com> Liszt; Huge directory of Internet discussion groups

<www.refdesk.com> refdesk.com; A vast listing of Internet sites on many topics, including the Internet

<www.tile.net/lists> Tile.Net/Lists; "The Reference to Internet Discussion and Information Lists"

Software

Microsoft *Internet Explorer* and Netscape *Communicator* browsers have newsgroup software built in

Women's Sites

Your business, its address, and your contact information can be listed for a small fee on women's business network sites like Field of Dreams <www.fodreams.com>; listed in the online directories of organizations to which you belong, such as the National Association of Women Business Owners <www.nawbo.org> or Women Incorporated <www.womeninc.com>; and partnered with others such as Womens Forum <www.womensforum.com>, or with industry associations that allow potential clients who are looking for assistance to search their sites.

Take advantage of as many of these online promotional opportunities as possible to get publicity and recognition for your business, whether it is off- or online.

CHAPTER EIGHT

The Internet in the 21st Century

The question of where the Internet is going and just how fast it will get there is giving headaches to economists, business owners, politicians, investors, consumers, and just about everyone who has attempted to predict what role the Internet will play in their personal lives and careers. Lauren Leifer, President, Compdisk, Inc. <www.compdiskinc.com> says, "It is a balance every business owner will have to achieve in this exciting but challenging Internet market."

Here are just a few of the growing trends that are beginning to emerge from present-day Internet statistics:

- Business-to-Business (B2B) transactions offer the greatest opportunities in e-commerce.
- Success comes to the Internet entrepreneur who decides what business model is best for her venture (B2B or B2C—business-to-consumer); who concentrates on customer service; who looks for ways to add revenue streams while cutting costs; and who finds and focuses on a niche market.

BUSINESS PROFILE: Lauren Leifer, Duplication and Replication Services and Development

What is your Internet venture?

Compdisk, Inc. <www.compdiskinc.com> provides clients with technology support and duplication services for CDRs, CDs, disks, and audiocassettes.

Is it solely an Internet business?

It is an established high-tech company with an online site.

When was the business started?

1967.

How did you originate the idea for your site?

From viewing other businesses' Web sites, I knew what I did and did not like, so I worked with a marketing person to design and perfect my company's site.

How do you think the Internet can help a business?

We started thirty-two years ago primarily as a local company, and gradually expanded nationwide. The Internet has provided us with new applications for product fulfillment and distribution, and has also opened worldwide markets for our services. The Internet can present women the world over with entrepreneurial opportunities they never could have had otherwise.

- Cybermillionaires are beginning to give back some of their wealth to the less fortunate.
- The more techno-savvy a person is, the better chance she has at getting a higher paid job.
- Governments will use the Internet to better communicate with their citizens.
- Products and services that help us to harmonize and integrate our lives with those of people from different backgrounds, cultures, and other countries will be well received.

With the Internet, I say my company has tried to stay on the "mundane" edge versus the "cutting edge." In that I mean that businesses should not rush headlong into using the Internet without some thought and planning how it will be used most effectively. At the same time, if companies move too slowly in taking advantage of the opportunities the Internet offers, they can fall behind their competitors.

Do you have any additional comments?

The Internet can also be used as an amazing "tool" to help others. For example, I have been able to take my love of jazz music and use it to help women jazz musicians promote themselves with another site I am presently having designed, <www.womenin jazz.com>. I also have other plans to use the Internet to help with public health information.

> *Lauren Liefer, president, Compdisk, Inc. is an*
> *active member of the National Association*
> *of Women Business Owners (NAWBO).*

- The Internet continues to improve communication between the citizens of different countries.
- Investors will expect Internet businesses to be profitable.
- Virtual education will continue to expand as more individuals get connected and have access to the educational resources of the Internet.
- In "Futurework: Trends and Challenges for Work in the 21st Century," the Department of Labor states that "improvements in computer technology signify that computers

BUSINESS PROFILE: Christina Blenk, Resources for
                                Women Business Owners

What is your Internet venture?

WomanOwned.com <www.womanowned.com>, "Dedicated to
Women Business Owners."

Is it solely an Internet business?

Yes, we are 100 percent Web.

When was the business started?

The first concept Web site went live in June 1997 as part of my corporate Web site. The purchase of the WomanOwned.com domain
and future site developments came soon after.

How did you originate the idea for your site?

I wanted a place where I could share my experiences as a woman-
owned start-up company and help others facing the same issues.
Visitors were so positive about the site that I decided that it would
become the prime location for women to learn about starting a
business and network with other business owners from around
the world.

How did you finance your start-up?

WomanOwned.com was started in my spare time and was never
financed through outside sources. All resources on the site are free
to visitors as well as the help I give through direct e-mail questions.
Advertising helps to offset some of the expenses and additional
services are being developed to build revenue for increased promotional opportunities.

will be an even stronger presence in the American workplace in the future."

- The U.S. government, led by President Clinton, this year
  (2000) proposed funding of $45 million for the Technology
  Opportunities Program run by the National Telecommuni-
  cations and Information Administration (NTIA) to bring
  the Internet to more people in communities who cannot
  afford Internet access, so that they might take advantage of
  its opportunities.

What resource helped you the most?

I learned that networking was the key to business success through my "real world" experiences. Besides the guidance gained through talking with other business owners, I found a wealth of information in my local library.

Can you offer any tips for creating a successful Web site?

Letting your personal style shine on your Web site is often the best feature possible. Content is necessary and community is great, but personality is even better. I write the articles on the site to inform the visitor and provide a "lighter" side to the dry business world.

Do you have any additional comments?

Understanding the Web technology is an asset that we had through our professional Web design firm. If your understanding of the technology and marketing strategies are not well developed, consider hiring the talent you need to get the job done. With parts of the project outsourced you can then focus on the creation of content and online networking opportunities.

Christina Blenk, president and
founder of WomanOwned.com.

Future Views of the Internet

When asked, "In your opinion, how do you see the Internet affecting women's lives in the future?" Christina Blenk, president, WomanOwned.com. responded, "I believe that the Web will help women level the professional playing field and will provide the resources to improve their daily lives. Women are driving the development of the Web more than they may realize."

Chuck Martin,* chairman of the Net Future Institute <www.netfutureinstitute.com>, a U.S.–based think tank focusing on the future of e-business and the Internet based in North Hampton, New Hampshire, was asked two questions:

How do you see women using the Internet to promote themselves and/or a business in e-commerce in the twenty-first century?

As the Internet becomes more and more ubiquitous, it will become more of a part of mainstream promotional life. A woman who is a better communicator will become exponentially better on the Net because of the tremendous reach and high degree of interactivity. It is this interactivity that will give a great communicator and great listener a competitive edge.

In your opinion, will they use the Internet in the same ways or differently from men?

The Net environment will reflect general demographics, so a woman who conducts business differently in the physical world will be allowed to do so in the networked environment, with much greater potential result.

Dr. Hazel Henderson <www.hazelhenderson.com>, an independent futurist and lecturer and author of *Beyond Globalization: Shaping a Sustainable Global Economy* (West Hartford, CT: Kumarian Press, Inc., 1999) and five other books, was asked, "How do you envision the Internet in assisting women in business ventures and/or promoting themselves in their professional careers?" She says:

---

*Chuck Martin is also author of the books *Net Future: The 7 Cyber Trends That Will Drive Your Business, Create New Wealth, and Define Your Future* (New York: McGraw-Hill, 1998) and *The Digital Estate: Strategies for Competing, Surviving, and Thriving in an Internetworked World* (New York: McGraw-Hill, 1998).

Because of my own experience (basically I am self-employed as a writer/consultant, and for the past 30 years I have been working for myself) it has been a boon to have a Web site, in so many ways.

First of all, the Internet enables you to get your message out to a larger group of people. People can find my books' titles, which are posted on my Web site. Instead of unnecessarily writing me letters or sending me e-mails to see if I am available for a speaking engagement, they can look at my schedule and pretty much see where I am going to be and if I would be available for a presentation without having to contact my assistant. That saves me time and unnecessary traffic.

As a member of NAWBO, I have conducted a number of presentations for them over the last couple of years, and I am just amazed how many women-owned businesses have been started. Because of the ease and low-cost entry the Internet gives, they can start small businesses on the kitchen table, and work at home—an almost ideal situation. Of course, what tends to happen with all entrepreneurs is that we tend to exploit ourselves and to work twice as hard, as we simultaneously manage child care, the laundry, and other tasks. Personally, I really rather prefer that kind of work setting where I make my own pace and don't have anyone watching my time. I think it is a much more holistic way to do a business, even though the women that I talk to do admit it tends to be a bit hectic. I think they really prefer that lifestyle than going to some 9 to 5 job.

The other thing I love about using the Internet is that you can go global even while you are still completely local. I live in a small town of less than 10,000 people so there are lots of good qualities of life, community, and all the rest of it, and yet, my work is global. I would say at least half of my time is spent in other countries and I fly out of Orlando, which is very convenient; yet I employ local vendors, and the money I earn comes home to the United States.

Another thing which has been guiding a lot of what I am doing right now is that I do believe that network markets reward cooperators. It is not the typical approach, of "competition to the death." Actually, the big opportunity is that you can build global market share in whatever it is you are doing, simply by cooperating and making agreements and figuring out how to share revenues and royalties. That, to me, is very, very exciting. Presently, I am partnering in a television network company, where we are building global market share by bartering and signing agreements with partner stations around the world.

I believe the Internet is helping to foster this partnering, and sharing, and cooperating, for which you do not need to raise much capital. You have a much more organic kind of operation; you can keep what I call your "cultural DNA" intact. Many of the women business owners I know are creating cooperative gains, and doing just as well. But I think we are measured differently, because the accounting firms are still figuring out how to measure goodwill, intellectual capital, and social capital.

This particular enterprise that I am very involved in helping develop, WETV and WETV.com, is based in Canada. WETV has partnered with 38 television stations around the world, in 31 countries, and it is all done by bartering air time and programming and making agreements with stations that share our cultural DNA, which is about "WE the people, and the Whole Earth." It is like a global C-SPAN and it is a public-private-civic partnership. "Oh my gosh," people say, "it is global TV, you are going to need $100 million." But we say, "Hey we're not in the 'bricks-and-mortar business,'" and we don't need to buy these stations, we just barter and make agreements. So I think this is the style that women are particularly suited to succeed in.

Barter is going to be the next big trend on the Net—a cross between E-Bay and Priceline, but the price is zero—and women will build value by cooperating. I am investor and advisor to Barter.com, one of the first and most innovative bartering sites.

Henderson, a "global futurist and evolutionary economist," who recently partnered with the Calvert Social Investment Fund in Washington, D.C., in a program to compile *The Calvert-Henderson Quality of Life Indicators of the USA* (Washington, D.C.: Calvert Group, 2000), which she says "is a book describing the new tools to measure national, economic, environmental, and social trends. That is the rest of the story and tells how we are doing on 12 aspects of the quality of life."

Gerald Celente is the author of *Trends 2000: How to Prepare for and Profit from the Changes of the 21st Century* (New York: Time Warner, 1997), and Director of the Trends Research Institute <www.trendsresearch.com> in Rhinebeck, New York. In answer to the question, "Is there a trend as it relates to women and the Internet overall that you foresee for the twenty-first century?" Celente says, "I will say that the glass ceiling will virtually disappear in the online world of doing business. Performance, intelligence, ingenuity, and creativity—not gender, race, or office politics—will help democratize the new millennium workplace."

When Jennifer Vallee, CEO of Pallaslearning <www.pallas learning.com>, was asked, "How do you see the Internet changing the way we learn?" she said, "With the right technology and pedagogical principles, online learning experiences can be dynamically designed in a manner that suits each individual's learning style. No longer will each learner be forced to learn in the same, perhaps mismatched, style as her 20 classmates learn. More than this, the unique ways in which women know and learn within the home, workplace, and community—ways that are ignored, subsumed, and devalued by society—can be embraced within the unbound forum of the Internet. The greatest change to the way women learn may very well become a social and political one. Our upcoming eBusiness Conference (to be held this Fall 2000) is bringing women from all business sizes together to discuss the direction of eBusiness."

BUSINESS PROFILE: Jennifer Vallee, E-Learning
                    Experiences for Women

What is your Internet venture?

Pallaslearning <www.pallaslearning.com

Is it solely an Internet business?

Pallaslearning is solely an Internet business, although some Pallasmembers are starting face-to-face Pallaslearning clubs in their local communities.

When was the business started?

We launched the site October 31, 1999.

How did you originate the idea for your site?

Pallaslearning is the matrix of my own interests, personality, and intellect. In essence, I've simply started the type of club that I've always wanted . . . smart, intellectual, ambitious, and challenging. Then I invited thousands of women to join.

Do you have a "vision statement" for your Web site?

Where women gather to learn, imagine, and explore.

How did you finance your start-up?

We are the ultimate rags to riches story, turning $200 into projected profits of over $3 million in our first year. In between that leap, we received private investment from friends and family. We have been approached by venture capitalists, but we turned them away.

"Hottest" Predicted Internet Business Ideas and Trends

In the March 2000 issue of *Philly Tech* <www.philly-tech .com>, writer Claire Furia Smith quoted in her article, "No Surprises," an Information Technology (IT) salary survey that was conducted by Dowden & Co., a professional compensation data group based in Drexel Hill, Pennsylvania. In 1999, Smith

What resource helped you the most?

Magazines. I buy *Business 2.0, Red Herring, Wired, The Industry Standard,* and *Fast Company* every month. I learned everything about this field from those publications. Essential books include *The E-Myth, Bulldog: Spirit of the New Entrepreneur,* and *Radical Marketing.*

Can you offer any tips for creating a successful Web site?

Find a narrow business niche and have the courage to maintain that focus. Too many Web sites overextend their brand by trying to "do it all."

Do you have any additional comments?

I enjoy the challenge of finding our own solutions. I think that many start-ups are spoiled by the millions they receive from venture capitalists. When we didn't have enough capital to pay course developers upfront, we devised a unique royalties-upon-sales model that everyone enjoyed because of our volume. When we didn't have a marketing budget, we secured major alliances that drove membership through the roof. Don't fall into the trap of big money. You lose all resourcefulness.

> *Jennifer Vallee is president and CEO of Pallaslearning, "Where women gather to learn, imagine, and explore."*

reports, in the Northeastern United States the average salary of a Web or IT integrator rose 10 percent, to $96,100, while the average salary of a Web application developer jumped 57.6 percent to $82,600.

It is obvious that for the time being, any job or business connected with the Internet will be in demand. Many of these IT professionals may and will go out on their own to start businesses. Experts predict the following Internet businesses to be popular into the next decade:

PRODUCT-BASED INTERNET COMPANIES

Art: Online galleries, photographs, graphic designs, clip art

Clothing: Sports, recreation, children's, women's, shoes, specialized

Collectibles: Collections and antiques

Entertainment products: Games, movies, videos; selling event tickets

Financial services: Retirement planning; online investing

Literature: E- and print books, booklets, poems, novels, cookbooks, reports

Music: Samples, music from new artists and bands, old music and record collections

Supplies: Crafts supplies, tools, party supplies

Technology and related equipment: Computers, hardware and software; home electronics

Travel services: Tickets, planning

SERVICE-BASED INTERNET PROFESSIONS

Computer consultant: A computer expert who assists individuals in learning to operate computer hardware and software to accomplish the work they wish to achieve

Computer LAN networker: A specialist who designs and maintains the network of computers linked together in a company

Computer programmer (independent): A computer specialist who writes programs for the internal workings of computers and programs that solve problems

Database manager: A specialist who sets up and maintains databases for companies and professionals

Desktop publisher: A computer and design specialist who lays out promotional materials, documents, reports, and other publications for individuals, companies, schools, and small businesses

E-commerce strategist: A person who plans a company's strategic e-commerce enterprises

Electronic publisher: One who publishes and often writes e-books, e-booklets, e-zines, e-newsletters for self-publication or for other businesses, which can be downloaded and sold over the Internet

Graphic artist: A professional artist or designer who creates designs for businesses and professionals and for online matter, using her talents and sophisticated software

Information broker: A professional who searches for data for companies needing information on products, competitors, trends, and other facts, usually specializing in a specific industry, trade, or profession

Internet marketing consultant: A promotional and advertising specialist to help virtual businesses drive traffic to their site

Multimedia producer: A specialist in using video, audio, graphics, and computer technology to create interactive devices for use in presentations and/or active Web sites or for the creation of CDs

Namespace consultant: Specialist who suggests the best keywords to lead people to a site when typed into a browser

Software developer: An engineer who creates and designs computer programs to perform functions and tasks for companies or for general sale

Systems analyst: A computer specialist who evaluates companies' computer networks and programs and makes recommendations for better efficiency or upgrading of their present systems

Technical support representative: A computer specialist who assists individuals or company employees with the operations of the hard- and software used in their personal or business operations

Translating service: A company that offers language translation services to businesses who do international trade, including sometimes advising the businesses on proper protocol for dealing with the culture and customs of other countries

Virtual assistant: A professional assistant working in partnership with an individual to provide support, without being physically present, learning their clients' businesses and working closely to help their clients become more productive and effective

Virtual instructor: An expert in a certain field or industry who offers teleclasses or instructs via online courses

Web designer: A specialist in graphic design, HTML, or other code programming and software who designs the Web pages of professionals and businesses

Web master: A specialist in high-level program languages that run Web sites who is responsible for site maintenance and upgrading

Writer (Web content, copywriter, technical): A word specialist for businesses' content and ad copy

As the Internet develops, so will new online businesses. The
process has just begun, and if you can be the first with a new
idea or "Internet model," you can do very well financially.
More important, as you begin to use the Internet to start or
promote a business or yourself, enjoy the process, and make
sure you give a helping hand to others along the way—share
the wealth!

RELATED RESOURCES

Books

*Blueprint to the Digital Economy: Wealth Creation in the
Era of E-Business* by Don Tapscott, Alex Lowy, David
Ticoll, editors (New York: McGraw-Hill, 1998)

Making Money in Cyberspace by Paul and Sarah Edwards
(Los Angeles: J P Tarcher, 1998)

GLOSSARY OF INTERNET TERMS

Bandwidth   The speed at which information is transferred over networks of the Internet.

Baud   The speed at which information is transferred over networks of the Internet.

Bookmark   Feature that stores your favorite sites' URLs in your Web browser for speedy access.

Bit   The smallest component of binary data.

Brick and mortar   The nickname used for traditional businesses operating out of a building or storefront.

Brick and click   The nickname of Internet ventures.

Browser   A software program such as *Microsoft Internet Explorer* or *Netscape Navigator* that enables you to read and navigate HTML Internet documents so you can "search" or "browse" for information.

B2B   The term given to Web business-to-business relationships.

B2C   The term given to Web business-to-consumer relationships.

Buzz   The latest news that is being bandied about companies, business owners, and/or new technology or products.

Certificates   Designations given to Web companies for meeting certain criteria in providing online customer services, such as electronic security forms or documents.

Chat   An online, present-time discussion group. Many Web sites invite chat guests to discuss certain topics and answer questions.

CSP   Commerce service provider like Yahoo or IBM, who handles all the technical aspects of your site (note that CSPs do not provide Internet connections, so you still need an ISP to connect to the Internet).

Cybercrime   Crimes that pertain to Internet abuse, ranging from illegal solicitations to harassment and cyberstalking.

Cyberlingo   Internet slang and often-used online language.

Cybersquatting   The act of registering a domain name for the sole purpose of selling it back to well-known companies with that registered name. Cybersquatting was outlawed by the Anticybersquatting Consumer Protection Act of 1999.

Desktop publishing (DTP)   The process of producing documents with a computer using software programs.

Domain   The word address of a Web server, a collection of connected computers, usually noted by a three-letter code—such as these common examples: .com, commercial site; .edu, educational institution; .gov, government site; .mil, military site; .net, network site; .org, nonprofit organization.

Electronic commerce (EC)   The technological exchange of business information and operations.

Electronic data interchange (EDI)   The computer-to-computer exchange of business information using a public standard. Since 1998, the federal government has made it a requirement that all its suppliers and contractors have EDI capabilities for submitting bids, invoices, and receiving payment.

Electronic software distribution (ESD)   The downloading of software or music directly over the Internet.

FAQ   Frequently asked questions; often listed on Web sites to supply answers to common questions related to that site or on a certain topic.

Firewall   A type of computer programming that is used for security so that the network user can see through the "firewall" into the Internet, but other Internet users cannot see through the firewall into your network. Online businesses who sell products or services over the Internet use firewalls to protect consumers' private information, such as credit card numbers.

Flame   A scathing comment in response to another person's comment in a news group, forum, or message board. A "flamer" is the angry e-mailer.

Frames   A Web page layout style that permits two or more pages to be seen simultaneously.

GIF   Graphics interchange format; a common file format for images.

Guestbook   The place on a Web site for visitors to sign in and give input.

Hacktivist   A computer hacker with an ideological mission.

Home networking   The connection of two or more home computers in order to share resources, information, and Internet connections.

Home page   The page your Internet browser loads at start-up; often refers to the first Web site document shown when you visit a new Web site or follow a link.

HTML   Hypertext mark-up language; the standard format for creating documents and pages on the Internet.

Hypermedia   A hypertext collection with pointers to other media—which may display images other than text, such as animations, sound, or images.

Hypertext   Text which is formatted so that related information can be accessed directly from the text.

Hypertext documents   The documents displayed by browsers.

Internet service provider (ISP)   The company that provides access to the Internet (local, or commercial access like AOL).

IP (Internet Protocol)   The common method by which data is sent over the Internet from one computer to another.

IP address   The number that identifies the location of a computer on the Internet.

IT   Information technology.

Killer App   A totally new concept, product, or service—"the ultimate business model" for a new idea that is very successful. Examples are Microsoft and Amazon.com.

Lurker   A person who logs into a newsgroup or chat but does not converse with anyone.

Market exchanges   Online marketplaces where service-business sellers can meet buyers who bid for their services using RFPs (requests for proposals).

Metatags   Part of a special code placed on your Web site's pages that enables search engines to index your site.

Netizens   Nickname for network citizens—those who use and take advantage of the resources of the Internet.

Portals   Web sites composed of integrated programs that provide a significant amount of specific information about a topic. They are associated with online communities that make use of chats, e-mail, forums, and search engines to discuss in depth all aspects of a particular subject.

Shopping Bots   Shopping agents—Web-based search tools—that can assist you in choosing which retailer has the prices, selections, delivery options, and warranties for the equipment, supplies, and other items you are looking for.

SOHOs   Small offices and home offices.

SPAM   Unwanted advertising solicitations sent via e-mail or posted to forums.

Spiders or crawlers   Search engines' electronic components that retrieve information from your Web site.

24/7   An online store, Web site, and/or technical support that is available 24 hours a day, seven days a week.

Uninterruptible power supply device (UPS)   A unit you can purchase to protect your vital electronic equipment if you should lose power or even if it just momentarily flickers. Essentially, it gives you some time to save your computer files and shut down your computer until your power is restored.

VAN   Value added network, pertaining to access and security in your online business transactions.

VPN   Virtual private network, pertaining to the type of access and security in your online business transactions.

WYSIWYG (pronounced "wissy-wig")   Acronym meaning, 'what you see is what you get'; used in reference to how a text printout will appear on paper as compared to how it looks on a computer screen.

Zine   An online publication. Also called e-zine.

RESOURCES

Unless otherwise noted, please send a long (business-sized) self-addressed, stamped envelope (LSASE) if you contact any of these listings through the mail.

Associations

BUSINESS OWNERSHIP AND INDEPENDENT CONTRACTOR ASSOCIATIONS

American Association of Home-Based Businesses
P.O. Box 10023
Rockville, MD 20849
Web site: www.aahbb.org

A national, nonprofit organization with free membership. Dedicated to the support and advocacy of home-based businesses. Does not sell or endorse any business opportunities.

Association for Enterprise Opportunity (AEO)
1601 North Kent St., Suite 1101
Arlington, VA 22209
Web site: www.microenterprise works.org

Information on the microdevelopment industry, special sections for state associations and SBA MicroLoan intermediaries.

The National Association of Women Business Owners
1411 K Street, N.W.
Washington, DC 20005
Web site: www.nawbo.org

"Approximately 7,000 members in 70 chapters around the country."

SOHO America, Inc. (SOHO Online)
P.O. Box 941
Hurst, TX 76053
Web site: www.soho.org

Free membership, articles, and information. "Can help you manage the challenges of working in a small office/home office environment."

Women Incorporated
333 South Grand Avenue, Suite 2450
Los Angeles, CA 90071
Web site: www.womeninc.org

A national, non-profit network of women business owners and

women in business. Various membership benefits.

Working Today
P.O. Box 1261, Old Chelsea
Box Station
New York, NY 10113
Web site: www.workingtoday.org

"A national nonprofit membership organization that promotes the interests of people who work independently."

INTERNET, COMPUTER, AND TECHNOLOGY-RELATED ASSOCIATIONS

The Association for Interactive Media (AIM)
1430 Broadway, 8th floor
New York, NY 10018
Web site: www.interactivehq.org

"The Association for Interactive Media is the largest nonprofit association in the world driven to maximizing the successful evolution of the Internet and Interactive media industries to further enhance the global economy. AIM serves the interest of companies and individuals focused on the business use of the Internet and interactive media to more effectively reach their respective marketplace. AIM's diverse corporate members represent interests from e-mail marketing, retailing, online marketing, content, e-commerce, research and

broadband access through the rollout of Interactive Television."

Association of Internet Professionals
Empire State Building
350 Fifth Avenue, Suite 3018
New York, NY 10118
Phone: (877) AIP-0800
E-mail: info@association.org
Web site: www.association.org

"The Association of Internet Professionals (AIP) is the premier professional association of the Internet industry. The AIP exists to unify, support and represent the global community of Internet professionals. The organization also serves as a forum for the ideas, people and issues shaping the future of the Internet industry."

Association for Women in Computing
41 Sutter Street, Suite 1006
San Francisco, CA 94104
E-mail: awc@awc-hq.org
Web site: www.awc-hq.org

An all-volunteer professional network devoted to the advancement of women in the computing professions. Members include (women and men) computer scientists, information systems developers and managers, technical writers, and others whose careers closely involve computers. Chapters exist in several cities and at some universities, plus it has an active network of independent members who communicate electronically.

HTML Writers Guild
Web site: www.hwg.org

"An international organization of Web designers."

Information Technology Association of America
1401 Wilson Boulevard, Suite 1100
Arlington, VA 22209
Web site: www.itaa.org

"Trade association representing the broad spectrum of the world-leading U.S. IT industry."

Institute for Women and Technology
3333 Coyote Hill Road
Palo Alto, CA 94304
Web site: www.iwt.org

"Works in areas that engage women and men in industry, academia, government, and communities to imagine, design, create, and deploy technologies that have positive impacts on women around the world, and partners with a variety of organizations."

International Webmasters Association
119 E. Union Street, Suite E
Pasadena, CA 91103
Web site: www.iwanet.org
"Global leader for the advancement of Web professionals."

Webgrrls International
Web site: www.webgrrls.com

"The Women's Tech Knowledge Connection." Forum for women interested in new technology and media.

The Web Host Guild
988 S.E. 9th Avenue
Pompano Beach, FL 33060
Web site: www.whg.org

Members include Web hosts who receive Guild certification for meeting the Guild's standards of reliability and support.

For additional associations related to the Internet, technology, and your industry and interests, check the reference section of your public or college library for the Encyclopedia of Associations, current ed. (Gale Research <www.gale.com>, Detroit, MI).

Awards, Conferences, Expos, Trade Shows

Electronic Commerce World's Conferences
Web site: www.ecomworld.com

Speakers, educational sessions, products for electronic business. Sponsored by ECOM WORLD, "The Online Magazine for EC Professionals." Register online.

TheStandard.com
Web site: www.thestandard.com

In conjunction with the weekly newsmagazine, The Industry Standard, "defines the Internet Economy" with its coverage. Also offers a dozen Internet Economy conferences, events, and seminars.

wbusiness Exposition and Conference
Contact: Cathy Walters
Web site: www.wbusiness.net

First international exposition for women business owners, Fall 2000. Also at this site, information about *wbusiness Magazine*.

***Working Woman* Entrepreneurial Excellence Awards, 2000**
Web site: www.working woman.com

These awards were cosponsored by BankOne and Working Woman magazine in conjunction with regional, half-day events, awarding outstanding women entrepreneurs. The women nominated for these awards are profiled in the booklet, *Wise Women: Success Strategies of Women Entrepreneurs* (Chicago: Bank One, 1999), coauthored by Vanessa Freytag, director of Bank One's Woman Entrepreneur Initiative. Bank One launched a special Web site <www.bankone.com/women>, in August 1999, as a financial resource and forum for women to share tips.

Books

COMPUTING AND INTERNET GUIDES

Smart Computing, Smart Computing Guide Series, Smart Computing Learning Series, and Smart Computing Reference Series

Web site: www.smartcom puting.com

Publications are available on newsstands and through their customer service department.

E-Commerce

Amazon.com <www.amazon
.com> provides an opportunity
for those interested in "cyberculture," to sign up to receive
e-mail notification of the latest
"cyberculture" books that are for
sale.

*Clicking Through: A Survival
Guide for Bringing Your Business Online* by Jonathan I. Ezor.
Princeton, NJ: Bloomberg Press,
1999.

*The Complete Idiot's Guide to e-
Commerce* by Rob Smith, Mark
Speaker, and Mark Thompson.
Indianapolis: Macmillan
Computer Publishing, 2000.
Web site: www.mcp.com

Creating Stores on the Web,
2nd ed., by Ben Sawyer, Dave
Greely, and Joe Cataudella.
Berkeley, CA: Peachpit Press,
2000.
Web site: www.peachpit.com

.comSuccess! by Sally Richards.
Alameda, CA: Sybex, 2000.

E-Business Roadmap for Success
by Ravi Kalakota, Marcia
Robinson, Don Tapscott.
Reading, MA: Addison-Wesley,
1999.

How to Start a Business Website
by Mike Powers. New York, NY:
Avon Books, 1999.

The Internet Business Guide by
Rosalind Resnick. Indianapolis:
SAMS, 1995.

*Starting an Online Business for
Dummies,* 2nd ed., by Greg
Holden. Foster City, CA: IDG
Books Worldwide, Inc., 2000.
Web site: www.dummies.com

*The Unofficial Guide to
Starting a Business Online* by
Jason R. Rich. Foster City, CA:
IDG Books Worldwide, Inc.,
2000.
Web site: www.idgbooks.com

General Business

*Business Know-How: An
Operational Guide for Home-
Based and Micro-Sized
Businesses with Limited
Budgets* by Janet Attard.
Holbrook, MA: Adams Media
Corp., 2000.
Web site: www.businessknow
how.com

*Homemade Money: How to
Select, Start, Manage, Market,
and Multiply the Profits of a
Business at Home,* 5th ed., by
Barbara Brabec. Cincinnati,
OH: Betterway Publications,
1997.

*The Small Business Start-Up
Guide,* 3rd ed. by Robert
Sullivan. Great Falls, VA:
Information International,
2000.

Educational Opportunities

E-COMMERCE COURSES

The following universities have e-commerce courses (check with your local college about existing or planned courses in your area).

MIT Sloan School of Business Management
Center for e-Business@MIT
50 Memorial Drive
Cambridge, MA 02142
Web site: http://mitsloan.mit
.edu

Price Center for Entrepreneurial Studies
Anderson School at UCLA
110 Westwood Plaza
Los Angeles, CA 90095
Web site: www.anderson.ucla
.edu
Ten-week certificate program offered twice a year.

VIRTUAL EDUCATION

Element K
Web site: www.zdu.com
A total corporate online university; training for computers, software.

Dell's "Educate U"
Web site: www.dell.com
Online university, 900 subjects.

EduPoint.com
Web site: www.edupoint.com
A database of more than 1.5 million courses from 3,000 educational institutions.

Jones International University
Web site: www.getmymba.com
"A University of the Web."
Fully accredited online MBA program.

Learn2.com
Web site: www.learn2.com
Online courses (tutorials, programming, graphics/publishing, others) to enhance your business skills.

NAWBO's Internet-Supplied Training
Web site: www.nawbo.org
Available through Tutorial.com from IBM.

Pallaslearning.com
Web site: www.pallaslearning
.com
"Where women gather to learn, imagine and explore." E-business courses and others, eBusiness Conference.

Smart Planet
Web site: www.smartplanet
.com
A division of ZD Net.
Computing, business, and other courses.

Internet Sites

GENERAL BUSINESS

BizMove.com
Web site: www.bizmove.com
"The Small Business Knowledge Base."

Business Know-How Online
Web site: www.businessknow how.com
"Advice, articles, message boards, tips and hints, and resources for building big profits from micro-sized businesses." Owner/author, Janet Attard (see Books, General Business).

imandi.com
Web site: www.imandi.com
"Reverse marketplace, delivering sellers to buyers." Has Small Business Services and Products sections.

The Small Business Advisor
Web site: www.isquare.com
A popular Web site that provides a variety of information for the entrepreneur and small business owner, including state-specific assistance, articles, tax information, and marketing tips.

The Business Resource Center
Web site: www.morebusiness.com

SmartBiz
Web site: www.smartbiz.com
Many free how-to resources for business owners.

INTERNET AND E-COMMERCE INFORMATION

Cloudwise.com
Web site: www.cloudwise.com
"Helps small businesses use the Internet to increase sales, lower costs, and develop better business practices. Business owners can build their own e-commerce Web site."

The E-Commerce Times
Web site: www.ecommerce times.com
A free online publication, "Everything You Need to Know about Doing Business on the Internet."

GoBizGo
Web site: www.gobizgo.com
"A one-stop solution for creating, launching, marketing, and growing your online business."

HotWired
Web site: www.hotwired.com
"The leading Web enthusiast's how-to site"; Part of Wired Digital (*Wired* magazine, HotBot.com).

internet.com Corporation
Web site: www.internet.com
"The E-business and Internet Technology Network is a leading provider of global

real-time news and information resources for the Internet industry and Internet technology professionals, Web developers and experienced Internet users."

InternetNews.com
Web site: www.internetnews.com
Daily, online publication covering Internet developments.

MarcommWise
Web site: www.marcomm wise.com
A Web portal of marketing communications.

Mucho.com
Web site: www.mucho.com
Online business solutions.

WOMEN'S BUSINESS

AFL-CIO
Web site: www.aflcio.org/women/index.htm
For working women's concerns.

AT&T's Women in Business
Web site: www.att.com/wib

Bank One
Web site: www.bankone.com/women
Launched in August 1999 as a financial resource and forum for women.

IBM's Women's Business Center
Web site: www.ibm.com/small business/women

WOMEN'S SMALL/ HOME BUSINESS

At-Home Mothers' Resource Center
Web site: www.athome mothers.com
Includes association and related print magazine.

Home-Based Working Moms
Web site: www.hbwm.com

Mothers' Home Business Network
Web site: www.homeworking mom.com

ParentPreneur Club
Web site: www.parentpreneur club.com
Home-business news.

Wahm.Com
Web site: www.wahm.com
For work-at-home mothers.

Women's Connection Online (WCO)
Web site: www.women connect.com
Online services to women business owners and professional women, some 1,100 pages of information, discussion groups, e-commerce.

The Women's Forum
Web site: www.womens forum.com
One of the leading online women's communities with over 60 partner sites.

Periodicals

BUSINESS AND SMALL BUSINESS

Enterprising Women
Circulation Department
1135 Kildaire Farm Road, Suite 200
Cary, NC 27511
6 issues/yr. $18.
"The magazine for women business owners. "

Entrepreneur.com
Web site: www.entrepreneur mag.com
Four online magazines: *Entrepreneur, Business Start-Ups, Entrepreneur's Home Office* (online only), and *Entrepreneur International.*

Home Business Magazine
Web site: www.homebusiness mag.com
Online site of print magazine. Includes resources, articles.

Smart Computing
P.O. Box 85380
Lincoln, NE 68501
Web site: www.smartcomput ing.com
12 issues/yr. $29.

Victoria
P.O. Box 7148
Red Oak, IA 51591
Web site: www.victoriamag.com
12 issues/yr. $19.97.
See their annual August entre-preneurial issue, "Passion into Profits," August 2000.
Entrepreneur Seminar in New York City.

Working Woman
Web site: www.working woman.com
See their June 2000 issue featuring their special report, "The Top 500 Women-Owned Businesses." A resource for business tools, offers annual entrepreneurship awards, and lists conferences.

E-COMMERCE

E-Company
Web site: www.ecompany.com
12 issues/yr. $19.99 (Canada $32.50C).

Inter@ctive Week
Web site: www.interactive week.com
Print and online; covers Internet business news.

Internet World
Web site: www.internetworld .com
Print and online.

NetGuide
Web site: www.netguide.co.nz
Net information.

Wired.com
Web site: www.wired.com
Owned by Wired Digital, which
has the search engine HotBot
<www.hotbot.com>.

WWWiz
Web site: http://wwwiz.com
"Everything Internet for
Business Professionals." Print
and online.

ONLINE ONLY

Entrepreneur's HomeOffice
Web site: www.home
officemag.com
Part of the Entrepreneur
Media group.

SmallOffice.com
Web site: www.smalloffice.com
From the editors of *Home
Office Computing* and *Small
Office Computing*.

Supplies and Equipment

COMPUTERS, SOFTWARE, AND RELATED EQUIPMENT

CDW Computer Centers, Inc.
200 North Milwaukee Avenue,
Vernon Hills, IL 60061
Web site: www.cdw.com
Print and online.

Cyberguys!
Web site: www.cyberguys.com
Catalog. Print and online.

Global Computer Supplies
11 Harbor Park Drive,
Department ZA
Port Washington, NY 11050
Web site: www.global
computer.com
Print and online.

MicroWAREHOUSE
Web site: www.warehouse.com
Computers, scanners, and much
more.

ELECTRONICS

Roxy.com
293 Boston Post Road
West Marlboro, MA 01752
Web site: www.roxy.com
Phones, digital cameras. Print
and online.

FORMS AND CHECKS

NEBS
500 Main Street
Groton, MA 01471
Web site: www.nebs.com

Miscellaneous

BUSINESS LOANS

Count Me In for Women's Economic Independence
Box 96064
Washington, DC 20090
Web site: www.count-me-in.org

A new organization that makes small business loans to women. Started by Nell Merlino (founder of Take Our Daughters to Work Day) and Iris Burnett.

RESEARCH INSTITUTE

National Foundation for Women Business Owners
110 Wayne Avenue, Suite 830
Silver Spring, MD 20910
Web site: www.nfwb.org

"The premier source of information on women-owned businesses . . . worldwide." This is a research institute—it does not have members.

WOMEN'S BUSINESS CENTER

Online Women's Business Center
Web site: www.onlinewbc.org

Funded partly by the SBA, the online site of Women's Business Centers that are located around the United States, the Virgin Islands, and Puerto Rico, specifically to assist women in business start-ups and management. The online site lists the location of these centers and offers extensive online instructions about business start-ups and a Technology Center with information about starting an online business.

YOUTH ENTREPRENEURSHIP PROGRAMS

The Consortium for Entrepreneurship Education
1601 West Fifth Avenue
PMB 199
Columbus, OH 43212
Web site: www.entre-ed.org

"Providing leadership for entrepreneurship education in America and the world." Workshops; networking information; conferences.

Resources for Persons with Disabilities

ASSOCIATIONS

Disabled Business Persons Association
9625 Black Mountain Road, Suite 207
San Diego, CA 92126
Web site: www.web-link .com/dba/dba.htm

Nonprofit organization.

INTERNET SITES

The Boulevard
Web site: www.blvd.com

Contains information on products, resources, publications, employment opportunities, and more.

The Cure Network, Inc.
Web site: www.cure.org

Jobs for the disabled.

Canadian Resources

ASSOCIATIONS

Canadian Women's Business Network
3995 MacIssac Drive
Nanaimo, British Columbia
V9T 3V5
Canada
Web site: www.cdnbiz women.com

Women Business Owners of Canada
97 Spence Street
Winnipeg, Manitoba R3C 1Y2
Canada
Web site: www.wboc.ca

BOOKS

Building a Dream: A Canadian Guide to Starting Your Own
Business, 3rd ed., by Walter S. Good (New York: McGraw-Hill Ryerson Ltd., 1997)

Internet Law and Business Handbook by J. Dianne Brinson and Mark F. Radcliffe (Menlo Park, CA: Ladera Press, 2000)
Web site: www.laderapress.com

Includes information about Canadian e-commerce laws.

GOVERNMENT

Canada Business Service Centers
Web site: www.cbsc.org

For business support and information.

INTERNET SITES

Canada.com
Web site: www.canada.com

"Canada's small business hub."

SteppingStones
Web site: www.stepping
stones.ca

Miscellaneous Canadian entrepreneur and small business
resources.

PERIODICALS

HomeBusiness Report
HB Communications Group,
Inc.
2949 Ash Street
Abbotsford, British Columbia
V2S 4G5
Canada

Phone: (800) 672-0103
Web site: www.homebusiness
report.com

4 issues/yr. $17.12 (U.S. and
other countries add $10/yr.)
Canada's premier print and
online magazine source of
information for the home-
based/small-business owner.
HBR's Web site provides free
articles online, an online bookstore, upcoming small-business
events in Canada, and links to
other small business resource
centers.

Profit magazine
Web site: www.profitguide.com

"The Magazine for Canadian
Entrepreneurs."

How to Contact the Author

If you have any questions, business ideas, suggestions, or comments
you would like to share, please send e-mail to:
pyhuff@hotmail.com.

INDEX